PENGUIN BOOKS

THE DEATH AND AFTERLIFE OF MAHATMA GANDHI

Makarand R. Paranjape is a critic, poet, novelist and public intellectual. He was educated at St Stephen's College, University of Delhi, and at the University of Illinois at Urbana-Champaign, where he earned a master's and a PhD in English. Currently Professor of English at Jawaharlal Nehru University, New Delhi, he was the inaugural Erich Auerbach Visiting Chair in Global Literary Studies at the University of Tübingen in Fall 2014 and the ICCR Chair in Indian Studies at the National University of Singapore (2010–11). His recent books include *Cultural Politics in Modern India: Postcolonial Prospects, Colourful Cosmopolitanism, Global Proximities, Making India: Colonialism, National Culture, and Indian English Literature* and *Swami Vivekananda: A Contemporary Reader*.

THE DEATH
& AFTERLIFE OF
MAHATMA GANDHI

Makarand R.
Paranjape

PENGUIN BOOKS

PENGUIN BOOKS

USA | Canada | UK | Ireland | Australia
New Zealand | India | South Africa | China

Penguin Books is part of the Penguin Random House group of companies
whose addresses can be found at global.penguinrandomhouse.com

Published by Penguin Random House India Pvt. Ltd
7th Floor, Infinity Tower C, DLF Cyber City,
Gurgaon 122 002, Haryana, India

Penguin
Random House
India

Published in Vintage by Random House India 2015
Published in Penguin Books by Penguin Random House India 2016

10 9 8 7 6 5 4 3 2 1

The views and opinions expressed in this book are the author's own and the
facts are as reported by him which have been verified to the extent possible,
and the publishers are not in any way liable for the same.

ISBN 9780143427599

For sale in the Indian Subcontinent only

Typeset in Adobe Caslon Pro by Manipal Digital Systems, Manipal
Printed at Replika Press Pvt. Ltd, India

www.penguinbooksindia.com

To
Madhav—

It's quite normal to want to 'kill' your dad now and again (especially with a lightsaber), but patricide is almost unheard of among the Hindus . . .

Contents

PART II
'My death is my message': Mahatma, the last 133 days

Preface to the paperback edition

Mohandas Karamchand Gandhi is a man we hate to love and love to hate. This paradox explains his enormous persistence, if not appeal, in India even seventy years after his assassination. Of his long, complex and inspiring life, no single aspect is probably more difficult, disturbing or debatable than its violent termination. The Mahatma's martyrdom and the bloody Partition of India constitute the twin traumas that scarred the birth of our nation. What is the meaning of the assassination of the 'Father of the Nation', that too at the hands of one of the Hindu 'sons' of Mother India? It is this question that still haunts us and this book tries to answer.

The Mahatma as a latter-day saint and apostle of peace has worldwide attraction, largely because this is how his life has been interpreted by the liberal West. But closer home, in the subcontinent whose recent history he gave his life to shape, his proximity is more uncomfortable. There is one primary reason for this: Gandhi challenges our core beliefs about who we are and what we should be. At the heart of our unease with him is the politics of identity, especially religious rage.

Those who broke away from India to found their own Muslim-majority state, Pakistan, have usually projected Gandhi as a Hindu leader. Indeed, Gandhi repeatedly declared himself a Sanatani Hindu. However, a sizeable section of those who ostensibly champion the interests of Hindus are also suspicious of Gandhi not only for supposedly favouring Muslim interests, but also consenting to, if not causing, the Partition. A small, but vocal, minority among them actually considers him a British collaborator and enemy of Hindus. According to this view, Gandhi's non-violence only weakened his own community, being tantamount to preparation for self-annihilation in a hostile and competitive world. Naturally, these votaries of Hindu ressentiment and counter-violence consider Gandhi to be their greatest obstacle and his 'principled' assassin a national hero.[1]

Apart from Hindus and Muslims, the other section of Indian society that has found Gandhi's legacy contentious are the Scheduled Castes, the former 'untouchables', who form an important political component in the Indian chessboard. They, along with other groups championing backward caste political mobilization and assertion, characterize Gandhi as the leader of upper castes. They pit Dr Babasaheb Bhimrao Ambedkar against Gandhi, constructing of the former as the revolutionary annihilator of caste, while all the while treating him as the god of reservations. Arguably, hereditary, caste-based quotas reinforce caste rather than annihilate it. Often, resulting in the reverse reinstating of hierarchies, they end up benefiting and perpetuating the 'creamy layer' among the Schedule Castes, while those at the bottom remain excluded. This, of course, does not mean that the genuine empowerment of depressed sections of society should be abandoned.

There are several other kinds and shades of Gandhi haters and Gandhi baiters.

Indeed, all those who benefit from divisive and aggressive identity politics find him troublesome, even abhorrent. The actual homicide of Gandhi is thus followed, over the years, by many similar symbolic and conceptual slayings. But, as I have suggested, a Mahatma may be defined as one whose afterlife is greater than his life. The latter may be cut short, but the former persists, even in adversity. Every attack on Gandhi, hence, invites us actually to re-examine, debate and discuss what he lived and died for. In that sense, not only his life, but his death is his message. This book has tried to decode that message.

I had been working on Mahatma Gandhi for over twenty-five years, but never thought of writing a meditation on the meaning of his death. In 2009, I spent the Michaelmas term at Oxford University as Shivdasani Visiting Fellow at the Oxford Centre for Hindu Studies (OCHS), giving a series of lectures on Gandhi. While there, I noticed several hardbound scholarly books that made up the OCHS Hindu Studies series. The titles were impressive, even forbidding, mostly on classical Hinduism. I thought, half wistfully, how apt it might be if the series had a book on Mahatma Gandhi, arguably, the greatest Hindu of modern times. In my more wishful moments, I even dreamed of being the author of such a book.

Just before my departure, I mustered the courage to broach the possibility with Professor Gavin Flood, then academic director of OCHS and series editor. To my surprise and joy, he seemed to think it a good idea. Not only did he encourage this project from the very beginning, but also supported it to its quite altered conclusion. For I had set out to write a different book, with the death and afterlife of Gandhi meant to form just one chapter. What happened, however, was that this topic consumed all my energy and interest. It is what the whole book became about.

Soon after my stint at OCHS, in the winter semester of 2010, I taught an MA course on Gandhi's writings at the Centre for English Studies, Jawaharlal Nehru University. I took the students in my class to the various sites of Gandhi's memorialization in Delhi, the national capital. At Gandhi Smriti, the erstwhile Birla House, where Gandhi was assassinated, we realized that the riddle of his slaying was left unanswered, like a horrific question mark looming in the air, above the very spot on the manicured lawns where Nathuram Godse's bullets had felled him. That sudden confrontation with the enormity of the Mahatma's murder became the real driving force of this book.

That first hardback UK edition of this book, published in the OCHS Hindu Studies series, has had a limited circulation, mostly confined to libraries. But the Vintage Indian edition, published by Random House in January 2015, not only sold better, but was also widely read, reviewed and appreciated. I am grateful to Namita Gokhale, friend for over two decades and fellow writer, who helped publish it. Meru Gokhale, my editor at Penguin Random House, proposed an impossible deadline, which her team, especially Fazal, Tarini and Richa, strove so hard to meet. It helped that the cover, designed by Tara, was so arresting that I immediately approved it. For this paperback edition, I am obliged to Meru, Tarini and Cibani for their efficiency and support.

My special thanks to Rajmohan-bhai, who not only read the manuscript, but graciously complimented me on it; to Professor Anthony J. Parel, one of the world's leading Gandhi scholars, for his continued good wishes and positive response to the text; and to Professor Douglas Allen, friend, philosopher and Gandhian, for his feedback and comments. I would like to acknowledge the colleagues, students and staff of the Centre for English Studies for their continued support, and the JNU administration for sanctioning leave for academic pursuits. I owe Manju, my housekeeper, for wholesome, regular meals, and the quietly devoted management of my home, much more than I can repay. Vipro, gardener (who can turn any garden into a jungle), plumber, handyman and friend, for his one-of-a-kind company and service, deserves special mention. Lastly and most importantly I wish to appreciate my mother, who at eighty-three still finds the book 'gripping' – how many lives she's lived in one so that she is a living treasure now – thank you for being there, Aai, through the worst and best of times.

This book argues that the overwhelming question no official history of Gandhi or India is willing fully to confront is what the murder of the Mahatma really means to Indians, especially Hindus. No understanding of contemporary India or Hinduism can be complete without addressing it. No attempt to fetishize or forget, venerate or re-execute Gandhi can cover up the great disturbance and unresolved shock that this event produced. Instead of trying to deny or displace this distress, we need to come to terms with it and realize its truly transformative potential. Only then can the twin birth traumas of the subcontinent – the Partition and Gandhi's assassination – be healed. I believe that this book tries to show the way.

Prologue[1]

In his Preface to Leo Tolstoy's 'Letter to a Hindoo', Mahatma Gandhi says,

> It is a mere statement of fact to say that every Indian, whether he owns up to it or not, has national aspirations. But there are as many opinions as there are Indian nationalists, as to the exact meaning of that aspiration and more especially as to the methods to be used to attain the end.[2]

This is quite true of us, even today. That is why Gandhi is so crucial. He forces us to interrogate our notions of nationalism and our aspirations for India even as he allows a wide plurality of such responses. This book is one such attempt to understand not only Gandhi's life and message but also the idea of India by inquiring into the meaning of his death.

Gandhi's death has been commonly viewed both as murder and martyrdom. Nathuram Godse murdered him but the Mahatma martyred himself. Gandhi was not a passive victim, but an active participant. He resisted tighter security at Birla House in spite of an attempt on his life. He continued to insist on the recitation of verses from the Koran in his multi-religious prayer meetings even after members of his audience protested and he was greeted by angry slogans such as 'Death to Gandhi' by irate refugees from West Punjab, now Pakistan. He kept asking Hindus not to retaliate against the wrongs they had suffered or vent their revenge on the Muslims of Delhi, who were not responsible for what had happened on the other side of the bloody border. He fasted to restore communal harmony in Delhi. It was only after all parties had pledged their support to such a truce that Muslims, who had chosen to remain in Delhi but had fled their homes and locked up their shops for fear of reprisals, returned to their abandoned properties. Against all calculations of strategic leverage against the invading Pakistan-backed mercenaries in Kashmir, he also insisted on and succeeded in the Government of India's repatriating Rs 55 crore of Pakistan's share of the national assets after the Partition. What is more, he refused to accept that Muslims and Hindus were two nations or that a nation could be formed on the basis of religion alone.

In the days leading up to his assassination, Gandhi repeatedly declared that he would rather die than countenance the destruction of the sacred freedom that so many had sacrificed so much for. In that sense, Gandhi's self-willed martyrdom was an offering, as he himself put it, a last and desperate *yajna* – sacrifice, oblation, sacred rite – to save India. The Arabic word for martyr, *shahid*, combines two senses – to be witness and to volunteer suffering unto death for a higher, spiritual or religious cause. The Greek origin of the word *martyr* and its connotations in the Christian tradition also attest to this dual meaning of bearing testimony and undergoing sacrificial death. Gandhi, in that sense, invited the nation to bear witness to his sacrifice, which was publically staged in the grounds of his prayer meeting in the heart of the capital of newly independent India. He himself also bore testimony to his faith in *ahimsa*, non-retaliatory love, refusing to succumb to the cycle of assured mutual destruction in reactive communal massacres. The Mahatma's martyrdom, in this sense, was a mighty and potent act of love-jihad – he died to stop hatred and bloodshed; he gave us life so that we would stop taking each others'.

But writing a book on him is not easy. Gandhi's presence, the force of his personality, the directness and power of his words, and his exemplary life make him difficult to engage with, especially for admirers. Conversely, for those who dislike Gandhi, his politics, and his personality, it is equally difficult to take him seriously or to stop reacting to him. Yet, Gandhi himself shows us how to deal with powerful influences. In the same Preface to 'A Letter to a Hindoo', a text that left him so moved that he translated it into Gujarati himself and published it in his paper, *Indian Opinion*, Gandhi says of Tolstoy:

> When a man like Tolstoy, one of the clearest thinkers in the Western world, one of the greatest writers, one who, as a soldier, has known what violence is and what it can do, condemns Japan for having blindly followed the law of modern science, falsely so-called, and fears for that country 'the greatest calamities', it is for us to pause and consider whether, in our impatience of English rule, we do not want to replace one evil by another and a worse. India, which is the nursery of the great faiths of the world, will cease to be nationalist India, whatever else it may become, when it goes through the process of civilization in the shape of reproduction on that sacred soil of gun factories and hateful industrialism, which have reduced the people of Europe to a state of slavery and all but stifled among them the best instincts, which are the heritage of the human family.[3]

The Preface was written on 19 November 1909, aboard the *S.S. Kildonan Castle*, where he also wrote *Hind Swaraj*, his foundational exposition on non-violent revolution and a far-reaching critique of modernity. The Preface to the latter was composed on 22 November 1909, just three days after he wrote the Preface to 'A Letter to a Hindoo'. Indeed, some key elements of *Hind Swaraj* are taken directly from Tolstoy, for example Gandhi's advocacy of non-violent resistance to evil, his belief that Indians are themselves responsible for their own enslavement by the British, and that India should not try to replicate the civilization of the West.

Though Gandhi quotes from Tolstoy, translates him, and adopts several tenets from him, putting them into practice to the extent of calling his settlement outside Johannesburg 'Tolstoy Farm', he still retains his independence: 'One need not accept all that Tolstoy says – some of his facts are not accurately stated.'[4] This, I believe, is the clue to reading Gandhi too: whether or not the latter's facts are accurately stated, one need not accept all that Gandhi says. But what is far more important is what Gandhi says of Tolstoy at the end of his preface:

> His logic is unassailable. And, above all, he endeavours to practise what he preaches. He preaches to convince. He is sincere and in earnest. He commands attention.[5]

Gandhi's logic too, for the most part, is unassailable; he too endeavours to practice what he preaches; he too preaches to convince; he is of course sincere and in earnest – quite contrary to some who consider him cunning and calculating. No wonder he commands attention. This book is a way to attend to his death, and through that catastrophe, to the life of the nation.

Part I

Birth traumas of the nation

1   Who killed Gandhi?

A book on the persistence of Mahatma Gandhi may well begin
with trying to make sense of his death. His death, or rather
assassination, marks the point of transition between his life and
*after*life. Ultimately, it is with the latter that I shall be more
concerned here. After all, a Mahatma, or great spirit, may actually
be defined as someone whose afterlife is greater than his life. But to
break out into that vastness, the actual event of transition is crucial.
In this context, that event is Gandhi's death, which is the subject
of this book. I use the word 'event' in an Eriksonian way, as a key
occurrence that helps us unlock a larger story. In his influential
and inspired study, *Gandhi's Truth: On the Origins of Militant
Nonviolence*, Erik Erikson shows us the need to retell Gandhi's
story from alternative perspectives: 'a presence such as Gandhi's,
in order to remain alive or indeed to become alive for mankind
beyond India, must be retold in terms of a new age'.[1] That is why a
study of the murder of the Mahatma, which was nothing less than
a catastrophe for a nation newly independent, marks a convenient,
almost statutory point of departure. Just as his life was far from the
ordinary, the Mahatma's death too was stunning.

While Erikson himself warns against the danger of
'traumatology' in its all-too-predictable application to the life
of a great man, it might still be useful to examine the trauma of

Gandhi's murder on the life of an infant nation. The purpose of such an exercise would be

> to discern not only origins but traumatic ones at that – trauma meaning an experience characterized by impressions so sudden, or so powerful, or strange that they cannot be assimilated at the time and, therefore, persist from stage to stage as a foreign body seeking outlet or absorption and imposing on all development a certain irritation causing stereotypy and repetitiveness.[2]

Without succumbing entirely to the dangers of either 'originology' or 'traumatology', the meaning and aftershocks of the slaying of the 'Father of the Nation'[3] may still be fruitfully examined, especially because, as I shall show later, a satisfactory understanding of Gandhi's death still eludes us.

When it comes to his life rather than his death, Gandhi's is one of the most well documented of any that we know, with his *Collected Works* extending into nearly a hundred large volumes, not to mention the scores of biographical and historical books written on him besides. What is, perhaps, not equally known is that his assassination, too, has been more closely examined than that of almost any other great man's.[4] Apart from the dozens of accounts and interpretations that are available, it was studied and documented by the Commission of Inquiry appointed by the Government of India and headed by the Justice Jeevan Lal Kapur Commission, whose six-volume report was published in 1970.

On the one hand, the Kapur Commission Report, invaluable as it is, attempts only to examine the killing of Gandhi, notably whether there was a larger conspiracy behind it than the one hatched by the motley, almost gormless, bunch that carried out the deed and was convicted for it. I am more interested, on the other hand, in the fuller ramifications of his death rather than the mere details and circumstances of his murder. What did Gandhi die for? What, moreover, is the significance of his death? Why is it still so crucial to understand it? The answers to such questions are critical if we wish to form an appropriate estimate not only of his life, but of the life history of the nation that he was instrumental in bringing into being. In trying to address these questions, we must, of course, also engage with the one that most commentators have asked, namely, 'Who killed Gandhi? Who was responsible for his murder?' But the larger concern, with the *meaning* of Gandhi's death, with its psycho-political implications for India and its people, is more demanding of our attention than merely the criminal conspiracy to assassinate him.

As a matter of fact, to all appearances, the question 'Who killed Gandhi?' is easily answered: Gandhi was killed by Nathuram Godse, a misguided Hindu activist, as the 'official histories' of the event would put it. However, were matters as simple as that? That there was a criminal conspiracy in which a large number of people were involved was fairly obvious even at that time. Several other conspirators, in addition to the main accused, were therefore charged and tried. But as Justice Kapur unearthed in his re-examination of the evidence and by recalling the available witnesses, the conspiracy to kill Gandhi was much wider than previously suspected. Robert Payne in *The Life and Death of Mahatma Gandhi* observes, 'The attentive reader of the voluminous trial reports soon finds himself haunted by the certainty that many others who never stood trial were involved in the conspiracy'.[5] Moreover, the persistence of the ideology that resulted in the Mahatma's murder, its conspicuous presence in our midst especially on the World Wide Web, and its championing by a section of one of India's leading political parties, to say the least, enlarges the circle of responsibility. Clearly Gandhi was not killed by a single individual. The individual was perhaps just an agent of history, but behind his murderous act were larger historical, political, and ideological forces.

Such a line of thinking, nevertheless, would appear to restrict the agency in Gandhi's assassination to a particular political group if not to one individual; but is the imposition of such a limit admissible? We know for instance that the Government was quite well aware of the conspiracy to kill Gandhi; in fact the killers had botched up a bomb attempt on Gandhi's life at the same venue, Birla House, just ten days earlier, on 20 January 1948. Of the team of assassins, Madanlal Pahwa, the latest recruit and weakest link, actually an angry and restive refugee from the just-created Pakistan, was caught by the police. He not only led the investigators to the Marina Hotel in Connaught Circus where Godse had stayed, but warned them that he would be back, with the ominous prediction, '*Phir ayega*' – he will come again. Between Pahwa's capture and the actual murder committed by the very same group a few days later is the story of an incompetent and messed-up police investigation, with gaps in communication, delays, misunderstandings, and erroneous conclusions, not to mention the stand-off between the Delhi and the Bombay police.

The story of this tragic bungling that cost the country its Mahatma has been documented in great detail by the Kapur Commission report and retold with the narrative verve of a thriller by Manohar Malgonkar. Surely, then, the Union Government led by Gandhi's chosen heir Jawaharlal Nehru, with Vallabhbhai Patel, so devoted to Gandhi as the Home Minister, not to speak of the Congress Government in Maharashtra, whose Deputy Premier, Morarji Desai, another of Gandhi's disciples and later to be India's Prime Minister, was directly involved in the investigation, are also responsible for being unable to prevent the Mahatma's murder.

Indeed, Government had been aware for some time of the threat to Gandhi's life. Several refugees from Pakistan, who had lost home and hearth, whose loved ones had been raped, kidnapped and murdered, had been enraged, shouting anti-Gandhi slogans, such as '*Mahatma Gandhi murdabad*' ('death to Mahatma Gandhi', or if it is not taken literally, 'down with Mahatma Gandhi') outside his prayer meetings. One of these slogans, as reported by Manohar Malgonkar was, '*Gandhi ko marne do, hum ko makan do*' ('As to Gandhi, let him die; as to us, give us homes');[6] another one was '*Marta hai to marne do! Khoon ka badla khoon se!*' ('If he so wishes let him die, what we want is blood for blood').[7] With a section of the public so angry and with credible intelligence of a threat to the Mahatma's life, why had the Home Ministry failed to prevent the second and, this time, successful attempt on his life within the space of ten days? Despite Madanlal's arrest, despite Dr Jain's warning to the Bombay Government, despite the failed assassination attempt on 20 January 1948 at Birla House itself, the police did very little to beef up Gandhi's security, let alone to foil the plot.[8] According to Payne, the total extent of the police *bandobast* (arrangement) at Birla House was only one assistant sub-inspector, two head constables, and sixteen foot constables;[9] clearly insufficient to keep at bay the throngs of slogan-shouting refugees outside or to watch over the milling crowds inside. Gandhi, whether he or Government knew it or not, was a sitting duck – or, if we were to be more metaphorically generous to his exalted status, *paramahamsa*.[10]

I am not suggesting that Patel or Desai were deliberately negligent in allowing Gandhi to die, but surely they are liable to bear some responsibility for the event. Worse, the complicity of the entire Congress Party in the Mahatma's neglect cannot be denied. After all, Gandhi's last will and testament, written the night before his assassination, actually called for the dissolution of Congress as a political organization:

> Though split into two, India having attained political independence through means devised by the Indian National Congress, the Congress in its present shape and form, i.e., as a propaganda vehicle and parliamentary machine, has outlived its use. . . . For these and other similar reasons, the A.I.C.C. resolves to disband the existing Congress organization and flower into a Lok Sevak Sangh.[11]

So intent was he on finishing this new 'constitution' – though it was more a dissolution – of the Congress that he told Pyarelal the previous day, 'My head is reeling. And yet I must finish this', and to

Abha, his young assistant, he remarked, 'I am afraid I shall have to keep late hours'.[12] This 'constitution' was published as his 'Last Will and Testament' in the *Harijan* of 15 February 1948, a fortnight after his death. In it, instead of enjoying the spoils of office, Congress workers were enjoined by Gandhi to fan out into the countryside and become a vast volunteer corps which would, in effect, serve as a comprehensive peoples' self-help network, almost an alternative government. Surely Gandhi's attempt to snatch away the rewards of power and pelf from Congressmen, just when they had started relishing such benefits, would have dismayed if not angered most Congressmen. That this was his considered opinion is evident from earlier remarks in this vein. For instance in a fragment of a letter written from Birla House on 14 November 1947, he said:

> My suggestion is that, in so far as the Congress was intended solely to achieve swaraj and that purpose has been gained – personally I do not think that what we have gained is swaraj but at least it is so in name – this organization should be wound up and we should put to use all the energies of the country.[13]

In addition, Gandhi's demand for the repatriation of 55 crore rupees which was Pakistan's share of the exchequer would have nettled the Congress Government as it incensed his right-wing opponents; some of the former would have liked to use it as a handle to rein in Pakistan's aggression in Kashmir, while most of the latter considered it the last nail in Gandhi's coffin, proving beyond a doubt his continuing partiality to the newly created Muslim state. Gandhi, old and feeble though he may have been, was surely a thorn in the side of the Congress establishment. As early as 1946, the Congress Working Committee had at his own insistence chosen to bypass him, if necessary, in the most vital of decisions pertaining to Partition and the future of India. After 15 August 1947 his irrelevance would have been all the more obvious to the Congress rank and file. That is why I would hazard to argue that though

Godse pulled the trigger and a larger group of Hindu nationalists cheered his act, many more people, including a sizeable section of the Congress Party, cannot be totally absolved of their liability in the crime. They may not have wanted Gandhi dead, they would certainly not have tried to murder him, but by marginalizing and bypassing Gandhi they had all but 'killed' him symbolically. Gandhi himself said to an unnamed correspondent on 18 December 1947, one-and-a-half months before he was assassinated:

> I know that today I irritate everyone. How can I believe that I alone am right and all others are wrong? What irks me is that people deceive me. They should tell me frankly that I have become old, that I am no longer of any use and that I should not be in their way. If they thus openly repudiate me I shall not be pained in the least.[14]

But had Gandhi really lost the plot or was he the only one still thinking clearly in these terrible times? In the same letter he says to his correspondent, 'seeing all this, people like you should take pity on an old man like me and pray to God to take me away',[15] a wish he repeated very often in his last days. The violence and carnage around him were so intolerable to him that he would rather die than watch helplessly; or, if he remained alive, God should give him the strength to make a difference, something he tried to do until his dying day.

Whatever the case may be, his death, if not often wished for and actually invited upon himself, was certainly preventable. Payne observes wryly,

> So Gandhi died, and there was no comfort in the knowledge that his death could have been prevented. In the eyes of too many officials, he was an old man who had outlived his usefulness: he had become expendable. By negligence, by indifference, by deliberate desire on the part of many faceless

people, the assassination had been accomplished. It was a new kind of murder – the permissive assassination, and there may be many more in the future.[16]

Tushar Gandhi, the Mahatma's grandson, who wrote a very long book on this subject, is even blunter:

> The Congress government and at least some of the members of the Cabinet were fed up of the interventions of the meddlesome old man. To them, a martyred Mahatma would be easier to live with. . . . The way the investigation was carried out, and the lackadaisical approach of the police in trying to protect Gandhi's life, leads one to believe that the investigation was meant to hide more than it was meant to reveal. The measures taken by the police between 20th and 30th January 1948 were more to ensure the smooth progress of the murderers, than to try to prevent his murder.[17]

That Gandhi was inconvenient is obvious: he had not only urged the disbanding of the Congress in his 'last will and testament', but he had opposed the Partition, threatened to walk across the border into Pakistan, asked for the Viceregal Palace to be turned into a hospital, and, of course, been conspicuous by his absence at the midnight hour when India kept its 'tryst with destiny', with Nehru sworn in as the first Prime Minister.

By a similar method we can widen the circle of responsibility of Gandhi's death to a much larger section of Indian people, including those whose rights he fought for, such as the dalits, the Muslims, the women of India, and ultimately even the Hindus whose leader he was according to Muslim separatists – thus amounting to millions and millions of Indians – all of whom turned their backs on him over a period of time. To that extent were not all of these groups responsible to varying degrees for his real and metaphorical assassination? This is the line of argument that a popular commercial movie such as *Hey Ram* ends up taking. The protagonist, unlike Nathuram Godse, is actually one of us, the so-called normal middle-class Hindu, who comes precariously close to murderous rage and violence before being pulled back into a safer, wholesome, 'secularist' position. *Hey Ram* seems to suggest that there is a Gandhi-killer lurking in the deeper folds of the psyche of the average Hindu. Or, according to the more sophisticated analysis of political psychologist Ashis Nandy, the 'real' killers of Gandhi were

the anxiety-ridden, insecure, traditional elite concentrated in the urbanized, educated, partly Westernized, tertiary sector whose meaning of life Gandhian politics was taking away. Gandhi often talked about the heartlessness of the Indian literati. He paid with his life for that awareness.[18]

Who really killed Gandhi? Are we not, all of us, in one way or another, responsible for his death? Jawaharlal Nehru, Gandhi's chosen heir and successor admitted as much when he said, in speech at Jallandhar on 24 February 1948, 'We are all responsible for this unprecedented tragedy'[19] and 'It is a disgrace that [the] people of India could not save Mahatma Gandhi'.[20]

2 The event

Before we confront questions concerning the meaning of Gandhi's death it might be useful to go back to the scene of the crime, to recall to our minds that fateful day when Gandhi proceeded towards his prayer meeting, his walk across the lawn abruptly terminated before he reached his seat. Despite the cataclysmic dimensions of this event, there are not many eye-witness accounts of it.[1] One of the best of these comes from Vincent Sheean (1899–1975), an American reporter and author, who, it seems, 'innocently went to India in 1947 to find out "something about life's meaning, purpose and significance"';[2] he was fortunate enough to interview Gandhi on 27 January 1948;[3] three days later he was also present when Nathuram assassinated Gandhi.[4] The advantage of Sheean's account is that, as an outsider, he is not partial to either the camp of Gandhi followers or Gandhi haters. He manages, moreover, to offer an account that is charged with immediacy and drama, despite the physical distance of some hundred metres between him and the assassination. The following excerpt is drawn from his book, *Lead, Kindly Light*, first published in 1949:

> I got a taxi and went out to Birla House in time for the prayer-meeting. . . . It was not yet five o'clock and people were still streaming in on foot, in cars and with *tongas*. As I came on

to the prayer-ground at the end of the garden I ran into Bob Stimson, the Delhi correspondent of the B.B.C. . . . He looked at his watch and said: 'Well, this is strange. Gandhi's late. He's practically never late.'

We both looked at our watches again. It was 5:12 by my watch when Bob said: 'Here he is.'

It was one of those shining Delhi evenings, not at all warm but alight with the promise of spring . . . the Mahatma advance[d] toward us over the grass, leaning lightly on two of 'the girls', with two or three other members of his 'family' (family or followers) behind them. . . . It was not a warm evening and he was wrapped in homespun shawls. He passed by us on the other side and turned to ascend the four or five brick steps which led to the terrace or prayer-ground.

Here, as usual, there was a clump of people, some of whom were standing and some of whom had gone on their knees or bent low before him. . . . Then I heard four small, dull, dark explosions.[5] 'What's that?' I said to Bob in sudden horror. 'I don't know,' he said. I remember that he grew pale in an instant. 'Not the Mahatma!' I said, and then I knew.

Inside my own head there occurred a wavelike disturbance which I can only compare to a storm at sea – wind and wave surging tremendously back and forth . . . I recoiled upon the brick wall and leaned against it, bent almost in two. I felt the consciousness of the Mahatma leave me then – I know of no other way of expressing this: he left me.[6]

Sheean did not actually see up close what happened, though he was on the same premises, but we do get a sense from his account of the atmosphere that fatal afternoon.

Manubehn,[7] his grandniece, who was actually by Gandhi's side when Nathuram fired the semi-automatic Beretta pistol, wrote a briefer, more dispassionate account that very midnight in her journal. What is truly remarkable is her tone of quiet detachment, something

Gandhi would have been very proud of in one of his closest associates in these last days of his life. Indeed, he had prepared and trained her for this eventuality through his repeated remarks and forewarnings after coming to Delhi on 9 September 1948.

Before proceeding towards the prayer meeting, Gandhi had been absorbed in a serious conversation with Sardar Patel, the Home Minister of newly independent India. In fact, he was late because no one wished to disturb this conference to remind him of the time. While talking to Patel, Gandhi also had his 'last supper' of one-and-a-half cups of goat's milk, the same quantity of vegetable soup, and three oranges.[8] He had also continued spinning during this time. The moment Patel's daughter, Maniben, informed him that he was already late for the prayer meeting, Gandhi got up. Manubehn picked up his pen, spittoon, and spectacle case, along with her notebook and prayer beads, and they 'set out for the prayer ground'.[9]

Manu tells us that Bapu, who had been such a stickler for time, had at last stopped living by the clock: 'You are my timekeepers . . . why should I consult a watch?'[10] Manu and Abha joked, 'Bapuji, your watch must be feeling quite neglected!'[11] After a while Bapu rejoined, 'I do not like being late for the prayer meeting. Today's delay is due to your negligence. . . . Even a minute's delay for the prayer causes me great discomfort'.[12] Manu, the author of this account, was to Bapu's right, his hand on her right shoulder as they walked.

When they had reached the prayer dais, 'a well-built young man, clad in Khaki clothes, tore through the crowd from the right,'[13] and accosted them. It was Nathuram Godse. He made a gesture as if of obeisance, joining his palms together. Gandhi was used to people touching his feet, though he didn't like it. This, Manu says, is what they assumed the man intended to do. Manu, stopping him from leaning forward, admonishes Nathuram: 'Brother, Bapuji is already late for prayers. Why are you bothering him?'[14] But Nathuram, quite roughly, pushes away Manu. All the things she is carrying, her notebook and prayer *mala*, Bapu's spectacles and spittoon, fall to the ground. Manu, at first, ignoring this, continues to remonstrate with Godse. But when her prayer beads also fall, she bends down to pick them up. Before she can retrieve them, 'Three deafening bullet shots rent the air'.[15] Before she can even begin to understand what is happening, it is all over:

> The shots had been fired at point blank range. There was sudden darkness, and the air was filled with smoke. The crowd began to surge forward. And in the midst of this sudden darkness, smoke and confusion, Bapu fell.[16]

We shall see how, as Bapu's body touches the ground, and crumples, it is as if an epoch has come to an end. Manu clearly says that Bapu's last words were '*He Rama! He Rama!*'[17] In fact, even as he falls, his hands are up, trying to reciprocate his assassin's 'fake *namaskar*'.[18] Manu comments on this gesture of the fallen Mahatma, 'And as he fell, his palms remained joined, as if pleading for forgiveness and mercy from the people'.[19] A guiltless man, even as he has been brought down, is still seeking to absolve his killers and those left behind alive. Taking everyone's blame upon himself, he seeks their forgiveness even as his life-breath ebbs away.

Manu relates how people rush to try to stop the Mahatma from collapsing, but to no avail. There he is, lying on the 'green lap' of Mother Earth. The time elapsed in this duration, according to Manu, is just three or four minutes:

> The bullets had been fired so near me, that for a while, my ears were deaf and I could not hear a thing. It took some moments before I could fully grasp the situation – so bewildered had I become. It is impossible to express our mental condition at that moment.[20]

The time on Bapu's watch, which he had stopped consulting, comes to a standstill at 5:17 p.m. His white khadi clothes are streaked with blood. No doctor is available. Another ten minutes pass before he is carried back to his room. Even his personal physician and close associate, Dr Sushila Nayar's first-aid box is found to be empty. There is, of course, no aid to the Mahatma's condition. He is dead. In any case, he had little use of medicines when he was alive; '*Rama nama*' (the Lord's name, chanted) had been his only doctor.[21] Manu says, 'And now no one but Rama could help him'.[22] The irony is that actually no one but Rama can help her and those left behind either; Gandhi himself did not need help any more. *Rama nama*, Gandhi's only medicine, worked as well in death as it did in life. It is the one unfailing remedy, whose action is identical, whether in this world or the next. Ferried across the ocean of *samsara* on the boat of *Rama nama*, the lifeless body of the Mahatma, in fact, is beyond human help, least of all from a doctor. Earlier, with his persistent cough for which he refused antibiotics, Gandhi may have needed *Rama nama* to cure himself. Now, having crossed to the other side, *Rama nama* has actually done its work; no more help is called for. Patel, the last major leader to have been with Gandhi, who has just reached his residence, now rushes back. Crowds have gathered as Gandhi's near and dear are sobbing inconsolably. Manu says that it was Bapu who had often comforted her when she cried in the past; after all, she is still just a teenager. But today, 'no amount of wailing . . . could induce Bapuji to open his eyes'.[23]

Just as no doctor is at hand and the first-aid box is empty, no hospital in the vicinity is able to send either a doctor or ambulance. When Brijkrishna Chandiwala, after failing to elicit any response on the phone, actually goes to Willingdon Hospital, he has to return empty-handed, unaccompanied by any doctor.[24] The Father of the Nation lies unattended till Dr Bhargava comes to examine him for the last time. At 12:30 that day, Gandhi had been trying to secure a building that would house Dr Bhargava's nursing home and orphanage.[25] Now the good doctor carries out a detailed examination only to pronounce the foregone verdict, which he does in the most humane and gentle way: 'Manu, child, Bapu is now no more!'[26]

Gandhi has been shot with the seven-chamber semi-automatic M1934 Beretta pistol bearing the serial number 606824. Godse, who had wielded the gun, fired three shots. The first passed through Gandhi's stomach, 'two and a half inches above the navel, and three and half inches to the right of the sternum'.[27] The second bullet 'pierced the chest at a spot one and a half inch[es] to the right of the breast-bone'.[28] Both bullets had emerged cleanly to the other side and fallen to the ground. The third bullet punctured Gandhi's right lung, and remained lodged there. There was a heavy loss of blood and Gandhi's face was ashen.

K. M. Munshi, Devdas Gandhi, Gandhi's youngest son, and Devdas's youngest son, Gopalkrishna Gandhi, also arrive. A while later, so does Jawaharlal Nehru. Manu says, 'And Panditji! He hid his face in Sardar Patel's lap and sobbed like a child'.[29] There are now tens of thousands of people thronging the grounds of Birla House. In the melee, Bapu's spectacles, which had fallen to the ground, and his sandals, have gone missing. Manu, who had clipped Bapu's nails in the afternoon while he had been talking to Patel, now does not throw them away: 'I carefully picked up these nails, and, as if they were precious jewels, I safely tucked them into my box.'[30] They remained with her. The Governor-General, formerly the last Viceroy of India, Lord Mountbatten, also arrives. Patel makes an announcement on the All India Radio. Nehru, who is to speak too, breaks into sobs, finally managing to complete his sentence, 'Our Bapu . . . Bapu is now no more with us'.[31] In the meanwhile, the throngs outside wish to have a last glimpse of Gandhi, so there is talk of moving him to the balcony where everyone can better see his body. Nehru, in a momentary lapse, says to Manu, 'Go and ask Bapu what arrangements we should make!'[32] Though Nehru and the other leaders of the Congress have always turned to Gandhi in their hours of crises, there is a poignant irony in asking him what to do with his own dead body, even as the crowds crave for a last glimpse. Manu bursts into tears as Nehru comes to his senses again.[33]

The Gita recitation, at K. M. Munshi's behest, has already begun. Now dignitaries from other lands, members of the diplomatic corps, seconded to the capital of the newly independent India, also start arriving. Not far behind are photographers and members of the press. All through, Bapu's face is utterly peaceful, body perfectly relaxed, as if he is 'in a deep, deep sleep'.[34] The body is moved to the balcony, placed in such a posture that it can be seen by the flocking crowds. A spontaneous cry rends the air, 'Mahatma Gandhi *ki jai!*' – Victory to Mahatma Gandhi. Manu says that the crowd thunders this slogan again and again, weeping, and showering coins and flowers on the departed Mahatma's body.[35]

At 2 a.m. on 31 January, the body is bathed in the waters of the Yamuna. The fallen prayer beads along with a garland of hand-spun yarn are placed around its neck in recognition of the role the latter had played in the fight for Svaraj. Bapu is then anointed with sandalwood paste, his forehead embellished with a *kumkum tilak*, the red auspicious mark[36] of victory. Near his head, in rose petals, are inscribed his last words, '*He Rama*', and by his feet, the sacred syllable, OM. The rest of Manu's narrative describes the most impressive, even glorious funeral procession; Gandhi's body placed in a gun carriage, pulled by both leaders and the masses on its way to its place of cremation, Raj Ghat, on the banks of the Yamuna. There were thousands of armed soldiers who accompanied the gun carriage carrying the body of the apostle of non-violence to his final destination, an irony certainly not lost on most commentators.

Yasmin Khan in her essay 'Performing Peace' shows that the newly formed Nehruvian state consolidated its hold on power and derived considerable legitimacy from Gandhi's assassination:

it was not only the fact of Gandhi's death itself but through the performance of the attendant rituals, ceremonies and the public and private manifestations of grief that Indian state sovereignty was consolidated and extended.[37]

The cremation rituals, distribution of ashes, and national mourning that followed all contributed to this process. Both Nehru, seen as his heir, and the Congress Party benefited because they were able to capitalize on the sympathy generated by Gandhi's killing. Such a pattern has been seen over and over again in the subcontinent so that the deaths of Indira Gandhi, Zulfikar Ali Bhutto, Mujibur Rahman, Rajiv Gandhi, Biju Patnaik, and others, ensured the rise to power of their political heirs and successors. But to dwell much longer on such details shifts our attention from Gandhi's death to the performance of the funeral and its after-effects on the Indian state. Given our main focus on the death itself, it is to this central event that we must perforce return.

3 The post-mortem

Gandhi was, of course, murdered; shot point-blank by Nathuram Godse who pumped three bullets into his chest with an M1934 Beretta semi-automatic pistol on the evening of 30 January 1948. This much is known or, at any rate, not disputed. Godse himself along with his accomplices stood trial. He and Narayan Apte were sentenced to death, and hanged on 15 November 1949 in the Ambala jail. They were cremated shortly thereafter in the jail compound. Then their ashes, mixed with soil, were immersed in the Ghaggar at an unmarked, undisclosed, and now therefore unknown spot.[1] The Government was careful that there would be no memorial to Gandhi's killers nor their relics ever used to strengthen the ideology they stood for. Godse's personality cult, not to speak of his ideology, were, however, promoted and perpetuated textually and extra-textually by his brother and fellow conspirator, Gopal Godse. It is, of course, an entirely different matter that Gandhi himself was against judicial killings, being an opponent of capital punishment. Not only Jawaharlal Nehru but also Gandhi's two sons petitioned against Godse's hanging. Nevertheless, the State following its own laws and principles, the Indian Penal Code being largely a British creation, sent the two condemned men to the gallows to hang until they were dead.

The two assassins had a relatively quiet death, except that Godse, if eye-witness accounts are to be believed, struggled for over 15 minutes at the scaffold while Apte went quickly. Their cremation and the immersion of their ashes were hushed up, but it was not as if the Godse legacy ended quietly there. Nathuram's younger brother, Gopal, was sentenced to life imprisonment for his role as accessory to the murder. After serving nearly 15 years, his sentence was commuted for good behaviour. On his release, he returned to Pune, his home town, where he was not only welcomed by his co-ideologists but, astonishingly, felicitated publicly on 12 November 1964 by a group of well-known citizens who still regarded Gandhi's assassination as a national service.

Reports of this felicitation were published in the press, notably in the *Indian Express* of 14 November 1965. G. V. Ketkar, Bal Gangadhar Tilak's grandson and well-known Pune resident, is said to have boasted that he knew of Nathuram's plans before the latter actually shot Gandhi. These remarks created a furore in Mantralaya, where the Maharashtra Legislative Assembly, then dominated by the Congress Party, is housed. Some Members of the House complained to the Central Government that the whole truth of the conspiracy to assassinate the Mahatma had not yet been uncovered, that actually the number of culprits and wrongdoers might be considerably larger. The Central Government took the matter seriously enough to appoint, albeit several months later in 1966, a retired Supreme Court judge, Justice Jeevan Lal Kapur, to investigate. The learned judge took three years to inquire into the matter, questioning and cross-examining several hundred witnesses. The result was the Report of the Commission of Inquiry, an exhaustive document in six volumes, the result of the recalling and examination of all those witnesses and participants who were still alive 20 years after the event.

But even after the Report of the Kapur Commission, the issue of Gandhi's death has not faded away. It has been remembered in book-length accounts and lengthy studies of several notable authors, the more recent of which have included those by Robert Payne, Ashis Nandy, and Gandhi's own grandson, Tushar Gandhi. The latter's retelling, *Let's Kill Gandhi*, is nearly a thousand pages in length. More controversial is Pradip Dalvi's Marathi play, *Me Nathuram Godse Boltoy*. The play was at first not found suitable for staging by the Maharashtra State Drama Scrutiny Board, but after the Hindu nationalist coalition of the Shiv Sena and Bharatiya Janata Party came to power, it was cleared in 1998. In a series of Marathi articles written in the same year and later collected as a book sarcastically entitled *Nathuramayan*, Y. D. Phadke offers a detailed and painstaking analysis of the distortions and inaccuracies in this play, which Dalvi had claimed was based on 'history'.

Phadke proves that the play, while pretending to be objective and balanced, tries to turn Godse into a hero and martyr instead of a misdirected assassin. One of the most egregiously insulting distortions in the play is that it shows Gandhi's grandson, Devdas, then the Editor of *Hindustan Times*, visiting Godse in Ambala jail, offering to appeal against his death sentence by representing Godse in the Supreme Court of India, as if convinced of the 'justness' of his father's murderer's case. Phadke shows that not only is there no record of Devdas visiting Nathuram in the Ambala jail, nor was there a Supreme Court in India then; this figment of Dalvi's imagination is meant only to show Gandhi's own grandson exonerating Nathuram, thereby suggesting that viewers may also do the same. The facts, as Robert Payne has pointed out in *The Life and Death of Mahatma Gandhi* (1969), are rather the opposite. It was Godse who wrote to Ramdas Gandhi, because the latter, who had wanted him to repent, was willing to have a dialogue with him. But, ultimately, Ramdas and Godse never met[2] because the latter's letter shows that he felt 'convinced' that he was right and that he could logically defend his action. He said he was more than willing to chant the Gita with Ramdas because he (Godse) believed that he had acted according to the Gita.[3] Ramdas, it would appear, had no interest in meeting such an unrepentant assassin, so convinced of the correctness of his actions.

In another attempt to glorify Nathuram, Dalvi invents a police inspector called Sheikh who is not only present at the assassination, but is later assigned to Nathuram on guard duty. This Sheikh is shown to have a daughter, Zubeida, who in Bollywood style, offers flowers at the spot where Nathuram sits in the courtroom and, what is more, prays for his well-being at the mosque each day. Why should Zubeida come to love Nathuram and pray for him so devotedly? That riddle is never solved. Zubeida, moreover, is pregnant; Nathuram sends her a message through Sheikh:

> If you really love this brother of yours, look after the baby in your womb. You will give birth to a son. Teach him my value. If another Gandhi is created on this soil, this country will need another Nathuram. We want Nathuram. Another Nathuram.[4]

This cry for more Nathurams, born though they be to Muslim mothers, to kill the Gandhis to come is an incredible piece of effrontery by a playwright who claims to be 'neutral' and 'objective' in his portrayals of both Gandhi and Godse.

Dalvi's play, Phadke demonstrates, is based mostly on Gopal Godse's various publications. These include not only Nathuram's own defence in the court, but also several 'histories' of the assassination that Gopal Godse penned after serving out his life-sentence as Nathuram's co-conspirator. Indeed, these books may be considered as constituting a coherent discourse not only justifying the murder, but also providing the ideological basis for continuing anti-Gandhism. Part of the Godse myth as perpetrated by these texts consists in portraying him not as a misguided fanatic or an ordinary criminal but as a well-intentioned, rational, and clear-headed patriot. As Dalvi shows in his play, Gandhi's assassin, Nathuram Godse, in fact made no attempts either to flee or resist arrest. Instead, he actually waited to be apprehended even as the crowd around Gandhi ran helter-skelter in the ensuing melee. This was indeed his historic moment: for him to run away, even if it were easy to do so, would have been self-defeating.

Godse, of course, was not alone; there was a conspiracy to kill Gandhi, as the Government had already uncovered. The conspirators were members or sympathizers of the Hindu Mahasabha, inspired by its president V. D. Savarkar. The latter himself stood trial and was acquitted for lack of sufficient evidence, but the suspicion that he was directly or indirectly involved in the murder lingers to this day.[5] Later attempts were made to link the assassination to the Rashtriya Swayamsevak Sangh (RSS), a right-wing Hindu organization, which was banned for a few years immediately after the murder; however it flourishes today, the ban on it having been lifted within a couple of years. Godse, himself, had been a member of the RSS for some time but left it later.[6] As Payne observes, 'The attentive reader of the voluminous trial reports soon finds himself haunted by the certainty that many others who never stood trial were involved in the conspiracy'.[7]

It was obvious then as it is now that Gandhi's assassins were Hindu nationalists who thought that he was the greatest obstacle to their goal to bring about a *Hindu Rashtra* or Hindu nation. India, although partitioned, had already become independent. Now they perhaps hoped that killing Gandhi would force the country to alter its ways to a course more favourable to their ideology, even if it did not convert it fully into a Hindu nation. These zealots hated what Gandhi stood for. They considered him the enemy of Hindu interests, holding him responsible for the Partition, which to them was an outcome of Gandhi's favouring Muslims over Hindus.

The book *May It Please Your Honour*, in which Gopal Godse published his brother's defence during the in-camera trial, is actually Nathuram's elaborate and lengthy justification of his action as it is a cogent charge-sheet against Gandhi. A detailed political dossier, it outlines Nathuram's own version of the history of the freedom movement and its ultimate failure to protect the interests of the Hindus. Much of this document is easily available on the Internet,[8] which demonstrates its continuing currency. From the number of hits and comments that Nathuram's indictment of Gandhi has attracted, it is clear that Godse still has many admirers, especially in the Indian diaspora. This attests not only to Nathuram's rhetorical skills but also to widespread ignorance of the facts of the assassination, despite extensive documentation over the years. Nathuram cleverly conceals some facts, distorts others, and tells outright lies from time to time to create an image of an irrational and stubborn false 'Mahatma', the 'Father of the Nation' who holds his country to ransom with his fads, whims and fasts. The 'victims' of the Mahatma's sins of omission and commission are, of course, the Hindus, whose self-sacrificing champion and saviour Nathuram projects himself to be. Gandhi's killing, according to this retelling of it, is not a murder but a heroic execution conducted on behalf of the Hindus by Nathuram. While it is fair to listen to both sides of the story, the continuing championing of Godse by Hindu communalists remains puzzling, if not distressing. Godse's whole argument hinges on how the removal of Gandhi was the sacred duty of any patriotic Hindu. Godse actually invokes Gandhi's favourite text, the Bhagawad Gita, to justify his actions. That the killers of Gandhi continue to occupy a space in India's political spectrum as well as civil society is also borne out by the fact that Radha Rajan's recent book, *Eclipse of the Hindu Nation: Gandhi and His Freedom Struggle*, reiterates many of Godse's accusations under the guise of a new history of the freedom struggle. The cult of Nathuram survives, even flourishes, thanks to the efforts of his brother Gopal Godse and the numerous Hindu nationalists who support the 'Godse thesis' against Gandhi.

4   The memorialization

The starting point of this inquiry into the wider and deeper ramifications of the death of Gandhi may be traced to a course I taught on 'M. K. Gandhi: Study of an Author' at the Centre for English studies, Jawaharlal Nehru University, in the winter semester of 2009. What I had felt intuitively about the significance of Gandhi's death gradually became clearer and clearer as the course progressed. But the turning point was the field trip to the various sites and institutions associated with Gandhi in Delhi. I scarcely understood it then, but this field trip turned into an interrogation of both the dead and the living Gandhi.

Gandhi's death was palpable, in more senses than one, most materially in the monuments that memorialized him but also less obviously in the decaying or moribund institutions founded or named after him, some of which we visited. Yet despite the all-pervasive atmosphere of decay there was something vital, even vibrant about his presence in the capital of India. More startling and unforgettable, however, was the unresolved cognitive discomfort generated by his actual assassination. It was this lingering, brooding sense of disturbance, even irresolvable distress that remained as the defining after-effect of the field trip. The assassination of the Father of the Nation, clearly, is something we have not been able to come to terms with. This book endeavours if not to resolve this crisis, then at least to address it comprehensively.

Delhi, destroyed and rebuilt several times, remains an imperial city – like Beijing, Tokyo, Seoul, Istanbul, Rome, Madrid, London, or St Petersburg. Though it is also one of the great cities of the world, a seat of power and majesty for hundreds of years, Delhi has always also been a city of tombs, cenotaphs and memorials to the dead. It is not as if the city itself conveys a sense of death, only that its grandest buildings usually commemorate some dead king or other. And how many such dynasties ruled Delhi, each leaving behind one impressive catacomb after another? From the mythical times of the Pandavas to the Tomara and Chauhan Rajputs, and thence, to the dynasties of Mamluks, Khiljis, Tughlaqs, Sayyids, Lodhis and Mughals, to the various Viceroys of British India, right up to the several memorials to our recent leaders like Mahatma Gandhi, Jawaharlal Nehru, Charan Singh and Indira Gandhi. Some of Delhi's grandest buildings are these tombs, of Altamash and Balban, Ghiyasuddin and Feroz Shah Tughlaq, Mohammad Shah and Sikandar Lodhi, Humayun and Safdar Jung, right down to Gandhi's Raj Ghat and Indira Gandhi's Shakti Sthal.

Interestingly, Delhi contains the mausoleums of not just kings and emperors but also saints and sages. All around Mehrauli, the first city of the Islamic conquerors of Delhi, are the tombs of many *fakirs*, *pirs* and saints, most of whose names have now been forgotten. Of those remembered, Delhi is a resting place of some of the greatest Sufi masters, especially of the Chisti order: not only Khwaja Qutubudin Bakhtiyar Kaki but the even more charismatic and popular Hazarat Nizamuddin, who is called *Mehboob-e-Ilahi* (Beloved of Allah), is buried here. The former was the direct disciple and successor of the founder of the lineage, Khwaja Moinuddin Chisti (Garib Nawaz) of Ajmer, and the latter the disciple of Bakhtiyar Kaki's disciple, the celebrated Baba Farid Ganj-e-Shakkar. The last great Sufi saint of Delhi, of the same lineage, was Khwaja Nasirudin *Chirag-e-Dilli* (the Lamp of

Delhi). The localities Nizamuddin and Chirag Dilli derive their names from these very saints. Indeed, the city is literally littered with hundreds of graves of Sufi savants.

But Delhi is famous not only for the graves of these sufis. Right beside Jawaharlal Nehru University is the shrine of Baba Gangnath, where the great Nath yogis are commemorialized. The Mehrauli area, even before Muslim conquest, was dotted with Jain temples, where similar statues of Tirthankars and Jinas, those who have conquered all their enemies and passed beyond the world of process, are enshrined. Not only is this city the final resting place of all these, it is the site of the martyrdom of the ninth Sikh guru, Guru Tegh Bahadur, for whom two gurdwaras, Sisganj in Chandni Chowk, and Rakab Ganj in Raisina Hill, at the heart of New Delhi, were built. More recently, the Delhi Government built another massive memorial to the Guru on the Singhu border of Delhi, handed over to the nation by Rahul Gandhi in July 2011. Interestingly, Rahul Gandhi's grandmother, Indira Gandhi, was murdered by her Sikh bodyguards; following her assassination, nearly 4000 Sikhs were killed in Delhi in anti-Sikh riots during the first days of her son and Rahul's father, Rajiv Gandhi's term as Prime Minister of India. The eighth Sikh Guru, Har Kishen, who was Tegh Bahadur's nephew, also died in Delhi of smallpox at the age of seven. The magnificent Bangla Sahib Gurdwara in New Delhi was built to commemorate his death. Therefore Gandhi comes at the end of a long line of holy predecessors and lies in good company.

To compare the tombs of emperors and saints, however, yields curious results. When one wanders through Mehrauli, Delhi's first Muslim city, one notices that the tombs of the kings are in ruins while those of the saints are centres of living pilgrimage and active social life. Ghiyasuddin Balban (1206–1287) ruled Delhi with an iron hand for 20 years, but today his tomb is a burnt-out pile of sandstone and mud, overgrown with grass and stubble. Just a stone's throw away lies the pristine and almost unchanged sanctuary of his older contemporary, Khwaja

Qutubudin Bakhtiyar Kaki (1173–1235). Attacked and damaged in the aftermath of the Partition, it was restored at the behest of Gandhi, who himself attended the Urs (annual feast) of the saint in January 1948. This shrine attracts hundreds of devotees every day and is still a centre for spiritual practices. Similarly, not too far from the Khwaja's *darga* are many more sites of the Jain religion, several of which had been demolished to build Muslim Mehrauli. One such shrine is the Dada Bari, where many Jinas and Siddhas (perfected beings) are represented in stoic and stereotypical postures signifying their transcendence of earthly demands and defilements. In the area that is now known by his name lies the grave and shrine of Hazarat Nizamuddin Auliya. Here at all times of the day, well into the late hours of the evening, devotees and supplicants flock to offer flowers and *chadars* (a ceremonial sheet of cloth), pray and fervently ask for boons. Such shrines are centres of worship and pilgrimage, with throngs of devotees. Similarly, all the gurdwaras associated with Guru Har Kishen and Tegh Bahadur continue to be active centres of devotion, with crowds of visitors and worshippers. The tombs of the emperors of Delhi, on the other hand, have not fared so well. The more obscure are in total ruin, while the famous ones are tourist attractions, maintained by the Archaeological Survey of India. Of these the most celebrated is Humayun's tomb, which today is a World Heritage site, recognized by UNESCO. This means that it has been restored at the cost of millions of dollars, with an entrance fee for visitors that is higher for foreigners than for locals. It was here that the last Mughal emperor, Bahadur Shah Zafar, defeated and deposed, had taken shelter with hundreds of his followers and dependents. Of course, he was not saved; his sons were hanged and he was transported to Rangoon, in Burma. The memorials to dead kings, were it not for some official patronage and management, would be vandalized and overrun by illegal occupants, as many ancient buildings in the space-starved cities of India have been.

Of the great dead and buried, only Tegh Bahadur and Gandhi have two or more memorials dedicated to them. This struck me during our class field trip to Raj Ghat, the 'royal steps' leading to the bank of the Yamuna river, the place where Gandhi's body was cremated, and where his ashes now officially lie in state. In addition to Raj Ghat, another famous complex memorializes Gandhi. This is the Gandhi Smriti (literally 'Gandhi Memorial'), just a few kilometres away, also in the heart of New Delhi's elite residential zone, which has some of the most expensive real estate in India. This was the erstwhile Birla House, the home of G. D. Birla, probably India's richest man at independence, and the place where the Mahatma was murdered by Nathuram Godse.

This double commemorialization makes Gandhi special; it is almost as if he combined in himself the majesty of temporal power, for which the state built a memorial, and the piety of a saint, for which he is remembered today at the site where he was felled by his assassin. Gandhi thus combined in himself both temporal power and spiritual authority. Before Gandhi, Guru Tegh Bahadur represented a similar confluence of '*miri piri*' (worldly glory and spiritual power); after being tortured at Aurangzeb's behest for refusing to change his faith, he was beheaded in Chandni Chowk, the great boulevard of medieval Delhi stretching from the seat of imperial power, the Red Fort, to the royal Fatehpuri Mosque. Where his decapitated head fell, many decades later, a great gurdwara was erected called Sis Ganj Sahib (*sis* meaning head). After his decapitation, it is said that despite the large posse of Mughal troops guarding his martyred body, some devotees managed to smuggle his remains away and cremate them in the vicinity of Raisina. On that spot a Gurdwara stands today called Rakab Ganj Sahib (*rakab* meaning body). This double commemoration is not surprising: the great Guru was both the temporal and the religious leader of his people, as Gandhi himself became 372 years later.

In one of the most eloquent tributes on his death, it was Sarojini Naidu, the poet and national leader, who noticed the strange appropriateness of Gandhi's death in the city of emperors and kings:

> I used to wonder very often during his many fasts in which I was privileged to serve him, to solace him, to make him laugh, because he wanted the tonic laughter of his friends – I used to wonder, supposing he died in Sevagram, supposing he died in Noakhali, supposing he died in some far off place, how should we reach him? It is therefore right and appropriate that he died in the city of kings, in the ancient site of the old Hindu empires, in the site on which was built the glory of the Mughals, in this place that he made India's capital wresting it from foreign hands, it is right that he died in Delhi; it is right that his cremation took place in the midst of the dead kings who are buried in Delhi, for he was the kingliest of all kings. And it is right also that he who was the apostle of peace should have been taken to the cremation ground with all the honours of a great warrior; far greater than all warriors who led armies to battle was this little man, the bravest, the most triumphant of all. Delhi is not only today historically the Delhi of seven kingdoms; it has become the centre and the sanctuary of the greatest revolutionary who emancipated his enslaved country from foreign bondage and gave to it its freedom and its flag.[1]

Sarojini, with her poetic gifts and vision, had long ago noticed how Gandhi was both kingly and saintly, how his death was at once both royal and saintly, how his commemorialization would therefore partake of both discursive traditions.

On Gandhi's death his anointed heir and successor, Jawaharlal Nehru, was also aware of the grave importance of the appropriate way to memorialize him. As Yasmin Khan observes,

> Nehru was strikingly self-conscious about Gandhi's memorialization and reflexive about the ways in which

Gandhi's memory could be usefully appropriated after his death. While wishing to honour him and to avoid opportunistic commemoration, Nehru astutely recognized the utility of Gandhi's death-memorials to the national cause. The importance of theatricality, performance, ritual and commemoration was as well understood by Nehru as by his viceregal predecessor – 'brick and mortar has its uses', he wrote on a proposed national memorial for Gandhi, 'and is desirable to give some solid and substantial shape to our work. This has a psychological importance and a permanence'.[2]

Despite such attempts to impose an authorized and official way of commemorating the fallen Mahatma, the more popular and vernacular attempts to remember him, as we shall see, could not entirely be suppressed.

Nehru, however, 'consistently attempted to define the limits of commemoration and to create a centralized monopoly on the project of Gandhi's memorialisation'.[3] First of all, he had to contend with those who, literally, wanted a 'piece' of Gandhi: ashes, relics, even a bit of the soil where he was killed or cremated. That is why he recommended the most 'modern' of materials, cement concrete, for the place of cremation. In an undated note that the Union Cabinet accepted on 3 February 1948, Nehru had recommended that 'The surface of the platform on which Mahatma Gandhi's body was cremated may be cemented in order that people in search of sacred earth from the spot will not be able to tamper with it'.[4] Khan, citing this note, remarks: 'Concrete, then, the ultimate symbol of the modernizing and developmental aspirations of the postcolonial state, could, quite literally, be used to seal Gandhi's memory and to limit people's interaction with his corporeal remains'.[5] Nehru also actively discouraged the indiscriminate proliferation of statues, especially ungainly and ugly ones.[6] Yet hundreds of statues did come up, some lending themselves to easy satirization as in the film *English, August*, which shows Gandhi's walking stick propping up one from the behind, almost as if suggesting 'up his ____'. Today, it is Bhim Rao Ambedkar's turn to be thus memorialized all over India, in a blue suit, holding a book, and pointing ahead.

Even if the state's investment in Gandhi's commemorialization was severely disciplined, if not curtailed, the two monuments in Delhi bear, albeit differently, its all too evident stamp. Yet the contrast between Raj Ghat and Gandhi Smriti may be seen as the difference between how state power and civil society tried to come to terms with this dual legacy of Gandhi. What do we make of this man, who was at once the tallest political leader and hero of his times and also the nation's conscience-keeper and public saint? It was therefore somewhat uncanny that when we went from Raj Ghat to Gandhi Smriti the first question that the Director of Gandhi Smriti asked was, 'Please tell me how you felt at Raj Ghat as compared to what you feel here?'

Intrigued, we quickly brought to our minds our experience of Raj Ghat. We had parked our bus in the official parking lot which contained many other tourist coaches. The first thing that struck me was how touristy and commercial Raj Ghat had become – a 'must-see' in the itinerary of every visitor to Delhi. Though it seemed like a quiet day, we still had many tourists, including busloads of school children, visiting along with us. We went around the niches that, almost like meditation chambers of some ancient monastery or the ramparts of a fortification, adorned the periphery of Gandhi's Samadhi. Each niche contained a quotation by Gandhi, written in the many different languages of India. We, this class, at a national university, made up of students from different parts of India, were moved to read these quotations, trying to decipher their different scripts and languages. We were from different parts of the country, spoke different languages, belonged to different religions and ethnicities, but Gandhi had helped to make us a nation. And because we were a nation, we were all together today, studying at one of India's better universities in the capital, open to admissions to students from all over the subcontinent and beyond. Somehow, Gandhi was central to our story, to who we had become.

We went to the central flame where a bhajan, not entirely euphonious, was in progress. Then someone commented that the place was bound to be spruced up if a foreign dignitary were to visit. Of course it was customary for every visiting head of state to place a wreath on the grave of the Father of the Nation, but I was glad that there was no such visit that day or this whole monument would be cordoned off for security reasons. Raj Ghat, on further reflection, did exude a feeling of being slightly unkempt that day, even somewhat derelict. As if no one really cared for the Mahatma except to pay lip service to his memory, certainly not to engage deeply with his words and deeds. There were broken tiles and sandstone masonry; in several places the paint had peeled off and some of the letters in the plaques bearing his words had been chipped off. True, there was no garbage lying about, but the gardens were not in perfect shape.

We left the *sarkari* (official) precinct to connect with Gandhi's spirit in a less conspicuous place nearby. Sitting in a circle on a grassy knoll, we commenced on an impromptu discussion on Gandhi, which later erupted into a series of multilingual songs on him and the freedom movement. I for one, was startled at the variety and range of talent present in our own small class, and was also surprised to find my students able to break free from their detached and dispassionate academic stance to something more spontaneous and involved. From being a sombre and sober reflection on Gandhi at the site of his Samadhi, our little gathering had almost turned into a celebration. The singing drew us together and our spirits soared, we broke into laughter, conversation, and song, without the least self-consciousness. Just then a large group of schoolchildren from a very modest government school seemed to surround us; they were a boisterous, carefree, and happy lot, tumbling down the grassy slope, noisily playing, chasing or fighting with one another.

At that moment I understood in a flash what being in a free country really meant. The most humble and ordinary citizens as well as their children could romp all over the very bones of the founding fathers of their nation. To be 'free' meant not so much that you could do as you pleased, but that you actually owned your country. In British India the forefathers of these children would have never dared to run amuck in the lawns around India Gate or in any of the exclusive environs of New Delhi. They were servants and outsiders in their own land, their movements and access restricted as the signboards in many places clearly indicated, 'Indians not allowed'.

But while I was thinking over my experience at Raj Ghat, Dr Savita Singh, the Director of the Gandhi Smriti, had gone on to answer her own question. Raj Ghat represents the death of Gandhi while Gandhi Smriti commemorates his life, she said almost triumphantly. She had a point, I thought, when I recalled to my mind the slightly sad and isolated samadhi, with the quietly burning flame, at the centre of a huge manicured lawn within a faceless government complex, frequented by visiting dignitaries and curious tourists. But she was only partially correct, because our own corroboree and the capers of the frolicking, unruly school children certainly suggested that Raj Ghat was not just a place of the dead but a favourite holiday destination, even a picnic spot, where life in its variety asserted itself in celebrating the freedoms which the frail old Mahatma had died to uphold. It seemed to me that Raj Ghat, 'tainted' by officialdom and dampened perhaps by the odour of death, nevertheless remained vibrant, attracting the living in their teeming and irresistible variety, represented not only by tourists, hawkers, unemployed youth, retired loungers and occasional pilgrims, but also by frisky children and furtive lovers. The vernacular appropriation and celebration of the monument had overshadowed its official script. Was there something intrinsic to Gandhi that defied the deadening clasp of state officialdom, or is this the common fate of any public monument in our country, not exclusive to Gandhi?

I was reminded of another memorial to Gandhi, in far off Pondicherry, where right in the middle of the promenade by the sea, stands his large, somewhat muscular statue, avuncular but larger than life. Under his white French-style canopy, the dark, bronze Gandhi looks to be smiling straight across at the smaller Nehru statue across the road. Not too far away is the solemn and silent samadhi of Sri Aurobindo and the Mother, beautifully decorated, bedecked with flowers, where thousands visit each day, and hundreds gather in hushed meditation after bowing down reverentially at the cold marble. Nearer Gandhi's statue and much more recently, another impressive memorial has been erected by the state, this time to Dr Babasaheb Ambedkar, the leader of the erstwhile untouchables. I see many admirers remove their footwear as they enter the premises to pay their respects. But unlike these 'sacred' memorials, marked by cheerless awe and sombre gravity, Gandhi's statue is surrounded by the concourse of ordinary life, hundreds of eating, strolling, talking, laughing, playing members of the public. His memorial is a favourite haunt of children, especially, who use its slopes as slides, playing catch around giant bronze feet. Of all religions, sizes and ages, they are free and irreverent around the Mahatma, totally relaxed as the children and future citizens of a free country ought to be. Likewise at Raj Ghat, outside of the actual Samadhi, the common people of the land have taken over Gandhi's memorial, overrunning it with an affectionate intimacy that all but erases the Government's official ideology stamped on the authorized national memorial to the Mahatma.

At Gandhi Smriti our experience is indeed different. This is the old Birla House on Tees January Marg, the street thus renamed to associate it forever with the day of the Mahatma's martyrdom, 30 January, 65 years ago. The large stately mansions of the native capitalist class, along a tree-lined, genteel avenue, surround the site where the Mahatma was felled. In those days of course the Birla clan, led by its redoubtable patriarch, Ghanshyam Das, himself

Gandhi's acolyte, was one of the biggest business conglomerates in India. This Birla home in India's new capital was handed over, after some reluctance and back-pedalling by its erstwhile owners – quite expected given the immense value of the property – to the Gandhi Smriti and Darshan Trust. Outside the gate sit hawkers, adjacent is a taxi stand, and the street is lined with auto rickshaws waiting for custom.

As we enter we feel a somewhat festive atmosphere with various stalls exhibiting Gandhian products, paraphernalia and memorabilia arranged to greet visitors. One of these stalls has an old man plying the *charkha*, the humble spinning wheel that Gandhi turned into a symbol of national self-reliance. Many of my students have never seen a real *charkha*, let alone someone spinning on one. So we crowd around this craftsman, fascinated by how he spins thread out of small balls of cotton. The director has arranged for us to be taken on a guided tour. We begin in Gandhi's own room, not too far from the entrance. I am struck by its stark simplicity, the absence of any furniture except a mattress covered in a spotless white sheet, beside which are Gandhi's spectacles, spinning wheel, sandals, a small, low desk and writing implements. The room is pregnant not only with Gandhi's presence, but with a message. Just as Bapu Kuti, his hut in Sevagram, Wardha, in backward and rural central India, tells a story, so does this room in the heart of opulent New Delhi. It takes a while to apprehend what the room means.

Gandhi was telling the world that he simply lived in the old Birla House, but he did not belong to, or in, it. It was just his Delhi camp office. He lived in it as he was wont to in his ashram at Sevagram. The truth was that Gandhi had made Birla House his Delhi headquarters quite reluctantly. His usual and preferred location for several years had been the untouchable Bhangi or scavenger colony. But he could stay there no longer because the Government had told him that his security could not be guaranteed in the open and unregulated slum, asking him, instead, to stay at Birla House. Gandhi was surprised at their choice of accommodation for him, as he said in his first prayer meeting in Delhi on 10 September 1947 from these premises. He had obliged because he did not wish to cause too much trouble. Bhangi colony, moreover, was overflowing with refugees from Pakistan. Gandhi had no official position, either in Government or in the Congress Party. Where, then, was he to put up? There was literally no place for him there, no room in a sense for the Father of the Nation in the capital of the newly independent India! As Gandhi himself put it: 'I have been brought to stay at Birla House because refugees have been accommodated in the Harijan colony. Their need is much greater than mine'.[7] That is why Bapu was conveying through his lifestyle and the arrangement of the single room he had chosen to occupy in the huge mansion that he would not allow Birla House to own him, nor would he be overwhelmed by its comforts or conveniences. As he told his unnamed correspondent in the fragment of the letter of 4 November 1947:

> I am in the midst of this violent conflagration. Although I am in a house as big as a palace in the grand city of Hindustan, I think of the plight of innocent children and thousands of women in this cold season. My heart bleeds but I do not cry. I do not believe in crying. In the end I have to do or die. I wish God grants this humble prayer of mine.[8]

Leaving the rest of the house to its own purposes, he had occupied a tiny corner of it, where he worked and slept on the floor, in the same simplicity and austerity that he was used to. Gandhi was simply in the Birla House, not 'of' it.

What strikes me suddenly is that if Raj Ghat cannot appropriate Gandhi, nor can Birla House. Raj Ghat represented the power of the state and Birla House the power of big business. Neither the state nor big business could own Gandhi: though he occupied centre stage in both these realms of temporal power, he resisted both with equal firmness, and it would appear, with comparable ease. He had marked for himself a special domain of his own where he was neither contaminated by the blandishments of political power nor the inducements of big business. Gandhi's room in Birla House, like his hut in Sevagram, was not merely a space of habitation but a symbol of who he was and what he stood for.

From Gandhi's room we are led to the back of the house down the steps to the lawn, onto the path he took on his last day, walking to the red sandstone platform from where he would conduct his prayer meeting. The actual steps he took have been marked, somewhat obviously, with sandstone replicas, embedded into the lawn. This means that visitors are almost literally forced to walk in Gandhi's footsteps. Abruptly the steps stop in the lawns, midway to the platform, almost as if those in charge had forgotten or simply abandoned the completion of the path. Then the design becomes clear. The steps stop midway because this was where Nathuram Godse had pumped three bullets from his revolver into Gandhi's bare chest – as Dr Singh put it somewhat poetically to us, 'He died with a garland of bullets around his neck.' I remember what his grandson Ramachandra Gandhi had once told me in a personal conversation, 'Gandhiji died like a true warrior of peace, taking the bullets of his adversary on his chest, not shot in the back, trying to run away or escape from his enemies'. From times immemorial, taking the blow on the chest rather than on the back has been the mark of a true Kshatriya or warrior.

As we know, Nathuram had first bowed to the Mahatma, pushing aside one of his two living 'walking sticks', Manubehn, his 19-year-old grandniece, before straightening himself to fire his fatal charge. Manu had stepped in front when Nathuram had leaped upon them to say, 'Brother, Bapu is already late.' As Manu fell to one side, the mortally stricken Mahatma had fallen on his other walking stick, Abha, the nearly 21-year-old wife of his grandnephew, Kanu Gandhi.[9] According to Abha, even as the

Mahatma collapsed, his head in her lap, he uttered, 'He Rama', the name of the Lord and his favourite deity, on his lips.

Thinking of Gandhi's dying words and recalling that sad scene, we then go to what used to be Gandhi's seat at the far end of the garden wall, now marked by a sandstone bench. After dwelling there in silence for a few minutes, we return to the Birla House through the exhibition mounted in tents pitched to our right. Inside once again, we enter at the start of the permanent photo exhibition on Gandhi's life arranged chronologically from his birth in Porbandar in 1869.

Later we are taken to a more interesting, ultra-high-tech, almost postmodern exhibition curated and designed by Ranjit Makkauni, which uses digital tools and toys to bring home Gandhi's message to a contemporary generation raised on laptops and mobile phones. The common objects of Gandhi's daily use are cleverly transformed into learning devices, lighting up screens, initiating interactive, often speaking images, to explain some aspect of his life or thought. One interesting exhibit is the circle of peace where we have to join hands in a group so as to light up the floor, suggesting that peace only comes from cooperation and solidarity. We have almost run out of time, the premises are shutting down with the staff locking up and asking visitors to leave. Our guided tour and interaction with the Director and with another scholar, Madhuri Santhanam Sondhi, whose parents knew Gandhi personally, has brought us much closer to a world about which we had only read in books.

On our way back in the minibus a most interesting discussion ensues over what we have seen that day at Raj Ghat, Gandhi Darshan, Gandhi Museum, Gandhi Peace Foundation and finally at Gandhi Smriti. One of the most insightful observations has to do with the Gandhi Smriti, the site of the assassination. As one of my students, Siddhartha Chakraborti, observes, 'You are taken to the place where Gandhi was shot. But then, that's it! You don't know what to do with what happened.' Indeed, despite all the information and gadgetry, they have given us no tools or means either to make sense of Gandhi's murder or to come to terms with it. Instead, we have just been led back to the old and by now worn-out story of his life in the same photo exhibition that has been similarly mounted, with the same pictures, in dozens of places all over India. This is the Gandhi story institutionalized by the state and its ancillary outfits, reproduced in Gandhi museums all over the country and abroad. As the discussion continues I feel as if we have stumbled upon something both disturbing and quite profound this afternoon. It will take me months to try to understand its fuller implications. Least of all do I know that it will impel me to write a book about it.

5 The repression

When I look back on that visit and the discussion that followed, I am convinced that, without quite realizing it, what we had blundered upon was nothing short of momentous. This was the discovery of the repression of Gandhi's death, or to put it more accurately, his brutal murder, or to use the description of those who considered the slaying an act of bravery and patriotism, his execution. This was not any ordinary killing; it was the assassination of the Father of the Nation himself. Nor was the killer any ordinary criminal. The killer was Nathuram Godse, a Brahmin from Pune, who used Gandhi's favourite scripture, the Bhagawad Gita, to justify his action. Suspended in those manicured lawns of the old Birla House was a question of gigantic proportions, one that had the potential to destabilize not just the modern Hindu psyche but the nation itself. To understand Gandhi's afterlife, what he really meant to India and Indians, was no less than to understand all the ramifications of that question. So threatening and destabilizing was it that the only way that either the state or civil society could deal with it was by repressing it, turning away the visitors' attention to the somewhat more well-rehearsed, if not banal, facts of his life. The question had to be papered over, swept under the rug, or deflected somehow. Just as we wish to forget some searing and incomprehensible childhood trauma, this event that had dumbfounded the newly born nation of India was one of the deepest wounds of its infancy. Though we wish not to remember or confront it, without its unearthing the nation, fractured from without and fraught within, could not be healed or made whole. In the solution to the riddle of Gandhi's assassination also lay the answer to India's future.

That is why the sandstone steps marking Gandhi's footprints on the grassy lawns of the old Birla House stop midway, leaving a looming question mark in the air. It is an overwhelming question pertaining to an act so heinous that the Hindu psyche has yet to fully come to terms with it. Gandhi has been called the Father of the Nation: his image adorns our currency; his name marks our streets, localities and towns; his statues stand sentinel in the public gardens and parks of our country. It is he who is above all the symbol of the nation, whether in India or abroad. But we killed him. This uncomfortable fact is what all the monuments and memorials to Gandhi wish to hide or escape from. So strong is this aversion to his assassination that the event has been elided out of school textbooks.[1]

In popular accounts, Gandhi's murder has often been called a martyrdom. The Hindi words for it that come to mind are *shahadat* and *balidaan*, but these are, once again, attempts to repress the most uncomfortable aspects of this killing, which are that a Hindu killed Gandhi; that the killer was neither demented nor out of control but perfectly calm, deliberate, and rational; that he was a well-read Brahmin who quoted the scriptures; that he stood for and articulated the anti-Gandhi sentiments of a sizeable section of the population; that the Government was negligent in preventing this tragedy; that the specious, if elaborate, reasoning offered to justify the murder still has adherents; and so on. But these discomforts are nothing compared to the one overwhelming horror: that the act was self-consciously committed as a patricide. It is this killing of the 'Father of the Nation' by one of his 'sons' that is so intolerable and shocking to the Hindu psyche as to demand its continued repression.

We do not need much imagination to interpret Nathuram's act as patricidal because he himself saw it as such, according to his own court statement:

> Gandhiji is being referred to as the Father of the Nation – an epithet of high reverence. But if so, he has failed in his paternal duty in as much as he has acted very treacherously to the nation by his consenting to the partitioning of it ... I stoutly maintain that Gandhiji in doing so has failed in his duty which was incumbent upon him to carry out, as the Father of the Nation. He has proved to be the Father of Pakistan. It was for this reason alone that I as a dutiful son of Mother India thought it my duty to put an end to the life of the so-called Father of the Nation who had played a very prominent part in bringing about the vivisection of the country – Our Motherland.[2]

From this statement it is clear that Nathuram considered it his sacred 'duty' as a 'dutiful' son of Mother India to kill the 'treacherous' Father of the Nation who had failed in his 'duty' and instead become the 'Father of Pakistan'. The repetition of the word duty is surely striking. It is a direct invocation of the Bhagawad Gita, the scripture that Nathuram quoted to justify his act. In common parlance, the Karma Yoga of the Gita is often translated into English as the doctrine of doing one's duty without desiring the fruits thereof. Here Nathuram's justification of his deed fails on two counts: not only does he hanker after the goal of 'Hindu Rashtra' but he is willing to go to any extent to attain it. Far from being desireless, his act is solely instrumental and directed at achieving a specific goal. In addition Nathuram, in characterizing his act as the carrying out of a 'duty' in order to punish or correct Gandhi's failure to do so, arrogates to himself the capacity to accuse, prosecute, judge, and execute his adversary. The Gita does not empower one to judge the failure of another to carry out his duty or to punish him for it; it merely enjoins one to carry out one's own duty without hankering after its fruits. How can a murder, carefully plotted and ruthlessly executed with the sole desire for the fruit of the action, that is to kill a political adversary, be seen as 'desireless action'? No wonder no scholar of the Gita has found it worthwhile to point out the doctrinal fallacies in Nathuram's arguments, nor any of his supporters thought it necessary to justify his act on scriptural or philosophical grounds. Clearly the constant reference to 'duty' and thus to the Gita is a red herring; no matter how Nathuram wished to view or legitimize his act, we must look elsewhere to understand its sources and effects. The real clue, as I suggested earlier, lies not in Indian classical sources, but in Western ones; not in the Gita, but in *Oedipus Rex*. The matter is not of doing one's duty as the Gita enjoins, but of patricide, something too heinous to contemplate for the Hindu mentality.

It is also crucial to see the link between the Partition and the assassination of Gandhi so explicitly clarified by Nathuram himself. The killing, coming less than six months after Partition, thus becomes a repressed dyad in my own analysis into the nation's unconscious. The repression of the Partition, following Frederic Jameson's argument in *The Political Unconscious*, signifies not just the failure of the national project as envisaged by Gandhi and his associates, but also the unacknowledged desire for a reunion some time in the future. The utopian impulse for a united India based on Hindu–Muslim unity may be repressed, but that does not mean that it is dead or will never come back. For noted philosopher Basanta Kumar Mallik (1879–1958), 'the two events of Partition and Assassination were interlinked: the former he [Mallik] had already described as the defeat of India and Gandhi; the latter's assassination put a seal on it'.[3]

Ashis Nandy in his essay 'Final Encounter: the Politics of the Assassination of Gandhi', an extended examination of the event in the book *At the Edge of Psychology: Essays on Politics and Culture* (1990), fails to detect or stress the Oedipal pattern of the assassination despite his being India's leading political psychologist. Though he quotes from Nathuram's court speech and identifies the parricidal[4] nature of the event, his reading continues his older thesis, first propounded in *The Intimate Enemy* (1983), of maladjustments and discontents of Indian masculinity, of which he considers both the celibate Nathuram and the womanizing Apte as examples. 'The womanizer and the homosexual', says Nandy, 'both articulate, through diametrically opposite kinds of sexuality, the same sensitivities',[5] the one wanting to prove he is a man, the other fearing women, and uncertain about his masculinity.[6] Nathuram, according to Nandy, the 'ascetic misogynist' and Gandhi's 'other',[7] murders the Mahatma driven by

> fantasies of a mother who becomes a victim of rapacious intruders, a weak emasculated father who fails in his paternal duty and collaborates with the aggressors, and an allegiant mother's son who tries to redeem his masculinity by protecting the mother, by defeating the aggressors in their own game and by parricide.[8]

Apart from this diagnosis of Nathuram's personal pathology, Nandy devotes a considerable portion of his analysis to the political psychology of the Chitpavan Brahmin community to which Nathuram belonged.

Indeed, the bulk of his essay is aimed at proving that the murder was

> a case of the dominant traditions within a society trying to contain a force which, in the name of orthodoxy, threatened to demolish its centre, to erect instead a freer society and a new authority system using the rubble of the old.[9]

Nandy claims that the killing was engineered by 'the main strain of Indian, particularly Hindu, culture' for whom Gandhi's 'political activism' was 'highly subversive'[10] because of Gandhi's 'continuous attempt to change the definitions of centre and periphery in Indian society' and his 'negation of the concepts of masculinity and femininity implicit in some Indian traditions and in the colonial situation'.[11] According to Nandy, Gandhi tried to 'de-intellectualize Indian politics'[12] through a 'process of de-Brahminization through de-intellectualization',[13] which is what made the upper-caste Hindus retaliate and seek revenge. Gandhi also gave importance to the 'rediscovery of womanhood', making the woman the model of the satygrahi: 'It would therefore seem that Gandhi's innovations in this area also tended to simultaneously subvert Brahmanic and Kshatriya orthodoxy and the British colonial system'.[14] Nandy asserts that 'Gandhi not only wanted to be a trans-secular *mahatma* or saint in the Indian sense; he also wanted to be a bride of Christ – a St. Francis of Assisi – in the Christian sense'.[15] Godse killed Gandhi because the former was not masculine or manly enough to defend Mother India from the aggressions of the British and the Muslims.

For Nandy, Gandhi was radical precisely because he claimed to be a traditionalist, a Sanatani Hindu, but who went on to upturn the traditional hierarchies and the centre–periphery relations: 'He mobilized the numerically preponderant non-Brahmanic sectors of the Hindus, the lower strata of society, and the politically passive peripheries: the low castes and untouchables, the peasants and the villagers'.[16] The danger that Gandhi posed to the greater Sanskritic tradition was in 'making its cultural periphery its centre'.[17] Therefore, Nandy argues that this group revenged itself on him through Godse. But if this were true, why did so many upper-caste and middle-class elites support Gandhi or become his devoted followers? And why did the dalits continue to distrust and denounce Gandhi as an upper-caste leader, who wanted to maintain the hegemonic, hierarchical structure of Indian society? Similarly, the charge that Gandhi was irrational and anti-modern was not confined to Godse or the Brahmanical groups alone, but was also famously levelled against him by Ambedkar himself.[18]

But Nandy is right to the extent that there was widespread resentment of Gandhi among the Hindu right, constituted mostly by Brahmins. Poona was one of the centres of such malice, but anti-Gandhism was rampant in other parts of India, including Rajputana, and Central Provinces and Berar. For instance, during a brief period from 19 April 1947 to 7 February 1948, when Dr Bhaskar Narayan Khare was the Premier, the small Rajput state of Alwar was the hotbed of right-wing Hindu ideology and politics. Khare, a disgruntled and dismissed member of the Congress and later member of the Constituent Assembly of India,[19] even pronounced a 'Brahmin's curse' on Gandhi during a public meeting.[20] After Gandhi's murder, Khare was immediately sacked and put under house arrest in Delhi, but though his sympathies with Gandhi's killers were well known, there was no material evidence proving his part in the conspiracy. Khare joined the Hindu Mahasabha on 15 August 1949, served as its President, and was even elected to the first Lok Sabha of independent India from Gwalior, which was also one of the seats of Hindu cultural nationalism. After all, it was in Gwalior that the Beretta used to kill Gandhi was obtained.[21]

If we examine the findings of the Kapur Commission, it is evident that there were at least three groups of overlapping Hindu nationalists who hated Gandhi:

1. Sections of the RSS and Hindu Mahasabha, who were also anti-Congress, anti-Muslim, anti-Partition, but did not have the mass support of the people.
2. Some princes, including Alwar and Gwalior, who were sympathetic to these elements and to the idea of a Hindu Rashtra; but these too lacked popular support.
3. G. V. Ketkar, Lokmanya Tilak's grandson and editor of the *Kesari* (saffron) newspaper, and the so-called '*Kesari* group' of Poona were also in favour of a more militant Hindu activism and regarded 'Gandhism-cum-False Nationalism as their enemy no. 1'.[22] However, this group did not like Savarkar either, and wanted to organize the Hindu right under a different leadership.

Several members of these groups boasted that they would kill Gandhi and Nehru, 'liberate' Hyderabad state from the Nizam, or even bomb the Pakistan Parliament, but they were not taken seriously and, indeed, nothing came of these boasts. Only Godse and his associates actually did what they intended; they killed Gandhi.

That a section of the Hindu right wanted Gandhi eliminated and that many of its leaders and cadres were Brahmins is correct. However, Nandy's thesis begins to falter when he chooses to indict the whole Chitpavan community for Gandhi's death, something that the Congress-supported rioters did after the assassination, burning homes, destroying property and targeting specific individuals and groups of Brahmins, especially Chitpavans.[23] Nandy resorts to large-scale stereotyping to show how this community was ideally positioned to assassinate the Mahatma. He considers Poona to be the symbol of the loss of Brahmanical power which was trying to strike back at Gandhi for dislodging them. Claiming that Chitpavans combined 'the traditional prerogatives of the priestly Brahmans and the kingly Kshatriyas',[24] he argues that they founded their 'anti-British nationalism' on the 'reconstituted and self-created tradition' of themselves as 'upholders of a tradition of Hindu resistance against the Muslim occupation of India':[25] Furthermore, 'They saw themselves as the previously powerful, now weakened, competitors of the British. So terrorism directed against the Raj came naturally to them. Their aim was the redemption of their lost glory'.[26] According to Nandy,

> [Gandhi's] constant emphasis on pacifism and self-control . . . posed a threat to the warrior cultures of India . . . by constantly stressing the feminine, nurturing, nonviolent aspects of men's personality, he challenged the Kshatriya identity built on fear of woman and of the cosmic feminine principles in nature.[27]

Thus Gandhi posed 'more or less the same kind of threat to India's martial cultures as to her priestly cultures'.[28] But if this were true, how is it that Vinoba Bhave, Gandhi's foremost disciple, belonged to the same community, as did his political 'guru', Gopal Krishna Gokhale, who was also from Poona, and a Chitpavan Brahmin? Incidentally, Y. D. Phadke, the historian whose expose of Dalvi's play I cited earlier, was also a Chitpavan. An entire community cannot, quite obviously, be attacked for the act of one individual. Nandy's ethnic profiling is thus not convincing: while it is true that Hindu right-wing ideologies continue to attract sections of this community, to tar all of the group with the same brush is unjustified.[29]

But why is Nandy unable to see the classical Oedipal pattern in Nathuram's act? Is it because, like Sudhir Kakar, he believes that in South Asia, it is the mother not the father who is the dominant figure in a child's infancy? Earlier in the book, Nandy says that South Asia produces so many female leaders because 'competition, aggression, power, activism, and intrusiveness are not so clearly associated with masculinity'; instead, these qualities are often associated with women in mythology and folk lore: 'The fantasy of a castrating, phallic woman is also always round the corner in the Indian's inner world'.[30] Nandy's otherwise fascinating and provocative reading thus misses the main point of patricide, dwelling instead on the political psychology of dispossessed and vengeful elites.

Writing several years after but following in Nandy's footsteps, Anup Kumar Dhar in his paper 'Survival of Violence: Violence of Survival' (2004), offers a psychoanalytic explanation of Godse's act using the latter's own account of events. His thesis is that Godse provides the prototype of an 'emerging Hindu self' that finds 'fruition' in the Gujarat riots of 2002. I shall not engage with this aspect of the argument because I am primarily interested in his reading of Gandhi's murder. Dhar advances the patricide angle a little further:

> Godse was looking for in Gandhi a somewhat *menacing abstraction of the paternal role as the possessor-protector of the*

mother and the place of the Law. Instead Gandhi happened to be the *effeminate internal other* of the nationalist Hindu self.... And this *foreclosure* of the *inassimilable internal* other could be done only in the name of the survival of a dying race.... Hence an *assassination* – an assassination that in turn sets up possibilities for a more violent encounter with the threatening other – the other as foreigner, as outsider – as the *external other* of hegemonic Hindu identity.[31]

I would argue that the enormity of Godse's deed leads to a collective repression precisely because it is, to use Dhar's appropriation of the Lacanian phrase, *inassimilable*. Patricide produces the tremendous *foreclosure* in the Hindu psyche, rendering it confused and incapable of understanding its continued sense of unease and neurosis in contemporary India.

6 The unbearability of patricide

Why is patricide so difficult to confront for Indians, especially Hindus? Why does it produce such massive repression in the Hindu psyche that no serious interrogation of the meaning of Gandhi's murder is possible? Why, in other words, have we still not come to terms with the event? Why is there a national compulsion, instead, to turn away from it to a recounting of Gandhi's life? Or to turn the murder into a martyrdom so as to be able better to cope with its after-effects? To examine the implications of these questions we shall have to go deep into the innards of Hindu mythology, that inexhaustible source of symbols and significations that still shed their light, however dim, on our benighted present.

The horror of killing one's father is unimaginable and intolerable to the Hindu mind. In all of Hindu mythology there are very few instances of the killing of the father or the mother. Though the status of the mother is primary, there is one rather famous matricide in the Mahabharata, but the catastrophe is reversed. Parashuram at his father Jamadagni's behest beheads his mother Renuka because the sage has detected in her an act of mental infidelity. But the story hints that Parashuram knows that his father's anger is only short-lived, so after carrying out his ghastly commission, he entreats its reversal. His prayer is granted; the sage restores his wife and Parashuram's mother back to life. Interestingly,

Jamadagni had commanded his other four sons to do the same: that they refused him one by one, knowing full well the consequences of their disobedience, attests to the heinousness of the crime. Indeed, they are burned to death by their extremely powerful father's angry look. When Parashuram, who has been away during this domestic disaster, returns, he finds his mother whimpering inconsolably beside the heaps of the ashes of his four incinerated elder brothers. The story, however, ends happily, as already mentioned.[1]

Patricide, too, is very scarce, if not impossible to find in Indian myths. If it is anywhere, the place to look for it is obviously the Mahabharata because, as the *Adi Parva* puts it, 'What is not found here will not be found elsewhere' (*Yannehasti na tadkavacit*).[2] The lone instance that occurs in the Mahabharata is Paravasu's killing of his father by mistake. In C. Rajagopalachari's abridged retelling (1978), it occurs in chapters 32 and 33, in the interlinked stories of Yavakrida, the son of Bharadwaja, and Raibhya, Bharadwaja's peer, who was also a *rishi* of great repute, and his two sons Paravasu and Aravasu. Yavakrida is jealous of Raibhya's sons and wishes to be the greatest Vedic scholar of his time. Undergoing severe austerities to reach his goal quickly, he violates the established order. He is persuaded many times to find a proper teacher to study the scriptures as other people do. But he persists stubbornly, even threatening to offer his limbs one by one as oblations to the sacrificial fire, to achieve his purpose. In the end the Gods grant him the wish. But he lacks the moral character commensurate with the wisdom he seeks and therefore grows vain. Even his father warns him to cultivate self-restraint and not to transgress the limits of Dharma. Unfortunately Yavakrida falls.

Chancing upon Paravasu's beautiful wife, he is so overwhelmed by lust that he drags her to a lonely spot and ravishes her. When Raibhya returns to his hermitage, he finds his daughter-in-law raped and heartbroken. Enraged, he creates out of two hairs from his head vengeful demonic energies to kill Yavakrida. Yavakrida is hunted down to the very entrance of his father's hermitage and speared to death. As Bharadwaja confronts his son's corpse he guesses that Yavakrida has offended Raibhya, which has led to his death. But unable to control his grief and anger, he curses Raibhya that he will die at the hands of his own son. That is why Paravasu unwittingly kills his father, thinking him to be a wild beast about to spring upon him. But his grievous error is prepared for by his own lust. While conducting the king's sacrifice, Paravasu wishes to visit his wife one night, the same beautiful woman whose rape had led to Yavakrida's downfall. Mistaking his deerskin-clad father for a wild beast he kills him. But he is the official priest in the king's sacrifice: though both horrified and ashamed, he requests his younger brother to expiate his doubly heinous crime, not just of killing a Brahmin, but his own father. Aravasu's penance on his brother's behalf however does not wash off the latter's sins because penance cannot be done, nor sins be washed away, by proxy. When Aravasu returns to the sacrificial assembly, Paravasu, jealous of his brother's lustre, defames him as a Brahmin-killer unfit to participate in the gathering. Aravasu, humiliated and distraught, repairs to the forest concluding that there is no justice on earth. After years and years of penance, however, he finds it in his heart not only to forgive his brother but to pray for the restoration of his father's life and the cleansing of his brother's sins. The Gods, pleased with his virtue and austerity, grant him his wish. Thus the cosmic order is restored through purity, forgiveness and compassion, not through vengeful retaliation.[3] In both of these somewhat seriously told stories, where the instances of matricide and patricide are real with visible distress and suffering, the crimes are shown, ultimately, to be reversible.

Other stories of patricide, again owing mostly to mistaken identities or curses, are in the variants or subplots of the Ramayana and Mahabharata sagas. In the Krittibas Bangla retelling, for instance, Lava and Kusha, Rama's estranged sons, not only defeat but kill their father unwittingly when he goes to retrieve the sacrificial horse from their custody. However, Valmiki, the 'author' of the story, who has contrived these events to reunite the family, revives Rama.[4] There is also the story of Arjuna's 'death' at the hands of his son Babruvahana in the *Ashvamedha Parva* of the Mahabharata. The episode is interesting because it shows a rivalry between Arjuna's two wives, the Manipuri princess Chitrangada, Babruvahana's mother, and Uloopi, the Naga princess, who is Babruvahana's nurse and stepmother. In this case Arjuna and Babruvahana recognize each other, but fight over the sacrificial horse. When Babruvahana's arrows kill Arjuna much to Chitrangada's horror, Uloopi revives Arjuna with a special gem, explaining how this 'death' was the only way to release Arjuna from the curse of the Vasus and expiate his killing of Bheeshma, the grandsire of the clan. Arjuna's own parricidal sin leaves him only after his mock death at the hands of his own son. Uloopi scores over Chitrangada, both in egging on Babruvahana to combat, and also in revealing the mystery of 'invincible' Arjuna's defeat in the curse, besides claiming the credit of bringing him back to life with her gem.[5] It would seem that there is no pure or irreversible tragedy in Hindu mythology!

If patricide is 'impossible' in Hindu thought, it is quite common in the Western tradition. There, the Oedipal myth is defining if not definitive, given the status of a master narrative by Sigmund Freud himself. Even prior to Oedipus, an Oedipal pattern is already established in Greek mythology, with a series of patricides – and infanticides – from Cronos to Zeus. Uranus (sky) was both the son and husband of Gaea (earth). He visited her each night, covering the earth with darkness. His son, Cronus (later worshipped as Saturn by the Romans), tore open the sky (his father) with assistance from his mother, Gaea, to rule the world with his sister-wife, Rhea. Gaea fashioned the stone sickle or scythe which he used to castrate his father. The latter's cut testicles were flung into the sea, where they caused the white foam from which Aphrodite was born. Gaea had warned Cronus that his own offspring would upstage and depose him. Therefore, he began to eat them – Demeter, Hestia, Hera, Hades and Poseidon – soon after they were born. There is a particularly gruesome painting by Peter Paul Rubens showing Cronus devouring the infant Poseidon; the terror in the latter's face is unmistakable. Rhea, however, saved Zeus, the youngest of her children, tricking Cronus into swallowing a stone instead of him. Zeus forced his father to imbibe an emetic whereupon he disgorged his offspring in reverse order. A huge battle called Titanomachy ensued in which the Titans were defeated by the Gods; the victorious Zeus assumed overlordship of the heavens while many of the routed Titans were relegated to Tartarus. This series of patricides from Cronus to Zeus – sons killing, castrating and ousting their fathers; fathers killing or devouring their offspring; and sons in turn killing or overthrowing their fathers – has no parallel in India.[6] The Oedipus complex, according to Freud, is of course the source of all neurosis, the name of the Father serving as the repressive interdiction of the son's illicit desire for his mother, leading to the primal trauma that is the cause of every civilization's anguish, a thesis most famously advanced in Freud's *Civilization and its Discontents*, which affirms the same repression of illicit desire as the defining action of civilization itself.

Ramanujan in 'The Indian Oedipus' sums it up quite succinctly: 'There are very, very few stories of actual patricide in Hindu myth, literature and folklore'.[7] He lists, very briefly, the 'few marginal instances' of 'Arjuna killed by his son, Rama killed by his sons, both in battle, both revived later'[8] and though he and the other Oedipus-seekers in India have missed the story of Paravasu's killing of his father Yavakrida, his conclusion stands. Precisely what is so shocking about Godse's deliberate and cold-blooded execution of the Father of the Nation is that it is not an act of ignorance, mistaken identity, or the outcome of a curse. It is a planned and deliberate patricide, which makes it all the more loathsome. Hindus complicit to whatever extent in this crime bear a perpetual burden of guilt. It is this guilt that produces the requisite defence mechanism in us whereby we repress and evade the fact of Gandhi's murder and our responsibility for it.

7 Oedipus in India

In his oft-quoted footnote added in 1920 to *Three Essays on the Theory of Sexuality*, Freud declared:

> It has justly been said that the Oedipus complex is the nuclear complex of the neuroses, and constitutes the essential part of their content. It represents the peak of infantile sexuality, which, through its after-effects, exercises a decisive influence on the sexuality of adults. Every new arrival on this planet is faced by the task of mastering the Oedipus complex; anyone who fails to do so falls a victim to neurosis. With the progress of psycho-analytic studies the importance of the Oedipus complex has become more and more clearly evident; its recognition has become the shibboleth that distinguishes the adherents of psycho-analysis from its opponents.[1]

Even earlier, in *Totem and Taboo*, first published in 1905, Freud had started calling the Oedipus complex 'the nuclear complex of the neurosis'.[2] The importance to Freud of the Oedipal complex is underscored by his repeated use of the word 'nuclear', thus emphasizing how central it is to psychoanalysis itself. For instance, later in the same book, he posits that the 'two crimes' of Oedipus correspond to the two 'primal wishes' of children that form 'the nucleus of perhaps every psychoneurosis'.[3] In his concluding section, Freud returns to the Oedipus complex, emphasizing how it 'constitutes the nucleus of all neuroses',[4] and how 'the simultaneous existence of love and hate towards the same object – lies at the root of many important cultural institutions'.[5] Again, in his *Introductory Lectures on Psycho-Analysis*, Freud repeats how 'the Oedipus complex may justly be regarded as the nucleus of the neuroses'[6] as he does in 'A Child Is Being Beaten': 'the Oedipus complex is the actual nucleus of neuroses, and the infantile sexuality which culminates in this complex is the true determinant of neuroses'.[7]

For Freud, the complex was universal. The curse on Oedipus is also upon us: 'His destiny moves us only because it might have been ours – because the oracle laid the same curse upon us before our birth as upon him'.[8] All of us, Freud believed, directed our 'first sexual impulse towards our mother and our first hatred and our first murderous wish against our father'.[9] No wonder in *Totem and Taboo*, Freud posited incest and patricide as universal taboos that were common to all civilizations, indeed as the primary constituents of all civilization, the source of conscience, morality and guilt. In the concluding section of this book, he avers:

> I should like to insist that . . . the beginnings of religion, morals, society and art converge in the Oedipus complex. This is in complete agreement with the psycho-analytic finding that the same complex constitutes the nucleus of all neuroses, so far as our present knowledge goes. It seems to me a most surprising discovery that the problems of social psychology, too, should prove soluble on the basis of one single concrete point – man's relation to his father.[10]

So convinced of this thesis was Freud that he never deviated from it.

In its own heyday, Freud's formulation was challenged by Bronislaw Malinowski, who, during extensive fieldwork in the Trobriand Islands, found no evidence of the Oedipus complex among the matrilineal Melanesians. He published the results of his study in German as early as 1924 and in English in his classic *Sex and Repression in Savage Society*. Malinowski concluded that the applicability of the Oedipus complex 'is restricted to the Aryan, patriarchal society'.[11] More importantly, Malinowski pointed out a fundamental problem with placing the Oedipus complex at the originary moment of civilizations. But how, if it is the cause of civilization, can it be read civilizationally in the first place? In other words, the taboo can only be imposed and internalized *after* the event, which, when it first occurs, cannot logically be read in terms of totem or taboo. The 'complex', thus, cannot come to be recognized as such until it has been interpreted in terms of totem and taboo, which occurs *after* its occurrence. As Malinowski puts it:

> I have pointed out repeatedly that the Great Tragedy has been placed by Freud at the threshold of culture and as its inaugural act . . . [I]t is important to realize that this is an assumption indispensable to their theories: all their hypotheses would collapse if we do not make culture begin with the Totemic Parricide.[12]

But, as Malinowski argued, this founding event is absent in matrilineal societies, thereby undermining it universal applicability.

Freud, however, was able to deflect from too literal a reading of the Oedipus archetype by explaining that

> The Oedipus complex has a merely 'symbolic' meaning: the mother in it means the unattainable, which must be renounced in the interests of civilization; the father who is killed in the Oedipus myth is the 'inner' father, from whom one must set oneself free in order to become independent.[13]

In effect, while Freud continued to insist on the universality of the complex, his moving it to the symbolic plane made it possible to look for cultural variations or local differences in how it was expressed or worked out.

This is precisely what India's pioneering psychoanalyst Girindrasekhar Bose (1887–1953) did. Bose wrote a PhD dissertation at Calcutta University in 1921 on the 'Concept of Repression', where he tried to blend insights from Hindu psychology with Freudian ideas. Bose's bold act of sending this thesis to Freud led to a 20-year correspondence, which Bose subsequently published.[14] Bose was also instrumental in forming the Indian Psychoanalytic Society in Calcutta in 1922. Some of Bose's ideas, including the importance of mothers rather than fathers to Indian children and the Indian male's wish to be a female, shaped the whole course of subsequent work by Indian psychoanalysts including Sudhir Kakar and Ashis Nandy. Christiane Hartnack's *Psychoanalysis in Colonial India* (2001) offers a detailed and fascinating account of this encounter, summed up in the very readable summary 'Freud on Garuda's Wings: Psychoanalysis in Colonial India':

> In his correspondence with Freud, Bose explicitly pointed to the importance of the maternal deities in his culture. Other Indian psychoanalysts even criticized classical Freudian psychoanalysis for being a product of a 'Father religion or Son religion.'[15]

Bose sent Freud 13 of his articles on psychoanalysis, underscoring his differences with the latter: 'I would draw your particular attention to my paper on the Oedipus wish where I have ventured to differ from you in some respects'.[16] In an essay presented in 1928 to the Indian Psychoanalytic Association, referenced in the *International Journal of Psychoanalysis* (October. 1929, Part 4), and later published in *Samiksha: Journal of the Indian Psychoanalytical Society*, Bose declared:

> The super-ego must be conquered and the ability to castrate the father and make him into a woman is an essential requisite

for the adjustment of the Oedipus wish; the Oedipus is resolved not by the threat of castration, but by the ability to castrate.[17]

Earlier in the same paper he also said, 'The desire to be a woman or its modification the castration wish is regularly discernible in all analyses'.[18] Commenting on how Freud himself might have taken these culturalist modifications of his theory, Hartnack wryly observes:

> Perhaps Freud, in the privacy of his diary, expressed a premonition that, like the statuette of Vishnu, psychoanalysis would not travel easily. In Bengali joint families in the early part of the twentieth century, the biological father was only one of several patriarchal figures, and the biological mother just one of several maternal authorities.[19]

Bose's important Indian modifications to the Oedipus complex force us to think not only of weak fathers and threatening mothers in the Indian context, but also of the desire to be a woman or to be castrated in Indian males. Perhaps Nandy's observations on Gandhi's androgyny may fruitfully be linked to Bose's hypothesis. Strong mothers and boys not with a castration anxiety but with a castration wish certainly mitigate the threatening or coercive aspect of the Oedipus complex that creates neurosis in the first place. Does this mean that Oedipus is neither as neurotic-making or anxiety-inducing in India as it is in Europe?

Without quite being aware of Bose's work, it was A. K. Ramanujan who carried out the most extensive search for the Indian Oedipus to answer such questions. Ramanujan published an early version of this essay in *Indian Literature* (1972); a decade later he expanded and rewrote the essay for *Oedipus: A Folklore Casebook* (1983) and revised it in 1984; finally the essay found its way into his *Collected Essays*. Ramanujan starts 'The Indian Oedipus' with this observation:

> Searching for stories of the Oedipus type (Tale Type 931) some years ago in the myth and folklore of the Indic area (i.e. India, Pakistan, Bangladesh, Sri Lanka), I found very little that looked like the Sophocles play, where a young man kills his father and marries his mother.[20]

Ramanujan was following in the footsteps of scholars like Philip Spratt, whose work he acknowledges: 'Others have searched before me (e.g., Spratt 1966) and concluded that Indian narrative has no Oedipal tales, and therefore, of course, Indians have no Oedipus-complex'.[21] After trawling in vain in not only through the Vedic and Puranic lore, the closest Ramanujan comes to finding anything similar to Oedipus in India is a Kannada folktale. But here it is the mother who is accursed with the knowledge that her son will impregnate her, something she tries very hard to avert but, in the end, cannot, and therefore kills herself. As Ramanujan observes, 'The most striking difference between the Kannada tale and the Greek myth is the absence of the father and hence of patricide. There are very, very few stories of actual patricide in Hindu myth, literature and folklore'.[22]

When Ramanujan's essay was first published in 1971, he had not read R. P. Goldman's paper 'Fathers, Sons and Gurus: Oedipal Conflict in the Sanskrit Epics' which was published in 1978. In the revised version Ramanujan, following Goldman, shows that the direction of the Oedipal conflict is reversed in Indian narratives, with violent and domineering fathers and submissive or obedient sons. But it is through the latter's very act of obedience or submission that they become heroes and thus 'constitute the ego-ideal for Hindu men'.[23] In several stories, such as Rama's, Bhishma's or Yayati's, 'the son willingly gives up (often transfers) his political and sexual potency'[24] to the father-figure. In the case of Ganesh, where his father, Shiva, beheads him, 'The Freudian implications of the father beheading the son or breaking off his tusk are obvious'.[25] In nearly all cases of intergenerational conflict, the elders usually win, forcing the younger challengers to eat humble pie. Consider the laying low of all the five Pandavas, for example, upon meeting with a superior adversary, a real or substitute father, who breaks their pride. When the younger hero does vanquish his elder, as in Arjuna's killing of Bhishma, it is only because the latter teaches him how to do so, thus sanctioning his own defeat or death at the hands of the younger hero. The only exception, as Ramanujan points out,[26] is Krishna's slaying of his uncle Kamsa, but Kamsa is *not* the father and Krishna is, after all divine, so quite above the rule. Indeed, it is Krishna who not only defeats Indra, the king of heaven, but also incites Arjuna to kill his elders in Kurukshetra, quite against the established trend.

Continuing his investigation, it is no surprise that Ramanujan finds in India a pattern rather at variance with the European:

> Instead of sons desiring mothers and overcoming fathers (e.g., Oedipus) and daughters loving fathers and hating mothers (e.g. Electra), most often we have fathers (or father-figures) suppressing sons and desiring daughters, and mothers desiring sons and ill-treating or exiling daughters or daughter-figures.[27]

Ramanujan's key conclusion is by now almost predictable: 'The structural matrix of relations and actors is the same, but the *direction* is in reverse'.[28] Speculating on the 'problem of psychoanalytic universals' Ramanujan concludes that relations between fathers, mothers, sons and daughters are 'not culture-free': 'While intergenerational competition . . . seems universal, the direction of aggression and desire, and the outcome, seem different in different cultures'.[29]

Ramanujan was not aware of another attempt made long before his study to prove that the Oedipus complex was in evidence in India. George Devereux in 'The Oedipal Situation and its Consequences in the Epics of Ancient India', an essay published in *Samiksha: Journal of the Indian Psychoanalytical Society* in 1951, argued that the great Indian epics 'seem to reflect in an almost undisguised form a cluster of attitudes and fantasies which center about the Oedipus complex, the primal scene, the latency period and the revival of the Oedipus complex during puberty'.[30] However, both of the examples he supplies, of Kalmashapada and Pandu, do not illustrate either incest or patricide. Therefore, his conclusions about the universality of the Oedipus complex do not seem tenable:

> This finding contradicts the criticism that the nature (as distinct from the form and content) of the basic Freudian mechanisms is culturally determined, or else that they are a response to the analyst's overt or devious suggestions.[31]

On the contrary, Ramanujan's findings suggest that the stories and their internal structures take different forms in different cultures.

Reiterating that 'In Hindu history no major instance (to my lay mind) seems to be recorded where a son overthrows or assassinates his father and usurps the throne',[32] Ramanujan asks if this absence is itself because of repression. After all, there are several such recorded instances in the history of Muslim rule in India.[33] Actually, there are a few instances in history of patricide, one of which is the belief that the Maghadhan king Bimbisara was imprisoned and starved to death by his son Ajatashatru. Similarly, Buddhist texts allege that Ashoka killed 99 of his brothers, sparing only one, Tissa.[34] In that sense, Ramanujan is right in wondering if the taboo against patricide was 'so great that Hindu historians have repressed any such instances?'[35] At any rate, Ramanujan reiterates that 'There are no Prometheus or Cronos figures overthrowing or defying the elder gods in Indian mythology'.[36] He wonders if that might change with 'changes in Indian family, child-rearing, economy and politics'.[37] While Ramanujan, quite modestly, admits 'I have no clear answer'.[38] I would like to suggest that Godse's unprecedented transgression is what makes it and him so *modern*. He has, in a radical sense, broken with thousands of years of history and culture to kill Gandhi. This is what makes his act so unbearable to the Indian psyche.

From this extensive review, it is clear that patricide is not only very rare in Hindu tradition but, in a sense, 'impossible'. This is underscored by how murderous father-figures, who are scared of being dislodged from power by the next generation, are transformed from fathers to uncles. The best example of such a child devouring 'father' is Kamsa, the maternal uncle or *mama* of Krishna. It is also interesting that another *mama*, Shakuni, causes the carnage at Kurukshetra by cheating at the game of dice to defeat the Pandavas and usurp their kingdom. Similarly Dhritarashtra, the blind uncle of the Pandavas, connives in the latter's banishment after the failure of an earlier plot, which he has approved of, to eliminate them in the house of lac. Uncles there may be, but there are no murderous fathers in India. This preponderance of evil uncles is clearly a kind of displacement: evil, scheming fathers are 'inadmissible' and such possibilities are repressed and displaced onto uncles. In addition, if the uncle is the mother's brother, then he also serves as a useful ally to her in her battle with her husband for dominance and supremacy.

In any case, there is no Hindu equivalent of Abraham, ready to sacrifice his first-born son to a jealous God. Both the idea of a fiercely possessive and omnipotent monotheistic deity and a father willing to kill his own offspring do not have their counterparts in Hindu myths. True, some fathers fail their sons, as Nachiketas's father does, sending the latter inadvertently to the world of Yama or death; but Nachiketas not only learns the secret of immortality from the God of Death, but also asks for the boon that his father will not miss him now that he is no more in the world of the living. Rama, too, hearing of his father's promise to the latter's favourite queen, Kaikeyi, betakes himself to the forest even before his father can utter the decree of banishment. It is, if anything, a voluntary exile and renunciation of the throne to honour a father's word. Even if fathers falter or fail, sons do not turn against them, let alone rise to castrate or kill them. Perhaps a largely benevolent father and a usually dutiful son are the Hindu norm, thus defying the Oedipal pattern. Kosambi, who considered Freud's theory inadequate and 'arbitrary from the ethnographer's point of view' agreed with Malinowski that the dynamics of the Oedipal complex changed in matrilineal or matrilocal societies. In the latter, 'when the maternal uncle occupies the position of authority in the house and over the children' instead of the father,[39] it would make perfect sense for the uncle to be killed instead of the father, as in Kamsa's case.

We thus see two distinct variations on Oedipus in India. First, following Bose's line, sons becoming men not by overthrowing fathers, but by resisting and overcoming the influence of domineering mothers. Second, following Ramanujan, domineering fathers who defeat sons or sons who voluntarily accept defeat or transfer potency to their aging fathers. In either case, though, patricide is rendered impossible. Instead, dutiful sons end up deferring to the authority of fathers.

In this light, we may attempt to gauge the enormity of Godse's crime. Nathuram's assassination of Gandhi may be seen in psychoanalytic terms as the dutiful son's revenge on an unfaithful father in order to uphold the honour of the wronged mother. It is, in that sense, very much an honour killing. The mother, defenceless and betrayed, who cannot act except through her son is, of course, not just Mother India but the Hindu *rashtra* or the Hindu nation itself. Evidently there is some gender trouble here, because the *rashtra* is a very masculinist construct while the idea of Bharat Mata, definitely feminine. The Mother Goddess, moreover, even in the form of the nation, is not only richly endowed, both with ornaments and weapons, but can by no means be considered passive and powerless, even at her most

benign. Nathuram's ideological and psychological confusion may
be seen in his notion that she, who is often referred to as 'he', is
powerless and weak, requiring him to protect her/his honour. In
such a narrative, Gandhi the Father of the Nation is untrue to
the Hindu *rashtra* and therefore must be punished for his act of
infidelity. Such an Oedipal reading of Godse's act may go some
way to explaining the horror that Gandhi's death induces in the
Hindu mind. It may also explain India's traumatic tryst with both
the nation and with modernity, the latter being inaugurated with a
series of heinous killings, starting with the colonial British power's
hanging of Nandakumar, the first such execution of a Brahmin,
to Nathuram's patricide. Nathuram is thus unwittingly not merely
a modern Indian, but also a product of colonialism, looking for
strong masculine authority figures who must protect Mother India,
now enfeebled by alien rule and Partition and betrayed by weak
men. But for most Hindus, patricide is still an unspeakable crime
and must be erased from the nation's collective memory. Hence the
unresolved question over Gandhi's death, with the epochal event
remaining never fully accounted for in the national imaginary, but
usually explained away as sacrifice or martyrdom. Hence all those
narratives on the Mahatma in museums and exhibitions are never
really dealing with the killing itself but always looping back in a
circular fashion to his life.

8 The pollution

In most societies, killing is considered highly polluting. Since Louis Moulinier's magisterial study of pollution, *Le pur et l'impur dans la pensée des Grecs d'Homère à Aristote*, the most comprehensive discussion of ideas of pollution among the ancient Greeks is Robert Parker's *Miasma: Pollution and Purification in Early Greek Religion* (1983). For the ancient Greeks all evil, crime, wrongdoing and violation of conduct tainted and defiled the perpetrator. Such miasma may at first be literal and physical, when a killer is marked by the blood of his victim, which he must wash off before he can be purified again. But soon the literal, physical aspects of the contamination turned into something much deeper and more severe, a sort of alienation from one's essence and separation not just from society but severance from the cosmic order. Indeed, it is difficult for us to understand just how serious the threat of pollution was. To be polluted was not only to be split from one's own inner essence, that which made one a human being and entitled one to the privileges thereof, it also debarred one from the afterlife, whether it was the world of the heroes or the manes.[1] Pollution, until cleansed, meant an alienation from self, society and nature.

The extent of the dread of pollution in the Classical world can be gauged by the horror that the Chorus expresses at Medea's imminent murder of her own children in Euripedes' eponymous tragedy:

Earth, awake! Bright arrows of the Sun,
Look! Look down on the accursed woman
Before she lifts up a murderous hand
To pollute it with her children's blood!
For they are of your own golden race;
And for mortals to spill blood that grew
In the veins of gods is a fearful thing.[2]

Similarly, when Jason discovers Medea's crimes of jealousy he cries out:

You abomination! Of all women most detested
By every god, by me, by the whole human race!
You could endure – a mother! – to lift sword against
Your own little ones; to leave me childless, my life wrecked.
After such murder do you outface both Sun and Earth –
Guilty of gross pollution? May the gods blast your life![3]

Once again, what is striking is not just the anger or the grief, but also the utter horror and unbearable sense of pollution caused by Medea's filicides and murders. As the Chorus says earlier,

Where kindred blood pollutes the ground
A curse hangs over human lives;
And murder measures the doom that falls
By Heaven's law on the guilty house.[4]

What might strike a modern reader is how Euripides repeatedly stresses pollution rather than evil, passion, madness, sorrow, or rage. As Parker shows, homicides in Greek society were considered highly polluted as far back as in Homer.[5] Since there are few traces of blood feuds among the Greeks, the logical conclusion is that murderers were forced into exile owing to the pollution caused by their action.[6] This way, the cause of the problem was removed, also obviating the need for retribution.

So high was the sense of pollution caused by manslaughter in primitive societies that in *Totem and Taboo*, Freud corrects what he considers a general assumption that 'savage and half-savage' races are ruthless killers. This misconception still persists in the popular representations, especially in the West. On the contrary, Freud says,

> the killing of a man is governed by a number of observances which are included among the usages of taboo. These observances fall easily into four groups. They demand (1) the appeasement of the slain enemy, (2) restrictions upon the slayer, (3) acts of expiation and purification by him and (4) certain ceremonial observances.[7]

In other words, a murder could not simply be left alone. It violated the natural order of things and therefore elaborate rituals and observances were required to counteract its baneful effects. Murder, killing and death thus implicate the whole of society in a complex of violation, pollution, purification, atonement and so on, traces of which persist to this day.

Historically speaking, it is likely that some of these ideas of pollution and atonement, prevalent in both pagan and Jewish cultures, migrated into Christianity, where the original sin may itself be construed as the pollution arising from the violation of a sort of incest taboo – in the sense that Adam and Eve were siblings, which is why sex between them was forbidden. The wages of sin, in Christianity, is not only death, but if the sin is mortal, then eternal damnation. Similarly, Cain's murder of his brother, Abel, polluted him; cursed and marked by God, he wandered the earth till he founded the earth's first city, which is why pastoral innocence is never associated with cities. Cain was not only the first man born of woman, but also the first murderer and fratricide. Originally a farmer, while Abel was a shepherd, Cain could no longer pursue his original calling because the ground, polluted by his slain brother's blood, became infertile.[8] The taint left by Cain's crime could not be wiped out until, quite literally, the last of his descendants was drowned in the great flood.[9] The pollution caused by blood is also the reason that women in traditional societies were considered impure during menstruation. To cleanse the pollution of Adam and Eve's 'original sin', however, the blood of Jesus Christ was needed, blood here being much more potent than the traditionally universal purifier, water. Indeed blood, which normally pollutes, is here turned into a super-cleanser because it is after all no ordinary blood, but the blood of the Son of God. The general pollution of (wo)man is thus expiated by the sacrifice of the Messiah. This form of atonement, as James Frazer and others have shown, is a variation of offering a substitute or scapegoat who carries away the pollution, thus cleansing the community. But in this exchange what is peculiar is that the affected party, the entire human community, has no agency in either the sin that they are charged with or its atonement; they are merely passive recipients of both the pollution and the cleansing, their agency confined only to whether they accept the saviour and commit themselves to abjure sin in his name. In the case of Gandhi's murder, however, we are responsible both for the pollution and for the possible cleansing through the appropriate form of atonement.

In Hindu traditions, in contrast to Christianity, there is no notion of original sin; instead, there is an idea of original purity. The self, *atman*, is incorruptible, quite identical in substance, and in some views even in form, to Brahman or the Absolute. No wonder there are many words like *nirmala, suddha, saucha, socha, medhya, puta, niranjana*, and so on, to denote the original purity of the self. In the moral code enjoined by dharma, many negative actions including killing (*himsa*), lying (*asatya, anrta*), stealing, sexual misconduct, hoarding and so on are polluting, causing a break in the individual's contract with himself. Such a self-alienating rift can have serious and harmful consequences not just for the individual but also for the family or community. To mitigate or counteract these ill-effects, the tradition provides for an elaborate system of *prayashchita* or atonement.

As P. V. Kane's monumental *History of the Dharmaśāstras* shows, the Hindus evolved an elaborate methodology of penance to counterbalance the consequences of wrong actions, reducing the guilt and cleansing the pollution that accrues from them. Manusmriti outlines several means of mitigating the consequences of sin. These include *anutāpa* (regret), *prāṇāyāma* (breath control), *tapas* (askesis), *homa* (offerings in a fire sacrifice), *japa* (repetition of prayers), *dana* (charity), *upavasa* (fasting), *tirthayatrā* (going on pilgrimages), and so on.[10] In Volume V, Kane also discusses *vrata*, or solemn religious vows and undertakings, a practice which goes back to the Rig Veda.[11] Incidentally, vow-taking was very important in Gandhi's praxis and informed his lifelong experiments in self-improvement.

There is some disagreement on the efficacy of *prāyaścittas* for intentional offences. According to Manusmriti[12] unintentional sins are expiated through Vedic recitation and intentional sins can be obliterated by performing various *prāyaścittas*:

> (All) sages prescribe a penance for a sin unintentionally committed; some declare, on the evidence of the revealed texts, (that it may be performed) even for an intentional (offence).
>
> A sin unintentionally committed is expiated by the recitation of Vedic texts, but that which (men) in their folly commit intentionally, by various (special) penances.[13]

In contrast, the Yājñavalkya Smriti supposes that intentional crimes and violations are not cancelled by *prāyaścitta*, but the act of atonement will re-allow social interaction with the guilty (3.226); given the linguistic property of Sanskrit to permit multiple meanings in the way words can be parsed, the same verse, however, can be interpreted to mean its exact opposite, that is, atonement will cancel the sins but not permit reintegration with society for heinous offences committed intentionally. In either case, atonement is not complete for intentional sins. There is also a distinction between the degree, kind and agent of wrongdoing, with complicated gradations and variations. However, very few crimes result in 'mortal' pollution, which in traditional Hindu society meant excommunication or loss of caste or being forbidden from social intercourse with others, which was tantamount to a kind of death or at least a loss of identity. These heinous sins (*mahāpataka*) include the murder of a 'holy' man and sexual misconduct with one's guru's wife, who stands in the place of one's mother. Here is one list of such crimes:

> Killing a Brahmana, drinking (the spirituous liquor called) Sura, stealing (the gold of a Brahmana), adultery with a Guru's wife, and associating with such (offenders), they declare (to be) mortal sins (mahapataka).[14]

But obviously this is directed at Brahmins; drinking liquor was allowed to other caste groups. It is also clear that associating with those who are polluted on account of having violated the prescribed code of conduct is forbidden until these offenders have performed the proper penance:

> Let him not dwell together with the murderers of children, with those who have returned evil for good, and with the slayers of suppliants for protection or of women, though they may have been purified according to the sacred law.[15]

Overall, grievous offences, including killing, are highly polluting. In fact, the Manusmriti[16] considers killing not just humans or animals as polluting, but even boneless creatures, insects, trees, shrubs, plants – indeed, almost *any kind of living being*[17] and prescribes penances to atone for it.[18]

From this overview, it should be unmistakable that Nathuram's assassination of the Mahatma, a case of deliberate and intentional patricide, puts a spell of symbolic 'pollution' on the whole nation, already stained with so much bloodletting during the violence and massacres of the Partition. Given the abhorrence, in fact, the *impossibility* of patricide to the Hindu mind, this act violates the very 'soul' or spirit of the nation from the Hindu point of view, fracturing its inner integrity and casting a miasma of horror and despair on its prospects as a newly independent nation.

To understand better the nature of this contagion, we might turn to Mary Douglas's influential, if commonsensical, study *Purity and Danger: An Analysis of the Concepts of Pollution and Taboo* (1966; 1984). Douglas stresses that 'pollution is a type of danger which is not likely to occur except where the lines of structure, cosmic or social, are clearly defined'.[19] Having shown at great length how the prohibition against patricide is extremely strong and well defined in Hindu society, we may regard the objection that traditional or mythic notions of pollution may not apply to modern societies or situations as not very convincing. On the contrary, the polluting consequences of Gandhi's murder would be evident to most Hindus; at least instinctively they would understand its implications, which would register on their unconscious, even if they did not associate it at first with patricide or did not care to remember it as such. In matters of this sort, not paying attention or 'forgetting' are both symptoms of the kind of collective repression that I have been positing, not of its absence.

Parker's synthesizing encapsulation of how pollution occurs, which he offers towards the end of his book,[20] shows how it is not merely guilt or anxiety that trigger pollution but fundamental breaches in the normal order. 'A culture's beliefs about pollution [do not] derive from anxiety or a sense of guilt', says Parker, but are instead 'by-products of an ideal of order'.[21] What ensues after such pollution, which violates the ideal order, is a state of 'abnormality', which demands appropriate 'ritual measures' to set it right.[22] That a son must not kill his father is part of the ideal order of the Hindus; patricide, if Freud is to be believed, is also a universal taboo. That Nathuram does perform such a deed makes him break not just the ideal order but also India's sense of continuity with its past. It marks his brand of Hindu nationalism as a fundamental rupture from the general Hindu tradition. It is thus a radically modern action by a radically modern Hindu. Hinduism, as it were, gatecrashes into modernity through patricide; or, to put it another way, this is a radically un-Hindu act. *Prāyaścitta*, it is clear, is not just for purging one's own soul of pollution; it is, necessarily, also for the restoration of order in the whole of society. Consequently, the atonement for this act, the circle of responsibility for which has already been enlarged to include all of us, has to be both social and collective; only then will the wound in the psyche of the nation be healed, only then will a breach in its soul-fabric be mended. Gandhi, we must remember, was not only Bapu, Father of the Nation, but a holy man; spilling his innocent blood is therefore highly polluting in a lasting, inauspicious sense, for the whole country and its inhabitants.

9 The haunting

Sarojini Naidu (1879–1949) was a close associate, even an acolyte and disciple, of Gandhi. She not only had a long correspondence, but enjoyed a witty, irreverent, and yet admiring friendship with him. For years Sarojini was also the unofficial ambassador of the Indian National Congress, travelling extensively to spread the gospel of the Indian freedom struggle under Gandhi's leadership. A child prodigy, she passed the Madras matriculation examination at the age of 12, wrote long poem at the age of 13, fell in love with a considerably older man at 15, went to England to study, but did not complete her degree at Girton College, Cambridge, returned to India to marry Dr Govindarajulu Naidu when she was barely 21, had four children in quick succession, but then grew disenchanted with the sequestered life of a Hyderabadi housewife, and plunged into the freedom movement at the behest of Gopal Krishna Gokhale, Gandhi's 'guru', going on to become the President of the Indian National Congress in 1925, and first woman Governor of India's largest state, United Provinces (now Uttar Pradesh), after independence.

But before she joined politics, Sarojini was already famous as a poet. She came in contact with the fin de siècle poets in English, whose leader was Edmond Gosse. Both Gosse and the British symbolist poet Arthur Symonds befriended her and championed her work. Sarojini's first collection of verse, *The Golden Threshold*

(1905), was published by Heinemann in London, to much critical acclaim. She published two other collections, *The Bird of Time* (1912), and *The Broken Wing* (1917), before poetic fashions changed decisively with the onset of modernism. Sarojini was famous as an Indian poet before Tagore, though the latter was a much greater writer and won the Nobel prize. She was called the 'Nightingale of India' and was renowned as an eloquent public speaker.[1]

In a memorable and stirring speech significantly titled 'My Father, Do Not Rest', broadcast on the All India Radio on 1 February 1948, Sarojini hailed the Mahatma's spirit, which she believed had risen Christ-like on the third day after his assassination: 'Like Christ of old on the third day he has risen again in answer to the cry of his people and the call of the world for the continuance of his guidance, his love, his service and inspiration'.[2] This seldom-studied speech is a crucial part of the evidence of this reading of Gandhi's death, for it is Sarojini who inaugurates Gandhi's haunting of India.

Sarojini, though full of sorrow and tears like all the bereft followers and admirers of Gandhi, imagines that Gandhi is not really 'dead'. It is her way of turning the colossal tragedy of the assassination into a sort of spiritual triumph, quite like Christ's resurrection:

> And while we all mourn, those who loved him, knew him personally, and those to whom his name was but a miracle and a legend, though we are all full of tears and though we are full of sorrow on this third day when he has risen from his own ashes, I feel that sorrow is out of place and tears become a blasphemy.[3]

According to Sarojini, the reason such a transformation is possible in Gandhi's case, is because all his life the Mahatma taught that the spirit is more important than the body:

> How can he die, who through his life and conduct and sacrifice, who through his love and courage and faith has taught the

world that the spirit matters, not the flesh, that the spirit has the power greater than the powers of the combined armies of the earth, combined armies of the ages?[4]

Sarojini proceeds to set up a contrast between the small and the large, the frail and the powerful, the physical and metaphysical, the material and the spiritual, this world and the other world:

He was small, frail, without money, without even the full complement of garment to cover his body, not owning even as much earth as might be held on the point of a needle, how was he so much stronger than the forces of violence, the might of empires and the grandeur of embattled forces in the world? Why was it that this little man, this tiny man, this man with a child's body, this man so ascetic, living on the verge of starvation by choice so as to be more in harmony with the life of the poor, how was it that he exercised over the entire world, of those who revered him and those who hated him, such power as emperors could never wield?[5]

Thus she constitutes a mythos of superior power and glory, the proof in life and death of the greater might of soul-force over brute force, the strength of truth and non-violence of one ordinary man over the falsehood of empires and armies.

Interestingly, as her narrative continues, Sarojini, gradually if unconsciously, begins to admit the great distance between Gandhi and the rest of us, in which she includes herself. Gandhi's life and action are not to be judged or understood in terms of the yardstick set by the common run of humankind. Indeed, though she seeks to represent him, explain and articulate his uniqueness to the world, she finds her inspiration flagging. Gandhi is not to be easily explained or captured in words; it is as if she begins to lose grip on her project to encapsulate him or arrest his essence for a stunned nation mourning his loss. A gradual distancing is thus evident as her peroration progresses:

It was because he did not care for applause, he did not care for censure. He only cared for the path of righteousness. He cared only for the ideals that he preached and practised. And in the midst of the most terrible disasters caused by violence and greed of men, when the abuse of the world was heaped up like dead leaves, dead flowers on battlefields, his faith never swerved in his ideal of non-violence. He believed that though the whole world slaughter itself and the whole world's blood be shed, still his non-violence would be the authentic foundation of the new civilisation of the world and he believed that he who seeks his life shall lose it and he who loses his life shall find it.[6]

Again, she takes recourse, in the end, to biblical allusion and phraseology to account for Gandhi's extremism, his impractical and persistent adherence to his beliefs in the face of impossible odds. It is as if she is tacitly admitting that Gandhi's stubbornness was misplaced if not mistaken, that the 'real' world was far too brutal and ugly for his idealism and purity.

Sarojini next goes to the root of the hatred that resulted in Gandhi's slaughter, the internal strife and division in the nation, not only between Hindus and Muslims, but between Hindus and Hindus, whose far-reaching consequence was not just the Partition of the country amidst untold violence and bloodletting, but the very killing of the Mahatma whose idea of the nation was predicated upon unity and brotherhood. More profoundly, Sarojini hints that violence directed outward also strikes inside a community – the problem of Hindu vs. Muslim could never be separated from the problem of Hindu vs. Hindu. The killing of the Mahatma was a great tragedy for the Hindus, who out of a mistaken notion of his partiality to the Muslims, had taken the extreme step of killing him. What greater irony could there be than the greatest Hindu of modern times not being recognized or understood by his own co-religionists?

> It was very evident that it was not any community but his that
> disapproved so violently and showed its anger and resentment
> in such a dastardly fashion. Alas for the Hindu community,
> that the greatest Hindu of them all, the only Hindu of our age
> who was so absolutely and unswervingly true to the doctrine, to
> the ideals, the philosophy of Hinduism should have been slain
> by the hand of a Hindu! That indeed, that indeed is almost
> the epitaph of the Hindu faith that the hand of a Hindu in the
> name of Hindu rights and a Hindu world should sacrifice the
> noblest of them all.[7]

Here, albeit in passing, Sarojini touches on the horror, the
pollution, the shame, the sorrow – indeed the unspeakability – of
Nathuram's crime. Again, we notice how unbearable the event is
so that it must not, *cannot*, be dwelled upon. Sarojini, too, passes
beyond it rather too hastily:

> But, as I say, it would be the act of faithless deserters if we
> were to yield to despair. If we were indeed to believe that he
> is dead, if we were to believe that all is lost, because he has
> gone, of what avail would be our love and our faith? Of what
> avail would be our loyalty to him if we dare to believe that all
> is lost because his body is gone from our midst? Are we not
> there, his heirs, his spiritual descendants, the legatees of his
> great ideals, successors of his great work? Are we not there
> to implement that work and enhance it and enrich and make
> greater achievements by joint efforts than he could have made
> singly? Therefore, I say the time is over for private sorrow.[8]

It is peculiar how Sarojini contrasts *private* sorrow with *public*
avowal of Gandhi's mandate, choosing the latter to overcome
the former.[9] Why does she not consider the possibility of public
sorrow and private avowal of non-violence and *satyagraha* as the
more logical way ahead? I think that is because the immediate task

is to deny mourning, to forbid sorrow, and to interdict a national soul-searching on what might be the meaning of Gandhi's death. On the third day after his death the more pressing task is to heal, to move forward, to fill the void caused by the Mahatma's demise.

Sarojini's next move is, therefore, to be expected: it is a call to action, to divert the mind from the loss and to engage it in meaningful work:

> The time is over for beating of breasts and tearing of hair. The time is here and now when we stand up and say, 'We take up the challenge' to those who defied Mahatma Gandhi. We are his living symbols. We are his soldiers. We are the carriers of his banner before an embattled world. Our banner is truth. Our shield is non-violence. Our sword is a sword of the spirit that conquers without blood. Let the peoples of India rise up and wipe their tears, rise up and still their sobs, rise up and be full of hope and full of cheer. Let us borrow from him, why borrow, he has handed it to us, the radiance of his own personality, the glory of his own courage, the magnificent epic of his character. Shall we not follow in the footsteps of our master? Shall we not obey the mandates of our father? Shall not we his soldiers carry his battle to triumph? Shall we not give to the world the completed message of Mahatma Gandhi?[10]

The call to action helps refocus the attention of the nation, to shift the polluting blot of the murder into a rousing mark on the forehead, a battle cry for non-violence that will resonate across the nations unto the high heavens:

> Though his voice will not speak again, have we not a million, million voices to bear his message to the world, not only to this world, to our contemporaries, but to the world generation after generation? Shall sacrifice be in vain? Shall his blood be shed for futile purposes of mourning? Or, shall we not use that

blood as a tilak on our foreheads, the emblem of his legion of peace-loving soldiers to save the world? Here and now, here and now, I for one before the world that listens to my quivering voice pledge myself and you, as I pledged myself more than thirty years ago, to the service of the undying Mahatma.[11]

In a sense, Sarojini is sowing the seeds of the afterlife of Gandhi in his dying moments, pledging herself – and her listeners – to his ideals, to service and sacrifice. The dead Gandhi has thus been apotheosized into 'the undying Mahatma'.

After so much Christian terminology, Sarojini now suddenly resorts to a gesture that is both autobiographical and quintessentially Hindu. She remembers her own father Aghorenath Chattopadhyay's dying words:

What is death? My own father, dying, just before his death with the premonition of death on him, said: 'There is no birth. There is no death. There is only the soul seeking higher and higher stages of truth.' Mahatma Gandhi who lived for truth in this world has been translated, though by the hand of an assassin, to a higher stage of the truth which he sought.[12]

The great tragedy and loss of the Mahatma's death has thus been deftly averted. He is not dead, but has been *translated* to a higher level of truth. It is not just that this earth with all its sorrows is not the ultimate reality, but that, as the Gita would remind us, death itself, like life, is merely a transition in an unending sequence of the soul's evolution to higher levels of truth.

There is also the question of who will reap the spiritual surplus that Gandhi has generated. Who will be the inheritors of Gandhi's mantle and mandate, who will harvest the enormous loyalty and sympathy generated by his murder? The answer is clear. As a loyal soldier of the Congress Party, Sarojini also anoints Gandhi's successors:

Shall we not take up his place? Shall not our united strength be strong enough to preach and practise, his great message for the world? I am here one of the lowliest of his soldiers, but along with me I know that his beloved disciples like Jawaharlal Nehru, like his trusted followers and friends Vallabhbhai Patel, Rajendra Babu, who was like St. John in the bosom of Christ,[13] and those others of his associates who at a moment's notice flew from all ends of India to make their last homage at his feet. Shall we not all take up his message and fulfil it?[14]

Nehru is the Prime Minister; Prasad the President, and Vallabhbhai Patel the Home Minister and Deputy Prime Minister of independent India, all leaders of the Congress Party, who rule, Sarojini implies, in Gandhi's name. Sarojini, also a beneficiary, although less spectacular, of the windfall that accrued to the Congress, was the Governor (or, as she sometimes said jokingly, the Governess) of India's largest state, the United Provinces.

But it is in the last lines of her soulful oration that Sarojini really performs her most stunning and creative manoeuvre. Instead of a conventional apotheosis or a translation to a higher state, in contrast to her earlier attempt to resurrect or immortalize Gandhi, she suddenly prays that he *not* rest in peace. She does not want, through her very act of memorialization, to dismiss and forget Gandhi; she does not want his bones to rest in peace and for the people who adored him to carry on as before; she does not wish to put an end to the Gandhian narrative. On the contrary, instead of laying him to rest, she turns him into a ghost who haunts the nation:

May the soul of my master, my leader, my father rest not in peace, not in peace, but let his ashes be so dynamically alive that the charred ashes of the sandalwood, let the powder of his bones be so charged with life and inspiration that the whole of India will after his death be revitalised into the reality of freedom.

My father, do not rest. Do not allow us to rest.[15]

Gandhi now becomes the 'ghost who walks' – not the Phantom of the US comic book produced by Lee Falk, which incidentally was the most popular comic in India for decades – but a peculiarly Indian sort of spirit who produces, as Rajkumar Hirani's lovable goon Munna says, a *chemical locha* (a chemical disturbance) in the brains of succeeding generations of Indians. Gandhi's life is over, but his afterlife will continue to move, disturb, and haunt us.

Sarojini ends by giving us some hints of what this afterlife will be like, even as she asks of the dead Mahatma the strength to keep her pledge:

> Keep us to our pledge. Give us strength to fulfil our promise, your heirs, your descendants, your stewards, the guardians of your dreams, the fulfillers of India's destiny. You, whose life was so powerful, make it so powerful in your death, far from mortality you have passed mortality by a supreme martyrdom in the cause most dear to you.[16]

The pledge, the bond which she wishes all Indians to have with the 'Father' of the nation is of course a sort of debt to be repaid. We have incurred the debt by being directly or indirectly responsible for his death; it is a crime or sin we should atone for, a pollution that we need to cleanse before we can be free or whole again, restored to our unbroken essential state. But it is also a debt in the sense of a gift which the nation's founding father has left us by virtue of his bequest to enjoy into perpetuity.

Hindus believe that they are born with debts and obligations – to the Gods, to the ancestors, to parents, and to teachers – similarly, contemporary, post-colonial citizens of India too have incurred debts from those who ensured that they would be born free in their own nation state. Sarojini hints that the only way to repay our debt to Gandhi is to contribute to the ongoing project of nation-building and society-formation, by giving back and discharging our responsibilities so that what we have inherited is neither wasted nor spoiled, but preserved and increased for the next generation. The power of the Mahatma is hereby augmented in passing from embodiment to disembodiment, his martyrdom to the cause dear to him, non-violence and the brotherhood of all Indians, serving as a trigger to his enhanced estate.

In the process of such a transformation, however, Gandhi's action is not over, his task not finished. Instead, he is to have no peace, no rest; like any idea that resonates after the death of its staunchest advocate, he too is to persist and continue beyond his ashy grave or magnificent memorials into the very hearts and minds of Indians for generations to come. Somewhat like the ghost of someone snatched untimely from life, Gandhi's calm and fully conscious confrontation with death turns him into a spectral presence haunting post-colonial Indians. There *is* a way to escape this haunting, this visitation, though Sarojini does not spell it out. It is by undoing the two-nation theory, by making peace between Hindus and Hindus, Hindus and Muslims, men and women, upper castes and dalits. That, to put it simply, would be Gandhi's way.

10 The guilt

In 1945, soon after the defeat of Germany and the end of World War II, Karl Jaspers delivered a series of profound and moving lectures on 'The Question of German Guilt'.[1] These were published in German as *Die Schuldfrage* in 1947, a few months before Gandhi's assassination, and in a widely discussed English translation in 1948 soon after. Jaspers begins by acknowledging that 'The temptation to evade this question is obvious; we live in distress – large parts of our population are in so great, such acute distress that they seem to have become insensitive to such discussions'.[2] Perhaps, a vast number of Indians also felt a similar sense of distress and apathy after the traumas, bloodletting, and displacement of the Partition. Under the circumstances, it would not be difficult to understand the evasion, if not repression, of their guilt not only in the enormous carnage and violence of Partition but also in the murder of the Mahatma which was somehow intrinsically linked to this subcontinental tragedy. Though the circumstances were so different, we may have much to learn from Jasper's exploration of German guilt over the atrocities against the Jews and the great bloodbath of the war.

Jaspers distinguishes four types and levels of guilt. First, there is criminal guilt, which concerns actual crimes and cognizable offences punishable under existing laws and juridical processes. Nathuram

Godse and Narayan Apte were tried, sentenced and hanged to death under this process. Several of their accomplices also went to jail after being convicted; some, like Savarkar, who were charged with criminal conspiracy, were acquitted for want of evidence. The re-examination of the case by Justice Kapur resulted in the unearthing of many more links and widened the circle of blame for Gandhi's murder, but did not result in any fresh convictions. To all intents and purposes, this brief account more or less spells out the extent of the criminal guilt in Gandhi's murder. But if we consider Gandhi's murder as intimately tied to the logic of the Partition and the two-nation theory, to the civil war between Hindus and Muslims, the internecine strife between Indians themselves, then the criminal guilt of the thousands, even hundreds of thousands, who committed murder, rape, arson, loot, pillage, destruction of public property, and all kinds of other crimes cannot be so easily exonerated or forgotten. That the law and order machinery had failed or that during mass rioting and mob violence the rule of law was defunct is no excuse for their culpability. Their criminal acts would never be tried, nor would they be brought to justice, but that is no reason to absolve them of their crimes. Their criminal guilt remains and, given the failure of the law to prosecute them, turns into moral and metaphysical guilt.

The second category of guilt according to Jaspers is political guilt. Its circumference, as far as India is concerned, is much wider. It extends not only to those responsible for Gandhi's security or for law and order in general, but the newly installed Government of India itself, at whose helm were Gandhi's own closest disciples, followers and associates. But political guilt, according to Jaspers, extends to all citizens of a state because they are responsible for the actions of the state: 'Everybody is coresponsible for the way he is governed'.[3] Even if we are 'alienated from politics'[4] or apathetic to political issues, we are still responsible. That is because political inactivity or non-participation in politics cannot save us either from political responsibility or from guilt: 'Politically everyone acts in the modern state, at least by voting, or failing to vote, in elections. The sense of political liability lets no man dodge'.[5] The only way to counteract political guilt is by supporting the right causes and by refusing to collaborate with evil regimes. That is because 'Every human being is fated to be enmeshed in the power relations he lives by'; we must therefore join in the 'struggle for power for the sake of serving the right'.[6] Failure to do so 'creates basic political guilt and moral guilt at the same time'.[7]

Thus we see how easily political guilt may also slide into moral guilt of some sort. When it comes to events leading to the Partition of India, political guilt must squarely rest on the shoulders not only of those who committed the criminal acts mentioned above but those who directed them and used them to create nations. The application of rioting, killing, raping, looting and so on to achieve political ends taints so many regimes, not the least of which is Pakistan, clearly one of the most violent states in the region. At its inception, there was violence with many ghastly incidents such as 'Direct Action Day', the Calcutta killings, the invasion of Kashmir by mercenaries and so on; the three wars fought with India, one of which culminated in the creation of Bangladesh after the failure of its genocidal oppression, and the continuing acts of terror against India may all be given as examples. But other states in the region including India, Sri Lanka and Nepal, who also have histories of violent civil strife, cannot be spared either. Each of these states has used the state and non-state actors to perpetrate acts of violence for political ends.

As if anticipating such possibilities, Gandhi clearly warned against the creation of belligerent states, in *Hind Swaraj* (1909). Acts of terror in the service of freedom from imperial rule, according to him, were sure to result in a state which would be violent and warlike itself. The citizens of all such aggressive states, whether victorious or defeated, must share in their political guilt. No wonder, the citizens of the United States, one of the most aggressive and warlike states in our world, cannot avoid their share of political guilt in its acts. Political guilt must also accrue from the structural violence and oppression within states, those systems of exploitation, inequality and discrimination that continue to best the poor and the dispossessed in our very midst. We are all guilty for the ill-treatment of the wretched of the earth, as Gandhi said to us over and over again. To some, following Jaspers, this may be an example of moral, rather than political guilt: 'Blindness for the misfortune of others, lack of imagination of the heart, inner indifference toward the witnessed evil – that is moral guilt'.[8] To Gandhi political guilt was no different from moral guilt, because politics to him was nothing but a form of morality.

Moral guilt is the third kind that Jaspers identifies. Its basis is simple, even self-evident: 'I, who cannot act otherwise than as an individual, am morally responsible for all my deeds'.[9] Therefore, even if my crimes escape detection or criminal proceedings, even if I am somehow not politically responsible for them, I cannot escape moral responsibility. There may, of course, be mitigating circumstances, but 'every deed remains subject to moral judgment'.[10] However, Jaspers is quick to point out that 'Morally man can condemn only himself, not another'.[11] This is because we cannot sit in judgement on others. Moral guilt, unlike criminal or political guilt, is a matter of one's own conscience. That is why Jaspers considers it 'nonsensical' to

> charge a whole people with a crime. The criminal is always only an individual. It is nonsensical, too, to lay moral guilt to a people as a whole. There is no such thing as a national character extending to every single member of a nation. . . . Morally one can judge the individual only, never a group.[12]

Ideas of 'collective guilt' are thus essentially political to Jaspers, not moral. Indeed he says, 'To pronounce a group criminally, morally or metaphysically guilty is an error akin to the laziness and arrogance of average, uncritical thinking'.[13] It was, after all the ascription of collective guilt to Jews that became the precondition for their slaughter; to brand all Germans guilty, as posters put up during the Allied occupation did, was also not sustainable. Indeed, it was to take the issue of German guilt head-on that Jaspers gave these lectures in the first place. That is why, though he admitted that 'Guilt . . . is necessarily collective as the political liability of nations', he was quick to clarify that it was collective 'not in the same sense as moral and metaphysical, and never as criminal guilt'.[14]

To avoid a purely solipsistic and isolated notion of moral guilt, however, Jaspers also provides for an engagement with others 'in the solidarity of charitable struggle'.[15] It is only when one makes 'common cause', in an arena of closeness with other actors that one might conduct the examination of moral guilt outside one's own solitary or personal space: 'moral guilt can truthfully be discussed only in a loving struggle between men who maintain solidarity among themselves'.[16] Though the jurisdiction for moral guilt rests with my own individual conscience, I can carry the dialogue forward 'in communication with my friends and intimates who are lovingly concerned about my soul'.[17] It is in this sense that one engages one's own countrymen and women in an exploration of the death of the Father of the Nation because it is a matter that concerns us all, taking us to the very heart of how we became a nation. As Jaspers puts it, 'we are free to talk with one another, insofar as we are in communication, and morally to help each other achieve clarity'.[18] This is what we are attempting here by exploring such a topic together.

However, there are times when we may not be involved criminally, politically, or even morally, but we feel metaphysically guilty. If the crime is as great as the Holocaust, then even the fact 'That I live after such a thing has happened weighs upon me as indelible guilt'.[19] That we are comfortable, secure, and well-fed while others are starving, homeless, or destitute may also fill us with a metaphysical guilt. For metaphysical guilt, Jaspers says, 'Jurisdiction rests with God alone'.[20] Indeed, 'If human beings were able to free themselves from metaphysical guilt, they would be angels, and all the other three concepts of guilt would become immaterial'.[21] It is in this fourth category of metaphysical guilt that Jaspers comes closest to traditional Christian theology, with its notion of original sin. By being human and participating in the collective human condition, with all its flaws and horrors, we are all 'guilty' metaphysically.

But what of those who don't care, whose hearts are hardened? As Jaspers says, 'tens of thousands, are beyond moral guilt for as long as they do not feel it. They seem incapable of repentance and change'.[22] Citing Hitler and his closest followers as examples, Jaspers concedes, 'They are what they are. Force alone can deal with such men who live by force alone'.[23] This is a revealing insight about the way the cosmic law seems to operate: those who live by the sword die by the sword. Jaspers' remarks, or indeed explorations such as these on the meaning of Gandhi's death, cannot be directed at such men, though Gandhi would say that no man has lost his humanity to such an extent as to be impervious to the force of non-violence or love. Yet, more ordinarily, 'moral guilt' for Jaspers 'exists for all those who give room to conscience and repentance. The morally guilty are those who are capable of penance'.[24]

That is why we must ask to what extent we ourselves condone or even approve of those who caused Gandhi's assassination. Such a question will reveal that part of us where the killer has already made his home. All those who had suffered the horrors of the Partition and wanted retribution, all those who believed that Gandhi was a nuisance, the enemy of Hindus, whose ideas had made us impotent, incapable of retaliation, therefore sitting ducks to militaristic Muslims, all those who wished secretly that the old man was better dead than alive, all such Indians surely have cause for introspection. Our guilt, despite its repression, will not leave us so easily. 'Only the forgetful can deceive themselves' Jasper says, 'since they want to deceive themselves'.[25]

But is it so simple? Does not the repressed return with a vengeance, troubled by a bad conscience: 'Many a young man or

woman nowadays awakens with a horrible feeling: my conscience
has betrayed me'.[26] And why must we do something to alleviate
our guilt – not only because that will free us from our neurosis as
a nation, but because 'The consequences of guilt affect real life,
whether or not the person affected realizes it, and they affect my
self-esteem if I perceive my guilt'.[27] What is more, we must learn
to atone for our guilt because we *love* India. As Jaspers says, 'The
fatherland ceases to be a fatherland when its soul is destroyed'.[28]
This may apply as well to our motherland, India, which will cease
to be itself if it continues to harbour hatred and ill-will not only
towards Gandhi, but towards some sections which make up its
very core components, whether these are Hindus, Muslims, dalits,
women, or some other subgroup.

From deep searching into the roots of guilt comes great and
transformative knowledge: 'The outgrowth of the moral guilt is
insight, which involves *penance and renewal*'.[29] If this is what an
analysis of moral guilt leads to, then metaphysical guilt 'results in
a *transformation of human self-consciousness before God*'.[30] Just soul-
searching may lead to a new life not just for individuals but for
nations. 'This self-transformation by inner activity may lead to a
new source of active life',[31] one in which our pride is shattered, we
grow in humility, and 'where arrogance becomes impossible'.[32] It is
towards such a transformation that our exploration of the death of
Gandhi logically leads us. This exercise is not about wallowing in
some sort of self-indulgent guilt trip; rather it is a process in which
we learn to 'analyze, judge and cleanse ourselves'.[33]

Jaspers speaks as astutely and candidly of how a large number
of the German people may have been tacitly complicit in the Nazi
regime by 'partial approval . . . by *straddling* and occasional *inner
assimilation* and accommodation'.[34] I think by similar processes,
a great number of Indians may have partially approved not only
the murder of Gandhi but also participated in communal hatred,
which in one form or another still continues. We need to remember
how Gandhi's death is not merely the death of one man, but also

the slaying of a dream, the dream of communal harmony. That his murder is an act of communal hatred, not of individual hatred, is what makes it a matter for the general populace to atone for.

We must also not confuse such hatred with a genuine desire or necessity to defend ourselves from aggression and violence. Here, Krishna's injunction to Arjuna may serve as a guide: we must fight for the sake of dharma, but not for hatred, anger, or desire. Gandhi himself said that a valiant's man's self-defensive violence was preferable to a coward's non-violence. But just as it was important in Nazi Germany to make an 'either-or' choice for or against Nazism, similarly we need to make an either-or choice – against communalism, the two-nation theory, and hatred for one another. We cannot camouflage our tacit approval for the crimes of nations and communities through 'convenient *self-deception*'.[35] If we do so, we 'would remain inwardly brittle otherwise, and inclined to further fanaticism'.[36] What Jaspers says of Germans may apply equally to Indians:

> Whoever took part in the race mania, whoever had delusions of a revival based on fraud, whoever winked at the crimes then already committed is not merely liable but must renew himself morally. Whether and how he can do it is up to him alone, and scarcely open to any outside scrutiny.[37]

Jaspers offers us a clear insight into how hatred is generated and renewed in repetitive cycles that reproduce themselves.

In this context, Jaspers quotes Kant, 'who called it a premise of international law that nothing must occur in war which would make a later reconcilement of the belligerents impossible'.[38] When we think of all the acts committed during the Partition, many, we would acknowledge, make later reconciliation extremely difficult, if not impossible. Of course, there was an older basis for the belligerence between the Hindus and the Muslims, which includes the much earlier invasions and conquest of India by the latter, with its history of great violence, genocide, conversion, vandalism, loot, pillage and destruction. Since there was no clear acknowledgement of these wrongs, let alone atonement for them, it is not difficult to reopen the unhealed wounds that were left in the national psyche. But, ultimately, 'the recapitulation of the others' actions does not have the significance of alleviating our guilt'.[39] We must find another way out.

This, clearly, is 'to purge ourselves of whatever guilt each one finds in himself, *as* far as this is possible by restitution, by atonement, by inner renewal and metamorphosis'.[40] Given how deep the taboo against and the horror of patricide is and how pervasive ideas of *prāyaścitta* (atonement), if not guilt, are in the Hindu psyche, penance and atonement would seem the only way to exorcise or lay to rest the haunting of the nation by Gandhi's ghost. According to Jaspers, we must accept not only our helplessness in the face of the enormity of an event such as Gandhi's murder, but 'guilt must be accepted', so that some sort of 'transmutation' may follow.[41]

In a short concluding section, Jaspers talks of the 'way of purification', bringing his discourse in line with our earlier speculation on the deeply polluting nature of the murder of Gandhi and of Partition violence. He advocates 'Purification in action' which means, 'first of all, making amends'.[42] We must make reparation, but how? The answer is rather straightforward: by resisting the misuse of religion for political ends in public life and resisting hatred within ourselves. Religious fanaticism and intolerance, we must realize, has the capacity to destroy us; we must therefore never succumb to it, regardless of the temptation and provocation. It would be utterly unfortunate and self-defeating to succumb to its appeal either in a vengeful spirit, in retaliation for real or perceived wrongs, or out of expedience and calculation, because it may help us achieve our political ends faster or easier. Like Frankenstein's monster, communal hatred has the capacity to turn around to devour its creators.

But reparation will not work, will not succeed, Jaspers insists, if it is 'not earnestly willed': it will not 'fulfill its moral purpose except as it ensues from our cleansing transmutation'.[43] In other words, reparation, making amends, and penance – none of these can be faked or performed merely as gestures of appeasement or mollification. These will remain token gestures, empty of content, if they do not emanate from inner transmutation and cleansing. It is not what we display to the world, but what we are inside that really matters. That is why enforced constitutional and other measures to remove social differences in India will not work without an inner change of heart. This was precisely Gandhi's line as opposed to Ambedkar's; the latter wanted legal and other guarantees to promote the rights of the untouchables. In the process, we have today another war zone within Indian society along caste lines, with continuing hostilities, resentments and cynicism. The problem has not really been solved because there has been no inner transformation, no genuine atonement, no real penance on the part of the upper-castes from crimes committed and wrongs done.

No wonder, like Gandhi, Jaspers avers that 'purification is an inner process which is never ended but in which we continually become ourselves'.[44] Like the struggle for Svaraj, atonement and purification are continuous processes. We can never fully arrive, ridding ourselves of all our guilt, whether it is moral or metaphysical. But without purification and penance there cannot be freedom either, for 'Everyone comes again and again to the fork in the road, to the choice between the clean and the murky'.[45] We definitely need to come to terms with Gandhi's murder and with the great violence of the Partition that preceded it and in preventing which the frail, old Mahatma gave his life. We have to confront this collective repression in the Hindu mind; we have to accept our share of the guilt that accrues from the extent that we participated or continue to participate in violent hatred against other communities and in religious intolerance. For, as Jaspers puts it, 'without purification of the soul there is no political liberty'.[46] It is only 'such purification' that 'makes us free'.[47] Connecting to this theme of guilt and redemption and recalling another German philosopher, Ashis Nandy in 'Adorno in India: Revisiting the Psychology of Fascism' ends by meditating on the value of genuine soul-searching for a society like India: 'Such a society does not have to turn psychotherapeutic. It has continuously to try to be humane';[48] in the very next sentence, he avers, 'there is not much difference between the two'.[49] This is the sort of transformation much hoped for in the subcontinent.

11   The unbearable modernity of patricide

We have seen how in executing the Father of the Nation Nathuram did what, in a sense, no Hindu had dared to before him. His action thus caused an almost unbridgeable rupture between India's past and its present. From another perspective, the significant but hardly studied philosopher Basanta Kumar Mallik[1] also regarded Gandhi's death as a watershed separating the old from the new in a decisive way. The old to him was the community-oriented way of life that Asian traditional societies once followed, but which was India's present, until the first half of the twentieth century.

Mallik spent a memorable weekend with Bapu when the latter was a guest at his in-laws' at Hazaribagh. After Gandhi was assassinated, Mallik circulated a note called 'Mahaprasthan', which later became the introduction to a small book, *Gandhi – A Prophecy* (1948). Madhuri Santhanam Sondhi, one of the few scholars to have engaged seriously with Mallik, calls it 'a mediation on the significance of Gandhi's death and the new direction to which it pointed both for India and the world'.[2] This remarkable book is also fascinating because Mallik calls it a 'prophecy'. It was written, Sondhi says, 'in a mood of prescience and insight . . . recording what Gandhi said';[3] in other words, Mallik thought that Gandhi's spirit was speaking directly to him, not entirely unlike Munna in the Bollywood blockbuster *Lage*

Raho Munna Bhai, to which we shall pay more attention to in a later section.

Mallik is drawn into an inquiry of the historical implications of Gandhi's death. He is convinced that Gandhi's assassination 'is not just another unfortunate tragedy, but an event that signifies a watershed in world history'.[4] 'In macro terms', this event for Mallik, 'signals the end of the era of tradition not only for India, but for the rest of the world'.[5] According to Mallik, the event had four major implications. First of all, Gandhi's killing was a 'rejection not only of Gandhism as narrowly defined, but through Gandhi of the Indian tradition in its entirety'.[6] The reason for such a conclusion is that though it was Nathuram who pulled the trigger, much of India had already rejected the Mahatma's message. For Mallik, this meant that 'no ideal or plan can ever come to fruition without the consent of those for whom it is intended'.[7] But the implications were far deeper: Gandhi's assassination showed the 'climactic failure' of 'the second restatement', after Ramakrishna's, 'of Indian tradition'[8] rearticulated for modern times, but retaining its classical form. For Mallik, Gandhi's death therefore marked a clean break with the past; it proved that 'after the nineteenth century it has not been possible to effectively restate the Indian tradition'.[9] That was the reason why Gandhi's call in *Hind Swaraj* for a return to the 'Moral State' of a traditional group society such as India had been for centuries had few takers; what the text proposed was, essentially, impossible. The death of the 'Gandhi-Indian tradition' was 'final and absolute at this particular point in history'.[10] One reason for this failure was that Gandhi's non-violence may have itself been coercive, and to that extent violent, placing 'an unnatural strain on the other's moral nature'.[11] Not surprisingly, 'Gandhi left behind no heritage, no bequest for humanity. When he died, his vision died with him'.[12] As Gandhi himself said, no one person would fully succeed him or embody his vision.

Secondly, according to Mallik, in the present condition of the world, it was impossible to solve the conflicts between major world

views and types of civilization, of which there were primarily three
types: the humanistic-individualistic, founded in ancient Greece,
one version of which was Western-style modernity; the Asian
absorptionist or mystical type, of which India was an example;
and the Abrahamic, dualistic type, based on monotheism and
strong group identity. In the present age, we notice 'conflicting
and opposed human purposes remain in a perpetual conflictual
see-saw of victory and defeat, until both sides together reach
frustration' says Mallik,[13] prefiguring Samuel Huntington's *Clash of
Civilizations* (1996). Both Gandhi and Jinnah had succeeded, but
only partially. Gandhi freed India from British imperialism but was
frustrated in his aspiration for a united or undivided subcontinent.
Jinnah, on the other hand, freed his Muslim followers from Hindu
majoritarian rule, but could not create a successful Islamic state.
Gandhi's great dream of 'restoring the group society' also 'remained
unfulfilled'; as Sondhi puts it:

> It may still be argued that with Gandhi's death there was an
> unprecedented simultaneous frustration of all types together,
> unprecedented for in the past any defeated scheme was always
> superseded by its victorious opponent or competitor.[14]

But in the present scenario it was not as if the failure to revert to
her ancient civilization meant that India's tryst with modernity
was successful:

> Although free India apparently took the path of individualism
> through the adoption of several 'modern', which Mallik
> had classified as European/humanist, institutions and
> knowledgeable-systems, i.e., appeared to supplant the
> group scheme with the individualist, Mallik looked upon
> it as an artificial transplant, doomed to rejection, as indeed
> political developments in post-independence India appear to
> confirm.[15]

The logical conclusion for Mallik was that the death of the Mahatma signified the 'onset of an entirely new era . . . an era struggling to be born and recognized'.[16]

The third significance of the death of Gandhi to Mallik was the persistence of suffering for individuals as well as societies. Somewhat like the Buddha, Mallik believed that 'there is no escape from suffering'.[17] This suffering, however, is not merely individual or existential, but also social and political. As Sondhi puts it:

> Mallik points to the illusion of agency in a world of intrinsic relatedness whereby we either create suffering in the clash and competition of contradictory values, either through one side inflicting frustration on the other or undergoing it when the reverse takes place.[18]

Thus we are at a time when no side wins clearly, but each has an illusory sense of agency. Action of this sort is without decisive outcome, dogged by competition and the clash of conflicting values, resulting in all-round frustration. This is a sort of 'world pessimism' because 'in the end', according to Mallik, 'nothing happens . . . The values and objectives remain equally unfulfilled'.[19]

Finally, given that there was 'no escape from the framework of the universe' in which 'conflict is inevitable',[20] the only way forward is not the 'restoration of old values' but 'the opening of a path towards discovery of new norms and organization'.[21] What these might be is not yet clear, even 60 years after the death of Gandhi. As Sondhi puts it,

> Today, Gandhi can no longer be regarded as a force in political life; he serves either as a model for selective imitation in non-violent protest movements . . . or as an example to be shunned, as by global and industrial modernizers and believers in realpolitik. . . . He is also often viewed, especially in his own

country, as an interesting curiosity belonging to an idealistic 'bygone' age but defying emulation in the present.[22]

Gandhi's sudden eclipse makes sense if we were to regard him, following Mallik's opinion, as 'the last major experiment in re-enacting the values of tradition'.[23] But the defeat of tradition and of Gandhi is actually 'the promise of a very different type of fulfilment' hinted at in Mallik's idea of 'Bapuji's society of beings'.[24] The fuller implications of this were, however, never spelled out by Mallik, but it seems to indicate the next stage of historical evolution, somewhat like Aurobindo's idea of the supermentalization of the earth. More immediately, the assassination was 'a radical break with past historical patterns. The world had now been catapulted into the fourth stage of non-triumphalism in which no traditional scheme could prevail by commanding absolute faith and allegiance'.[25] Given that a 'simple return to India's Moral State' as advocated by Gandhi in *Hind Swaraj* was no longer possible, nor was a 'cross-civilizational leap into a humanistic or Legal State', what India had to do was to try 'to search for the basis of a new "World State" dominated neither by group nor individualist values, mediated neither by authoritarian nor libertarian methods'.[26]

As Sondhi concludes, 'For Mallik the two events of Partition and Assassination were interlinked: the former he had already described as the defeat of India and Gandhi; the latter's assassination put a seal on it'.[27] Godse's act of supreme and ruthless individualism brought the era of the collective social relations of India to an end; it represented the partial victory of anti-traditional modernity. Individualism, which was modern Europe's signature, had at last made decisive inroads into India. We may also regard Nathuram's act as supremely modern because he was able not only to break an age-old taboo against patricide, but because his cold, deliberate, premeditated assassination made him an agent of a special kind of instrumental rationality that is uniquely modern. That he tried to legitimate his actions by referring to the Bhagawad Gita is somewhat misleading. This does not make him a traditionalist at all; his Hinduism, on the contrary, like Savarkar's, was pragmatic, semiticized and quite modern. This was a defensive and anxious Hinduism, worried about its survival in the world. Paradoxically, it still saw as its principal enemy medieval Islam, not having overcome the hatred and phobia of the long period of Muslim rule in the country.

Godse's was a Hinduism that seemed more to subscribe to the Mosaic law of 'an eye for an eye' than the Hindu ideal of *ahimsāparamodharmā* (non-injury is the highest imperative). Godse's greatest grouse against Gandhi was that the latter was weakening Hinduism by destroying its fighting spirit. He did not hesitate to kill Gandhi to express his disapproval. Gandhi was seen as the stubborn obstacle to militarizing the Hindus so that they could also turn belligerent in the face of threats from others. Hindu fanaticism of this sort, like Islamic jihadism later, was a peculiarly modern phenomenon. Godse's proud patricide was a fundamentally un-Hindu act, implying the negation of age-old taboos in favour of a coldly calculated exercise in realpolitik.

There is another sense in which Gandhi's death marks a finality, a break with the past, an irreversible step towards a new social, political and religious consciousness. Gandhi's was the last, even though failed, attempt to reconcile Hindus and Muslims in a traditional spiritual brotherhood. Another way of saying this was that he tried to invent a new but a faith-centred national religion, which was not merely civic or secular, but truly interdenominational and spiritual. He called it, after Vinoba, *sarva dharma samabhava*, an equal disposition to all faiths. The ingredients of this religion included the study and, to an extent, practice of other faiths than one's own; non-judgement and non-criticism, but respect of others' beliefs; in times of conflict, accommodation rather than provocation; non-belligerence; eschewing the desire to dominate or convert others; believing in one God, but also in God as Truth rather than as some theological construct; and solidarity between all people, regardless of their religion. He tried to institute such a religion in his ashrams, especially in Sevagram, where worship took place in an open space under the skies, without the symbols of any faith or any structure that could be identified as a temple, mosque, or church. The worship consisted of reciting passages from various scriptures and singing communal hymns and bhajans. Gandhi's new 'national' religion was meant to remove religious causes of competition or conflict between contending groups. It was, in a sense, a bit like Akbar's Din Illahi, the interdenominational faith that the emperor invented to give all his subjects equal rights. However, like Akbar's experiment, Gandhi's failed too. After his death, most of its adherents reverted to their traditional faiths, in fact, to even narrower versions of these.

While Indian secularism continues to show respect rather than an indifference towards all faiths, the fact is that religion, along with caste and community, have been highly politicized and exploited in post-independence India. Other attempts at forging a national culture using Gandhian ideas of religion, such as Svadhaya's tenet of *sarva dharma sveekar* (the acceptance of all faiths) are successful largely in Hindu majority areas. Whether they can be applied at a larger scale is not clear. With a recrudescence of religious intolerance the world over, what is the future of Hindu–Muslim relations in the subcontinent? Pakistan's state policy of promoting Islamism under Zia-ul-Haq has rebounded upon them, making that country one of the most strife-ridden and violent places in the world. With the Taliban still active across the porous border, the spate of killings by religious extremists continues on both sides. The chances of the revival of Gandhi's formula of a religious or spiritual union of hearts seem rather remote in our times. Instead some sort of secular or civic rapprochement might have greater chances of success. In India, the economic and social success of the majority appears to have split the sizeable Muslim minority into those who wish to participate and join in the Hindu majority-led Indian narrative, and those who are recalcitrant and counter-systemic. There is still another even smaller set of strategists who, believing that Muslims are essentially inassimable into any other religious or social formation, dream of a reunited subcontinent in which their numbers will give them sufficient leverage to rule. In the meanwhile, they are working to make their votes count in those areas of India where they can swing the votes one way or another, determining who actually comes to power. Such calculations, to Gandhi, would have only been a cynical use of religion and identity politics. Not that he was alien to it in his own life. Whether it was the issue of separate electorates for the depressed classes or the creation of Pakistan, he had seen at first hand a rejection of his call for an understanding of religion that was uniting, rather than divisive.

12 The Mahatma's endgame

A study of Indian myths and legends, as we have already seen, indicates that no matter how strong the younger challengers are, the elders always win in the end. As Ramanujan plainly states, 'we must note that the son never wins, almost never kills the father figure. . . . The power of the father-figure is never overthrown'.[1] We have previously discerned how Nathuram's symbolic patricide is thus unprecedented. It is the magnitude of its violation of settled beliefs and mores that has made it unspeakable to Hindus, who still continue to repress it. That Gandhi was also the Father of the Nation makes this repression not just personal but collective and national. His murder is the nation's dark and shameful stain that must not be openly acknowledged. But could it be that Gandhi, as all powerful patriarchs in Hindu tradition, did not lose after all, finding a way to turn his death into Godse's defeat?

As Nandy suggests, Savarkar served as the assassin's ego-ideal;[2] in that sense, Savarkar was the good father, the 'real' but thwarted father, the proper father to partner the Motherland, one who would save and protect the mother from the aggressive and polluting infidels who had already despoiled her. A strong, masculine, even militant father figure like Savarkar would put an end to centuries of pillage, rape and humiliation that the Motherland had undergone. All the alternative 'ego-ideals' to Gandhi – Jinnah, who became the 'father' of Pakistan, Savarkar who couldn't become the 'father' of India, Bose, another 'dutiful' son like Godse who also failed, and Ambedkar, the 'father' not so much of the Indian constitution as of the dalit nation – were all 'modernizers' and, to varying degrees, Gandhi-haters. They distrusted and disliked Gandhi precisely because he refused to become modern, refused to buy into realpolitik, refused to subordinate morality to the quest for power; Gandhi stubbornly refused to allow the end to justify the means. Gandhi's great, almost single-handed rejection of the dominant political culture of his times was voiced in his radical critique of modernity, *Hind Swaraj*. That is why *Hind Swaraj* was founded on a civilizational discourse, one which actually spelled out the clash of civilizations thesis long before Huntington, albeit in a totally different manner. Gandhi pitted the traditional, virtue- and liberation-oriented Indian civilization against the modern pleasure and consumption-driven civilization that was threatening to engulf India. He clearly saw that India's freedom struggle would be as good as lost even before it was begun if India imitated the civilizational goals of the West and modelled its nation on Western ideals; equally, he felt that India's freedom would be lost even if it was won if India achieved its aim of political independence through a violent overthrow of the British empire. Writing in the *Young India* of 12 February 1925, Gandhi had said,

> I hold that the world is sick of armed rebellions. I hold too that whatever may be true of other countries, a bloody revolution will not succeed in India. The masses will not respond. A movement in which masses have no active part can do no good to them. A successful bloody revolution can only mean further misery for the masses. For it would be still foreign rule for them.[3]

A freedom so won would only spell India's moral degradation; it would be no freedom at all, but only a mimicry of Western ideas of freedom and nationhood. Such a freedom would continue to oppress and exploit the vast mass of Indians who continued to live in the old manner.

For Godse, dispatching this recalcitrant but irritating Mahatma was one way to secure India's future as a modern, Hindu state, which took its decisions rationally and pragmatically, not hampered or handicapped with self-defeating ideologies like *ahimsa* or morality. Gandhian politics, according to Godse, 'was supported by old superstitious beliefs such as the power of the soul, the inner voice, the fast, the prayer and the purity of mind'.[4] This was not only a grave error, but an extremely harmful one as far as India was concerned. Politics was, after all, about seizing power and holding on to it, whatever the cost; it was high time that the Hindus had an unabashed will to power. Whatever stood in the way of their attaining power had to be shoved aside. Godse 'wanted Indian politics to be "rational", "power-oriented", "normal" politics. He felt that the elimination of Gandhi from the Indian scene would remove the Gandhian constraints on mature statecraft and hard *realpolitik*'.[5] So what if it meant the killing of the Father of the Nation? The nation could 're-marry' a more suitable ideologue, someone who better embodied the values of supremacist Hinduism. Unfortunately Savarkar, whether from astute practical considerations or from a well-worked-out strategy for self-preservation, was utterly cold to Nathuram during the long-drawn trial, hardly deigning him a nod, let alone a look of recognition. That the 'good' father on whose behalf he had carried out the coup of killing the 'bad' father was so aloof must have hurt Nathuram, heightening his sense of isolation and alienation. The brave son remained unacknowledged, ever the pariah, irredeemably polluted.

But did Godse really succeed? Or did the Mahatma, even in his own death, turn the tables on his assassin? In order to address such a question we must at last consider the responsibility of the one person we have not suspected in this inquiry over Gandhi's murder – Gandhi himself. It is at last worth asking if after considering and exhausting all other actors the needle of suspicion does not, after all, quite decisively point at him? I am not by any stretch suggesting that Gandhi's murder was actually a self-inflicted suicide. That would be too simplistic. It was not that Gandhi deliberately stationed himself in the way of an assassin's bullets because he 'knew' and willed his own death, but, to put it in a slightly different way, just as Nathuram was looking for answers, so was the Mahatma. He was also wondering why India had turned out so differently from his plans. Why had the Partition, with all its carnage and brutality, happened? Where did India go wrong? Where did *he* go wrong? What was the way out of the horrors that had engulfed India's freedom? Why was the end so bitter? The bloodshed and false freedom that he had warned his readers against in *Hind Swaraj*, why had that very same fate overtaken his country, despite his efforts to lead a non-violent struggle to independence? If he could only locate the malaise, put his finger on it, he might do something to stem the tide, if not to overturn it. He wanted to heal the wounds that had gashed his nation's heart and sundered its body politic even in its very first throes of freedom and its very first birth pangs. As Payne documents, during the last days of his life Gandhi was not only searching for answers to such questions, but also gradually becoming reckless of his own safety and almost inviting a violent death and martyrdom, even as he was working for peace and taking Bengali lessons at 78.[6] As many have suggested, moreover, he seemed to have premonitions of his own end. How responsible, then, was he for it?

It is Nandy who provides us the best clue to this conundrum: 'Every political assassination', he claims, 'is a joint communiqué. It is a statement which the assassin and his victim jointly work on and co-author'.[7] T. K. Mahadevan writing in the *Times of India* goes even further, using references from Hindu mythology which assert the special, even divinely ordained missions of both the Mahatma and his assassin:

Godse was to Gandhi what Kamsa was to Krishna. Indivisible, even if incompatible. Arjuna never understood Krishna the way Kamsa did . . . hate is infinitely more symbiotic than love. Love dulls one's vision, hate sharpens it.[8]

This puts the whole murder in a slightly different perspective. What if Gandhi 'knew' or sensed that his end was near, what if he had already understood, deeply and unconsciously, if not consciously and deliberately, what the 'real' root of the deadly poison that was spreading its tentacles across the land was; what if he had, with the unerring instinct that he was famous for, also 'decided' to offer the supreme sacrifice of the last and only thing he had left, his life, his remaining energy, and his last breath to arrest the contagion? What if, unbeknownst to him, Nathuram had been 'chosen' and 'prepared' for this final showdown of the Mahatma with his adversaries, this final act of courage and self-assertion, of *satyagraha* or truth-force, the ultimate denouement, before the curtains fell on his remarkable life? What if, to put it simply, the Mahatma had, after all, scripted his own exit?

That there is sufficient evidence to suggest this cannot be denied. Manubehn, Gandhi's grand-niece, and one of his closest confidants, offers us a remarkable if tantalizing peek into those fatal final days in *Last Glimpses of Bapu* (1962). Just two days before his assassination, he told Manu:

> If I were to die of a lingering disease, or even from a pimple, then you must shout from the housetops to the whole world that I was a false Mahatma. . . . If I die of illness, you should declare me a false or hypocritical Mahatma. And if an explosion took place, as it did last week, or somebody shot at me and I received his bullet on my bare chest, without a sigh and with Rama's name on my lips, only then you should say that I was a true Mahatma.[9]

Another version of the same passage is found in Manubehn's *The End of an Epoch*, translated from Gujarati by Gopalkrishna Gandhi, but in this account Gandhi says these words the night before the murder:

If I die due to a lingering illness, nay even by as much as a boil or a pimple, it will be your duty to proclaim to the world, even at the risk of making people angry at you, that I am not the man of God that I am claimed to be. If you do that, my spirit will have peace. Note down this also that if someone were to end my life by putting a bullet through me, as someone tried to do with a bomb the other day, and I met this bullet without a groan, and breathed my last taking God's name, then alone would I have made good my claim.[10]

These remarkable passages show that Gandhi was not only aware of how serious the threat to his life was, but also that knowing of the failed assassination attempt by the same group of conspirators, he had done nothing to increase his security or take any measures to prevent its recurrence. Indeed, receiving bullets on his bare chest unflinchingly with Rama's name on his lips was exactly as he actually died, almost foretelling in an uncannily precise manner how his end would come. He even had a sense of what kind of man his killer might be: 'If I am to die by the bullet of a mad man, I must do so smiling, God must be in my heart and on my lips'.[11] That his murderer would be some sort of 'madman', indeed that the turning of his beloved country into the killing fields of Partition was also nothing but a bout of temporary insanity that engulfed the country was also perhaps evident to him. Perhaps it was against this madness that he had taken his final stand. The drops of his own blood, so precious and few, would somehow staunch the wounds of his country, preventing any more bloodletting. These would be the purifying drops of blood that would end the contagion and pollution that all this killing had caused. That is why he was unequivocal in telling Manu, 'And if anything happens, you are not to shed a single tear'.[12] There was to be no mourning not just because the Mahatma had led a full life or that his death was, as his life had been, quite 'beautiful', but because it was no accident in the first place, no ordinary murder or crime, but a strange and complex ritual, so necessary to his final transformation; therefore the ultimate manoeuvre of the Mahatma, so to speak. No wonder, on the eve of the fateful termination of his life, Manu portrays him quoting an Urdu poem: 'Short lived is the splendour of Spring in the garden of the world'.[13]

How morbidly prescient of Gandhi, therefore, jestingly to scold Manu on the morning of his death day even as she is busy making his throat lozenges for the evening, 'Who knows what is going to happen before nightfall or even whether I shall be alive? If at night I am still alive you can easily prepare some then'.[14] Early that morning, less than 12 hours before the event, he says to Manu: 'If someone fires bullets at me and I die without a groan and with God's name on my lips, then you should tell the world that here was a real Mahatma'.[15] Gandhi's biographer D. G. Tendulkar notes that on that same fateful morning Gandhi tells a co-worker, 'bring me my important letters. I must reply to them today, for tomorrow I may never be'.[16] Pyarelal in *Mahatma Gandhi: The Last Phase* also documents a similar incident. A few minutes before he is shot, he instructs his assistants to tell two men who want to see him, 'Tell them to come after prayer; I shall then see them – if I'm alive'.[17]

In fact, according to Pyarelal, Gandhi's will to live, which was normally so robust that he wished to go on for 125 years, was now weakening; Gandhi, Pyarelal observed, was anxious, even depressed: 'I watched day after day the wan, sad look on that pinched face, bespeaking an inner anguish that was frightening to behold'.[18] To one reporter Gandhi said, 'I have lost the hope because of the terrible happenings in the world. I don't want to live in darkness'.[19] Historian and biographer B. R. Nanda wonders 'whether he had a presentiment of an early end' or whether such remarks 'were no more than occasional glimpses of the torture of mind and spirit which he suffered during this period'.[20] By December 1947, a little over a month before he was murdered, Pyarelal felt that Bapu 'was literally praying that God should gather him into his bosom and deliver him from the agony which life had become'.[21] Accustomed to mobs shouting 'Death to Gandhi', he had, according to Nandy, become 'a self-destructive depressive'.[22]

Unlike the claims of some of these scholars, I believe that Gandhi, instead of yielding to despair, was actually deeply aware of the kind of death he wanted: 'There is an art in dying', he wrote to a correspondent, 'As it is, all die, but one has to learn by practice how to die a beautiful death'.[23] His whole life had been one long preparation for this moment, which would be of his own choosing, not that of his assassin's. Gandhi, the supreme life-artist, was still in charge, even in the manner in which he scripted his own death. As Nandy theorizes, 'No victory is complete unless the defeated accepts his defeat'.[24] Despite the horrors of Partition and the apparent failure of non-violence, Gandhi never accepted defeat. Just as he had not accepted that the British, superior in military might, had defeated India. As always, Gandhi changed definitions, thus giving the defeated a new way to see themselves and their vanquishers. 'Militant nonviolence . . .' as Nandy puts it, 'totally refuses to recognize the defeat in violent confrontation to be defeat'.[25] Similarly, Gandhi refused to let his assassin vanquish him. He turned the tables on Nathuram.

It is not as if the possibility of such a twist to the tale went entirely unnoticed. As Payne says,

> For Gandhi, this death was a triumph. He had always believed that men should be prepared to die for their beliefs. He died as kings die, felled at the height of their powers, and Sarojini Naidu was right when she said that it was appropriate that he should die in Delhi, the city of kings.[26]

Gandhi connived at his own assassination because he hoped, in his violent death, to bind the nation to his memory more radically in death than in life: 'Gandhi knew how to use man's sense of guilt creatively'.[27] This bonding with the nation through his martyrdom was his way to continue to haunt the nation that he had fathered, never letting it go in a direction that would destroy it – unlike Pakistan which, without such a moral anchor or haunting, went, as some would say, to rack and ruin. Gandhi, who had shunned the label of Mahatma through most of his life, seemed, thus, to embrace it in death. In her perceptive essay 'From Mohandas to Mahatma: The Spiritual Metamorphosis of Gandhi', Karen E James says, 'He had accepted his public and spiritual role as a Mahatma, and he realized that only death at the hand of an assassin would finally complete and confirm his life's work'.[28] Gandhi, then, had crafted his own death as he had his life. James considers the death to be the validation of his life, the proof that he was not a 'false Mahatma'.[29]

Of the many reflections on the meaning of his martyrdom, Nirmal Kumar Bose's bears recollection. Bose, an eminent scholar and teacher, had served as Gandhi's interpreter in Bihar and Bengal during the latter's peace marches. In the conclusion of *My Days with Gandhi* he says,

> But that martyrdom which brought his life to a finale which is comparable to the Greek tragedies acted as the touchstone which gave new meaning and new significance to the words which had so long sounded commonplace or strange in our heedless ears. . . . India is blessed because she gave birth to one who became Gandhi, and perhaps, blessed again that, by dealing him the blow of death, we endowed his life with an added radiance which shall enrich the heritage of humankind in all ages to come.[30]

The death, to Bose, endows the life with an extra glow, but as we have seen at such great length, that is not strictly speaking true. The halo was added by his admirers and followers, but Gandhi's purpose in 'choosing' such an exit from the world stage was entirely different. It was not to enhance his prestige or burnish his image for posterity. That was not the work of the Mahatma as he saw it. The work of the Mahatma was nothing less than to trigger the transformation in the hearts and minds of his countrymen and women. The death was meant to flag and foreground the task as yet unaccomplished, the purging in the hearts of Indians of hatred, healing the wounds in the nation's psyche, challenging Hindus to look closely into their own minds for precisely those fanatical ideals which they saw so clearly in their fellow countrymen. The work of the Mahatma was to show us that our own purpose as a nation was far from done despite our political independence.

James offers a different, more obviously Christian interpretation, which turns Gandhi into a saint. That this reading is based on ideas of sin and redemption is not surprising:

> In retrospect, Gandhi's violent death is the only logical culmination of his life's work, and especially of his last years. During his last phase, Gandhi accepted himself as a true Mahatma, and thereby accepted the responsibility for India's fate and for her sins. An introspective, depressed state of mind is concomitant with the carrying of such a burden. At the same time, the depth of his conviction that his path was the right one, and that God would show him the light, was also to be expected. Without such beliefs, the burden he carried would have crushed him. Only a man of intense spiritual conviction could attempt to face the communal problem as Gandhi did.[31]

James also brings in the personal dimension in which such an acceptance of his destiny was the only way that Gandhi could cope with the failure of his project. Once again, it is not his public role, but his private quest for liberation and self-realization that is crucial. Whether or not Gandhi could 'save' others, he certainly had to do this to redeem, if not prove, himself. It is not that Gandhi's blood can wash away all our crimes; on the contrary, he invites us to follow in his footsteps by accepting responsibility for our actions as he did. That he atoned for the sins of others with his own life and blood may be true, but his saintly sacrifice does not absolve us from our own accountability. Gandhi's sacrifice does not offer us an easy way out of our guilt; rather, it forces us to confront it and take on the unfinished project of self and national transformation. James returns to her Christian reading when she says, 'In life he aspired to suffer for India. It was fitting that his death should complete that suffering'.[32] But Gandhi's 'suffering' was not a proxy for ours; it was for the sake of truth, for non-injury.

It was almost as if Gandhi, by dying in this manner, was making it impossible for us to forget him or disregard his life's message. Over and over again, Indians and non-Indians alike who had occasion to encounter his life and works would be perplexed and challenged by his death. They would, in a sense, be compelled to make sense of it, to try to understand its true significance. Gandhi was daring us to be content with the false propaganda of Nathuram and his intellectual descendants – as if saying, believe that if you will be content with it or embark upon the journey to discover for yourselves what really happened, what this face-off between two Hindus was really about. If Gandhi had died quietly it would have been easier to ignore his ideas, but his murder created a permanent disturbance in the mind of Indians, especially Hindus, which made him and his mission unforgettable. Gandhi chose this death not to crown himself with martyrdom or sainthood; on the contrary he did so to make it impossible to forget him or what he stood for.

That is why even the controversy over his last words is not only somewhat less important but also provokes us, as his death does, to find out the truth for ourselves, to take sides. Gandhi's critics and opponents reject the claim that his last words were indeed '*He Rama*'. The accounts of Manu and Abha who both aver that he did say '*He Rama*' as he collapsed are not only reliable because they were closest to him, but are also corroborated by a whole range of sources. On 'the other side', Godse and his followers maintain that the last sound to escape from Gandhi's lips was merely a guttural cry of pain, not the name of the Lord. Nathuram, who pulled the trigger, may not have heard what Gandhi said because the explosions were deafening; Gopal

Godse, his brother and justifier, was not present, but is responsible for averring that Gandhi did not say '*He Rama*'. According to Manohar Malgonkar, Gurbachan Singh, a businessman from Panipat, also verified that Gandhi's last words were '*Hai Rama!*' while Karkare said that all he heard was a 'cry of pain, a guttural rasp, "Aaah!"'.[33]

The issue was important to both sides partly because both swore by the Bhagawad Gita, which pays a great deal of importance to a dying man's last words or thoughts. According to the Gita, anyone with God on his mind goes to God after death, while those whose minds are elsewhere lose that opportunity. The implicit idea is that only those whose lifelong devotion and concentration are on God can have Him on their mind till their dying moment; the others, by force of habit, will be distracted by other thoughts and desires, which in turn will influence their next birth. Even if Gandhi's last sound was a gasp, not the name of his *ishta devata* or favourite deity, Rama, there's no denying the possibility that his mind may have been on the Lord. So this controversy serves little purpose. The historian Vinay Lal sums up Gandhi's challenge to present-day Indians even in his dying words:

> When Gandhi uttered the words 'He Ram', he was doubtless true to himself; but, politically speaking, he managed to confound, as he does so down to the present day, both the Hindu militants who falsely declared him a traitor to his faith and so showed only their own miserable conception of Hinduism, as well as the secularists whose conception of both religion and politics is much too narrow to accommodate the creative ecumenism of true dissenters like Gandhi.[34]

Whether we are Sanatani Hindus or secularists, Gandhi, ultimately, forces us to meditate on both his life and death. He does so by co-scripting his murder with Nathuram, thus negating or subverting the latter's design to wipe out what Gandhi lived and, quite deliberately, died for.

13   Gandh*ism* vs. Gandhi*giri*

The life and afterlife of the Mahatma[1]

As he approaches the end of his monumental monograph on *The Life and Death of Mahatma Gandhi*, Robert Payne concludes somewhat wistfully,

> The years passed, and the murder of Gandhi became a fact of history, strangely remote and strangely final. The case was closed, the murderers have been punished, many of the witnesses were dead, and it seemed hopeless to revive an inquiry which must in the nature of things remain incomplete and insubstantial.[2]

I have, quite in contrast to Payne, endeavoured to show that the case is far from closed, that the Mahatma's death continues to haunt and tantalize us. The almost compulsive return to this topic, witnessed in the number of books and studies on it decade after decade is only one proof of this fact. Another, perhaps more substantial, corroboration of this is the spurt of interest in Gandhi from the most unexpected of sources, Hollywood and Bollywood. Though there have been many celluloid depictions of Gandhi, two stand out as being especially notable: Richard Attenborough's *Gandhi* (1982) and Rajkumar Hirani's *Lage Raho Munna Bhai* (2006).[3] Of the many attempts to capture Gandhi on celluloid, I consider these two feature films to be not only the most successful and spectacular, but also the most inviting of our special consideration. That is because they stand for two different narrative modes and mimetic styles of representing Gandhi, thus, albeit unintentionally, complementing one another with uncanny symmetry.

Movies had already become the world's newest and most powerful medium during Gandhi's life. He himself was filmed several times, starting with some American news and documentary companies' attempts to interview him for Western audiences. One of these early efforts is commonly available on YouTube. This – supposedly the earliest – talkie on Gandhi was shot by Fox Movietone in May 1931 at Borsad, near Anand in South Gujarat, on the eve of the Second Round Table Conference, which took place in London. It begins with the journalist unloading his heavy cinematographic equipment from a bullock cart after he arrives through the Borsad ashram gates. This rather self-conscious self-representation, it would seem, is as required to familiarize the audience with the new medium of film as it is to show viewers the great efforts, no expenses spared, that the American has made to reach and film Gandhi. Gandhi speaks very softly, in a whisper, while the journalist tries his best to draw him out. Earlier, Gandhi has insisted that his interviewer walk with him during one of his constitutions, so as not to take up too much of his time or cut too much into his schedule. The journalist finds Gandhi walking too briskly for his (the journalist's) comfort. Eventually, the two end up on the floor, Gandhi, bare-chested, as he talks, while his interlocutor, quite uncomfortable and overdressed, tries cleverly to 'trap' Gandhi with some of his questions. Gandhi, on the other hand, already a past master at this game, not only disarms him with his humour but, when required, evades answering directly or being drawn into saying anything controversial. Without actually knowing it, Gandhi is revealed to be quite media savvy.

Called *Gandhi Talks*, the film shows a still-sprightly if ageing Mahatma of feeble voice, quite averse to being photographed. As he said in the *Harijan* of 21 September 1947, opposing the proposal to make his statue in Bombay, 'I must say that I have dislike even for being photographed; nevertheless, photographs have been taken of me'.[4] To return to this first talkie on Gandhi, except for the dynamic opening sequence, the film is rather static, with the two figures almost frozen on the floor. Gandhi, we quickly realize, is rather easy to exoticize to the West: prohibition, child marriages and sartorial peculiarities – all become grist to the journalistic mill. Of course, to add to his exoticism, Gandhi does not sit still, but plays with his toes as he talks. His interviewer asks him whether it would be proper for him to dress as he does when attends the Round Table Conference. Gandhi replies that he should be uncomfortable wearing anything else than his customary attire, which, of course, is also a political statement in that it represents how a majority of the masses of colonized India dress, in bare essentials, upper bodies bare. Politics and piety, the two themes of Gandhi's life – civil disobedience and *satyagraha* – form part of the exchange, which is marked by the wit and humour so typical of Gandhi. When asked if Government will yield to his demands, Gandhi says he doesn't know. 'But you are hopeful?' Gandhi replies with a smile, 'I am an optimist.' On the other hand, what if he is imprisoned? 'I am always prepared to go to jail' retorts the clever Mahatma. Indeed, the exchange shows how carefully he measures his words. When the journalist attempts to plant words into his mouth, Gandhi returns, 'That is more than I can say.' Quite prophetic and essential to our inquiry is the unexpected question, 'Would you be prepared to die in the cause of India's freedom?' At that time, in the early thirties, Gandhi does not seem to be too pleased: 'It is a bad question' he says, neither negating nor affirming its implications. Perhaps, somewhere deep inside him he *knows* but does not wish to face up to that knowledge.

While Gandhi was often filmed speaking to the press, it was functional rather than artistic as far as he was concerned. He simply wanted to get his message across and did not hesitate to do so through the new medium. Gandhi's attitude to feature films, however, was somewhat antediluvian and not very positive. In June 1944, after his wife Kasturba's death, Gandhi spent some time with a prominent Porbandar business family, the Morarjees, in their Juhu mansion. His hosts arranged for him to see the movie *Mission to Moscow*, the special screening of which was attended by about a hundred prominent Bombayites along with Gandhi. The film was a big hit in those days. Sarojini Naidu was also present. It seems that Gandhi objected to the low dresses of the ladies and to couples in a close embrace.⁵ He thought that such films would have a negative effect on public morality. He also saw *Ram Rajya*, a mythological, which he liked better, but, according to Payne, 'to the end of his life he showed a deep dislike for films and cameramen'.⁶ I am not quite sure that this is true because whether it was the radio, which he used quite effectively, or movies, Gandhi, the great communicator, was not averse to trying the latest media. He knew the advantage of reaching millions through them.

One way to enter into the question of how Gandhi was depicted in the movies is to examine these three images, which signify three different attempts to frame Gandhi on the silver screen:

All of them, obviously, resemble the Mahatma, but which one is the 'real' Gandhi? On looking closely, we will be able to identify these images. Figure 12.1 below is from Richard Attenborough's *Gandhi*, while Figure 12.3 is from *Lage Raho Munna Bhai*. In both these movies, Gandhi is played by actors: the then unknown but now famous Ben Kingsley, and the still-obscure Dilip Prabhavalkar respectively. But what of the photo in the middle? That image represents Gandhi as himself. But the question remains: why is that representation more 'real' than the other two? Is it because in it Gandhi plays himself while in the other two he is portrayed by professional actors? Playing himself, however, we may not forget, is also a form of portrayal. Any representation, even *self*-representation, is also re-presentation; there is no way to get to the 'real' Gandhi without some process or the other of mediation. Even a photo of Gandhi, so accurate and life-like to all appearances, is a text that invites interpretation. In this case, the 'real' images of Gandhi that were crafted during his own lifetime later become the sources of cinematic depictions, thus basing the 'reel' Gandhi on the 'real' Gandhi. But the cinematic Gandhis also depart in significant ways from the documentary Gandhis. All, in the end, invite interpretations, including comparisons between them. The documentaries serve as a rich archive of images which are later adapted for a variety of purposes, including sculpture and portraiture. But this ensemble is itself subject to interrogation in the manner in which it seeks to frame and signify the Mahatma's life.

FIGURE 12.1 *Gandhi* (1982) (Source: *Gandhi*. Directed by Richard Attenborough. [Film still] USA: Columbia Pictures.)

FIGURE 12.2 A Portrait of Gandhi as Himself (*c.*1930) Alle pinkiwinkitinki (flickr) CC-BY licence

FIGURE 12.3 *Lage Raho Munna Bhai* (2006) (Source: *Lage Raho Munna Bhai*. Directed by Rajkumar Hirani. [Film still] India: Yash Raj Films.)

Of the various attempts to portray the 'real' Gandhi on 'reel', the most thorough and extensive instance is clearly *Mahatma: Life of Gandhi 1869–1948* (1968). This is a hugely ambitious, comprehensive, and painstaking assemblage of a vast array of audio-visual material to constitute possibly the longest of biographical documentaries ever. Made in 1968 by the Gandhi National Memorial Fund in cooperation with the Films Division of the Government of India, it was scripted and directed by Vithalbhai Jhaveri, who also recorded the audio commentary that runs through it. This 30,000-foot documentary is divided into 33 reels. The initial 6 reels cover a little over the first half of Gandhi's life, until he is 45. These years include the 21 he spent in South Africa. The remaining 33 years of his life from his return to India in 1915 to his murder in January 1948 extend over some 27 reels that also depict important facets of the history of India's freedom struggle. With a total length of about 330 minutes, the film is over six-and-a-half hours long. It also includes the earliest filming of Gandhi, in 1912 during G. K. Gokhale's visit to South Africa. Overall, *Mahatma: Life of Gandhi 1869–1948* embodies the most carefully collated and reliable visual archive on Gandhi. As such it is a 'source' of most other cinematic representations of Gandhi, including the two I shall discuss.

The three photos serve to remind us not only of the relationship between the two fictional accounts of Gandhi, Attenborough's and Hirani's, but also how they engage with the historical figure that we have come to know through similar processes of mediation. That is why, without trying to gauge the 'reliability' or 'authenticity' of the two feature films or evaluate their truth-value or mimetic accuracy, it might be instructive to juxtapose the two modes of representation, two narrative grammars, and two ways of recuperating Gandhi's legacy that the films stand for. The first question that strikes us is the challenge of filming Gandhi. From Jhaveri's text, we realize that though photographed a lot, Gandhi was not filmed as often. Actual 'talkies' of him are even fewer. From scant live records in the first half of his life when he was relatively less famous to later cinematic depictions is thus quite a leap.

That is one reason why Richard Attenborough's *Gandhi* becomes so important, even epochal. For a variety of reasons, it is *the* ultimate biopic. An expensive multinational effort, combining expertise and actors from five continents, the film achieves a verisimilitude and historical feel that has seldom been equalled. Indeed, it became somewhat controversial precisely because it was filmed with Government of India support and investment, which is what gave the director and crew unprecedented access to locations, material and facilities in India such as no normal, commercial venture would have enjoyed. Quite naturally, India-detractors, not to mention Gandhi-baiters, dismissed it as propaganda. Longer than most Hollywood movies, it stretches to three hours and eleven minutes, thus requiring special screening times all over the world.

It is a lavish production in 70 mm, with six-track sound. Shot on a massive scale, often on actual locations, specially made available by the Indian Government, it not only featured world famous actors and an international star-studded cast, but also thousands of extras, that made up crowds, mobs and background fillers. *Gandhi* was a great success, with worldwide impact. Nominated for nine Oscars, it won the Academy Awards sweepstakes, bagging eight awards, including one for best picture. Its global collections exceeded $100 million; the film is still in circulation and continues to move international audiences. One of its greatest contributions was that it made Gandhi a global icon 35 years after his death.

Attenborough's *Gandhi*, I would argue, is very much about the *life* of Gandhi, seen through Western eyes. As Attenborough himself put it in the companion book published when the movie was released, 'We were attempting to discover, and then dramatise, the spirit of this extraordinary man'.[7] Indeed, Attenborough's retelling removes the Mahatma from a limited, exotic, anti-colonial context and reterritorializes him as a twentieth-century saint. As Darius Cooper in a review of the film observes, 'Attenborough's three-hour film on Gandhi concentrates primarily on the Mahatmaness of the man, obliterating most human nuances that made Gandhi the unique person that he was'.[8] This is true, barring, of course, those few obviously human touches, such as his pushing his wife out of the house in anger when she refuses to clean the toilet. But these insertions are humanizing in an obvious sort of way. Otherwise, the narrative follows Christian hagiographical conventions, making it essentially the vindication of a saintly life. No doubt, such an interpretation is possible, in the first place, because Gandhi's remarkable life – and death in martyrdom – lends itself so readily to it. In what was one of the most astute obituaries on him, George Orwell, who rejected sainthood as an ideal, famously quipped that 'Saints should always be judged guilty until they are proved innocent' but went on, in the end, to pronounce a favourable verdict on Gandhi.[9]

Attenborough, after all, was following an already established paradigm when interpreting Gandhi. The image of the old Mahatma as a modern-day saint is a common, even predominant, though not exclusive example of how he came to be seen, even during his own lifetime. Markovits shows how Gandhi was iconized in a bewildering, sometimes contradictory, array of portraits: 'as a Bolshevik, a fanatic, a trouble-maker, a hypocrite, an eccentric, a reactionary, a revolutionary, a saint, a renouncer, a messiah, an avatar. He was likened both to Lenin and Jesus Christ, indicating the whole scope of representations'.[10] These various perceptions, however, settle into two major tropes after his death: within India, he was the 'Father of the Nation' and 'an apostle of non-violence outside'.[11] The growth of the latter iconography of the saintly Gandhi in the West, Markovits shows, had many contributors, including the Rev. Joseph J. Doke, an English Baptist missionary in South Africa, who wrote a book eulogizing Gandhi as early as 1909. Doke did not stop short of comparing Gandhi with Christ.[12] In an essay significantly titled 'Saint Gandhi', Mark Jurgensmeyer traces the canonization of Gandhi in the West as a saintly figure in the Christian tradition. A Unitarian pastor, Rev. John Hayne Holmes, declared in a sermon in New York in April 1921 that Gandhi was not only a saint, but a saviour.[13] Earlier, Willy Pearson, another English clergyman, was the first to proclaim Gandhi's sainthood, comparing him with St Francis of Assisi,[14] and later Romain Rolland's immensely influential book, *Mahatma Gandhi* (1924), translated into many European languages, was to confirm such a canonization.[15] Attenborough's cinematic hagiography clearly belongs to this tradition.

Of course, Attenborough used Hollywood film-making conventions, staging his scenes elaborately, as other makers of cinematic 'epics' such as David Lean had done before him. *Gandhi*, though hagiographical, follows a mimetic style of film-making in which cinema, the visual image itself, is supposed to portray or reflect 'reality'. Cinematic realism is shored up by accurate set and costume design, painstaking research, art direction, method acting, shooting on location, adherence to 'unities' of time and space, and documentary-style camera work and editing. No wonder that Bhanu Athaiya's excellent art direction for the movie won her an Oscar.

When Attenborough discussed the project with Nehru way back in 1963, the latter told him that 'the spirit and fundamental truth of Gandhiji's life should be apparent in all that we might attempt to convey'.[16] Later, Indira Gandhi, who actually sanctioned the funds for the film, was also keen that Government not interfere with the script, but 'merely satisfy themselves that, related to the subject matter, the manner in which the film was envisaged was a proper one'.[17] After she had seen the film, a satisfied Indira Gandhi publicly declared, 'The film has captured the spirit of Gandhiji'.[18] Attenborough's own aims were also clearly stated at the start of the film: 'to try to find one's way into the heart of the man', and to be 'faithful in spirit to the record'.[19] Yet, in his review of the film, a noted historian of South Asia, Stephen Hay, shows how the film often took liberties with history, compressing, amalgamating, exaggerating, inventing, as the narrative need arose.[20] Attenborough himself was quoted in the *New York Times* as admitting 'we cheat[ed] like mad' in compressing and combining historical events.[21] But though the film was riddled with inaccuracies, it came across as being historically accurate and psychologically credible.

The most devastating critique of Attenborough's *Gandhi* came in a review by the same title from the vitriolic pen of Salman Rushdie, first published the year following the release of the film and later re-printed in *Imaginary Homelands*. Rushdie claimed that the film satisfied the 'exotic impulse' of the West, especially its longing for a saintly figure 'dedicated to ideals of poverty and simplicity' and, even more conveniently, for its desire for revolutions that 'can, and should, be made purely by submission, and self-sacrifice, and non-violence *alone*'.[22] Britain needed a Christ-like figure so that the 'history of one of the century's greatest revolutions' could be 'mangled'.[23] 'This', observes Rushdie wryly, 'is nothing new. The British have been mangling Indian history for centuries'.[24] For Rushdie, one of the film's greatest failures was its depiction of Gandhi's assassination, which is important enough to be placed at the beginning and the end of the film. But the film does not emphasize or even clearly identify who Gandhi's killer is, ignoring his ideological or political affiliations: it would seem that the 'mob threw up a killer'.[25] Bose, who might have 'provided another sort of counterweight' to Gandhi, is excised from the narrative; 'All counter-arguments are therefore rigorously excluded'.[26] The biggest irony is that Attenborough's extravaganza is 'an incredibly expensive movie about a man who was dedicated to the small scale and to aceticism'.[27] Rushdie dismisses the film by a withering last dig, 'rich men, like emperors, have always had a weakness for tame holy men, for saints'.[28]

Of course, Gandhi was no tame holy man or convenient saint, something that *Lage Raho Munna Bhai* (2006) brings out rather well. The Bollywood counterpoint, if not rejoinder to Hollywood hagiography is not even about the Mahatma's life at all though it is most certainly about his *afterlife*. We might also consider it a hugely successful and popular attempt to represent Gandhi, but from a totally different style of film-making than Attenborough's. Some might dismiss it as another Bollywood potboiler, with an improbable plot, full of strange happenings.[29] Yet, as we shall see, the film has much going for it. The basic story concerns the transformation of a lovable Bombay hoodlum called Munna, whose normal business is threat, extortion, 'protection', and other such illegal activities. However, he falls in love with the voice of Jahnavi, a radio show host of a popular programme called 'Good Morning Mumbai'. On the occasion of Gandhi's birthday, she decides to run a special quiz on the Father of the Nation. Munna, wishing to impress her, kidnaps several professors and forces them to give him all the right answers. The result is that he wins the quiz and is invited to Jahnavi's show.

There, believing his bluff that he is a Professor of Gandhian studies, Jahnavi unexpectedly requests him to speak on Gandhi, his 'favourite' topic, to some seniors in the 'Second Innings House', where she resides too. Munna now realizes that he must read up on Gandhi or face not just embarrassment or exposure, but also lose the chance to win Jahnavi's favour. In the process of spending three days and nights at a Gandhi library, which no one else frequents, he begins to 'see' Gandhi. This figure of Gandhi, whom he first thinks is a ghost, also supplies him all the answers to his and others' questions. Gandhi now promises to help him out during his talk at the Second Innings House. Of course, only he can 'see' Gandhi, so his secret is not revealed. But unknown to Munna, his sidekick and friend, Circuit, has accepted the commission to clear the Second Innings House for an illegal takeover by a real estate tycoon and the villain of the movie, Lucky Singh. This is how the plot unfolds, gradually 'forcing' Munna to adopt Gandhigiri (the Gandhian way) as opposed to Gundagiri, or the gangster's way of doing things, all in order to woo his lady love.

Despite such an improbable plot, I believe this film needs to be taken seriously for a variety of reasons. A purely practical one is its great impact factor. It is among the highest grossing Indian films, with a revenue of over 100 crores, or a billion rupees according to Box Office India figures.[30] Audiences all around the world, not only in India, loved it, going to view it several times. It won several national awards and was shown tax-free in Mumbai and Delhi. It now has regular reruns on TV and during flights, having become something of a classic. That its subject is Gandhi obviously distinguishes it from other hits that performed similarly at the box office. That a Gandhian film could do so well is thus not just noteworthy, but invites further analysis. It was as if it became India's answer to Attenborough's *Gandhi*, but offered a new way of 'doing' Gandhi in our times, suggested by the neologism it coined, 'Gandhigiri'. The film, moreover, inspired copycat instances of this method, with several reports of how one of its techniques, sending roses to adversaries, was successfully duplicated in many parts of the world. According to newspaper reports, the film caused a spurt in the sales of books on Gandhi, and several schools organized group screenings.[31] Summing up its unusually strong impact, Sudha Ramachandran quoting from *Outlook* magazine, says, '*Lage raho Munnabhai* marks the magnificent, fun-filled return of Gandhi to mass consciousness'.[32]

The film was well received and reviewed not just nationally, but also internationally. Amelia Gentleman in the *International Herald Tribune* lauded the film's special appeal and achievement; *Lage Raho* caused 'real excitement' and became 'the unexpected box-office hit of the year':

> With its big Bollywood soundtrack and dance routines, the movie brings Gandhi firmly into the mainstream and theaters have been packed for the past three weeks. The Congress Party recommended that all party members see the film. The Delhi authorities declared that tickets to the film would be sold tax free because of its assiduous promotion of Gandhian values.[33]

Similarly, Mark Sappenfield of the *Christian Science Monitor* pointed out how the film was not piously preachy but a hands-on way of engaging with Gandhi: 'Gandhi gets his hands dirty. He appears as an apparition only visible to the wayward gangster, counselling him on how to help others deal with everyday problems'.[34] Swati Gauri Sharma in *The Boston Globe* wanted a version of Gandhigiri in the United States which 'encourages people to take up Gandhigiri, Kinggiri, or Kennedygiri. If it worked for Bollywood, it could work for Hollywood'.[35] A few months after its release, a special screening of the film was arranged on 10 November 2006 at the United Nations. Introduced by the then UN Under-Secretary Shashi Tharoor, this was the first Hindi film to be shown at the UN. Director Rajkumar Hirani, writer Abhijat Joshi, and actor Boman Irani were present as the film met with thunderous applause.[36] As the Indo-Asian News Service (IANS) reported, 'An evening that had started with massive security arrangements in the sombre UN setting, concluded in a festive atmosphere in the lounge of the UN with diplomats from other tables joining in raising a toast for the film'.[37] Eventually, the Prime Minister of India, Manmohan Singh, also got to see the film. He said it 'captures Bapu's message about the power of truth and humanism'.[38] The following year, on 15 June 2007, the UN General Assembly unanimously adopted a resolution declaring 2 October, Gandhi's birthday, as the 'International Day of Non-Violence'. [39] The film was also a great hit at Cannes and has been shown in university campuses all over the world.

But what is also remarkable is that it seemed to have been made with the conscious attempt to recuperate Gandhi for contemporary India, as its director Rajkumar Hirani said. He was shocked at how little Indians knew about Gandhi and thought of doing something about it. Hirani narrates an incident during the filming which to him was symptomatic of this ignorance. The boy who served tea on the sets kept asking for the name of the film, which was then the still tentative 'Munnabhai Meets Mahatma Gandhi'. When informed of this by the music director, Shantanu Moitra, the boy said, '*Munnabhai to theek hai, yeh Mahatma Gandhi kaun hai?*' (Munnabhai is fine, but who is this Mahatma Gandhi?).[40] Hirani continues:

> So this is the sad state of affairs today. I was shocked. And it's not just the *chai-wallah*. A few days ago on TV a lot of politicians were asked India-related questions on the news channels, and I can't believe a lot of them don't know October 2 is Gandhiji's birthday! Many didn't know his first name. They kept saying, 'What's in a name, we respect his ideals', but come on! How can you not know his name?[41]

Hirani plays on these incidents in the quiz in the movie where viewers are asked the name of Gandhi's mother. Given the constraints of the medium, Hirani could not be overtly didactic; instead he had to create a story that would enable him to interpret and expound his own ideas of Gandhi:

> If I stop you and say something about Mahatma Gandhi, you'll brush me off saying 'boring.' To preach is very boring, and nobody wants free advice. But if it's entertainment, then this changes. If you explain something to a kid through an interesting story, he'll be hooked. [42]

Yet there is no doubt that given his sense of purpose, Hirani was repaying a traditional Hindu debt not just to his forefathers but also to the Father of the Nation. His act of remembering Gandhi was a way not just to pay tribute to, but in a way to revitalize the Gandhian spirit so as to reiterate current-day India's connection with the Mahatma.

The writer of the film, Abhijat Joshi, himself a Professor of English and Creative Writing at Otterbein College, Ohio, spent several years researching Gandhi before working on the script for *Munna Bhai*. Joshi, growing up in Ahmedabad and imbibing a good deal of Gandhian ideas, actually wrote a screenplay for a TV series on Gandhi called 'Post-dated Cheque'. This was a phrase that Gandhi himself had used to describe the promises of Dominion and autonomy in the Simon Commission's proposals in March 1942, which he likened to a 'post-dated cheque on a failing bank'. [43] Unfortunately, Joshi could not encash his post-dated cheque; the project had to be abandoned. But he persisted in his pursuit of Gandhi, inspired by some of the surviving freedom fighters he had interviewed in 1997: 'These people fought hard for the country's freedom. They are also witness to the present sorry state of the nation, but they refused to give up hope'. [44] When it came to *Lage Raho*, Joshi shared the concern of the producer Vidhu Vinod Chopra and the director Rajkumar Hirani that the film not become too solemn: 'It was important for us to dispel the myth about Gandhi being a sedate, ascetic person. We wanted to show his other side – witty, humorous, light-hearted and creative'. [45] Thus, unlike some typical Bollywood film, *Lage Raho* is well researched and has a serious academician as its scriptwriter.

Bollywood, no doubt, does not pretend to be realist cinema; instead, it is sentimental, not mimetic but mythic, aiming at simulation (also stimulation), not fidelity. Hirani quotes one of his own lead actors, Boman Irani, who played Lucky Singh, about the kind of movie he was trying to make:

> Boman put it very well that day, when he said that there are some comedies described as 'Leave your brains at home when you go to watch this film.' He said, 'No, for this film take your brains with you; it'll touch you.' And take your heart along too.[46]

That is why *Lage Raho* is as much about Bollywood as it is about Gandhi.

The film was a sequel to the immensely popular *Munna Bhai M.B.B.S.* The main character and his associate were already well-known, as was the antagonist, played once again by Boman Irani. Given the compulsions of the star system, the main character could not be Gandhi at all, but the already popular Munna Bhai, the petty Bombay gangster, with a heart of gold. Gandhi, in that sense, is almost an 'extra', in this case quite literally a poltergeist if not extraterrestrial. He haunts the lead character as a 'ghost' or apparition, as I have argued he has done the whole nation since his death, only in this film, the haunting is made literal, actually shown on the screen in the form of Prabhavalkar, who plays this role. The hero pretends to be a Gandhian, an expert on Gandhi, a professor; the whole film therefore is a Gandhian tutorial, disguised as mass entertainment. Bollywood, as I have always maintained, is not just a cinema of entertainment, but of edification.[47] Gandhi as a haunting presence in a corrupt post-colonial nation becomes an instantly recognizable and powerful tool for the director to bring out the ills of society and to propose a solution. Gandhi, as the film shows, is not so much an iconic external presence, but a 'chemical *locha*' (dissonance); an internal, conscience-arousing, destabilizing force in the body politic. Such a representation brings to mind Sarojini Naidu's eulogy on Gandhi's death that I discussed earlier:

May the soul of my master, my leader, my father rest not in peace, not in peace, but let his ashes be so dynamically alive that the charred ashes of the sandalwood; let the powder of his bones be so charged with life and inspiration that the whole of India, will after his death be revitalised into the reality of freedom. . . . My father, do not rest. Do not allow us to rest.[48]

A Mahatma is not just a great soul, but someone who may be defined as more active and powerful after his death than when alive.

When we compare *Lage Raho* to *Gandhi* we see that the Bollywood blockbuster is not hagiographical, but practical; it is not about Gandhism, but *Gandhigiri*, a new coinage that signifies *doing* Gandhi in the real world. It shows how Gandhi the exemplar resists appropriation but invites transformation. The film is by no means naive. It squarely shows modernity's challenge to Gandhi. As the scenes with the psychiatrists are meant to ask, is Munna's Gandhi merely a hallucination, easily dismissed as the hero's pathology? Is the rest of corrupt society sane, while Munna is clearly in need of medical attention? Or is Gandhi much more than a hallucination – is he actually Munna's and the nation's 'conscience' which, once awakened, will never be silenced like Gandhi's own still small but extremely insistent and powerful inner voice? Going by the action of the movie, Gandhi's ghost cannot so easily be exorcised. Gandhi is not merely an illusion or a figment of Munna's imagination, because he produces a chain reaction not only in Munna but in several other characters. Gandhi is a positive force for change – the conversion of Lucky Singh (a tribute to Bollywood's power of make-believe) is his final triumph.

The import of this entertaining 'tutorial' on Gandhi is thus nothing short of an inquiry into Gandhian praxis through a rejection of both *Gundagiri* (gangsterism), Munna's original vocation, and Gandhism (*Gandhivaad*), Munna's fake profession of Gandhian values. Through actual praxis, Munna makes Gandhi his own lived experience and reality, rather than merely spouting the Mahatma's

words. Munna becomes a neo-Gandhian himself, fighting Lucky
Singh and the whole Indian establishment, which uses money and
muscle power to rule over and exploit the disempowered masses.
That is why, in the end, Jahnavi calls him the 'best Professor ever'
because Munna, like Gandhi practises, instead of merely preaching.
In the film, both the instrumental use of violence and cynical lip
service to Gandhi are rejected in favour of a genuine '*satyagraha*';
insistence on the force of truth. In the end we realize that Gandhi
is neither ghost, nor apparition, but an idea that will not be easily
killed. In a deeper sense, Gandhi cannot be 'framed', boxed,
contained, or packaged, even as the film testifies to his continuing
relevance: 'I was shot down many years ago', says his character in
the film, 'but my ideas will not die by three bullets, my thoughts
will create a chemical imbalance in some mind or the other. Either
you put me inside a frame and hang me up on your wall or think
over my thoughts.' Doing Gandhi (*Gandhigiri*), the film suggests,
is the way that a new generation must think through Gandhi or
put his ideas into practice. Indeed, this is the only way to exorcise
his disturbing presence in our midst. Munna's transformation is
not from gangster to decent bourgeois, law-abiding citizen; it is
from a violent thug to a viable *satyagrahi*, who also questions and
struggles against bourgeois complacency and reaction. It is this
demonstration of the viability of *satyagraha* in contemporary India
that gives the film its more serious underpinning. Gandhism vs.
Gandhigiri is actually doxa vs. praxis, therefore going to the very
heart of the Gandhian project.

The appeal of *Lage Raho* is so special because it does not
fetishize Gandhi but liberates him from statues and portraits,
thus recuperating his energy to real-life struggles. Hirani does
so in the comic as opposed to Attenborough's solemn mode,
thus humanizing and familiarizing Gandhi – hence Bapu, term
of endearment, not Mahatma, a distancing honorific, is used
throughout the film for him. Gandhi's legacy is thereby harnessed
to critique postcolonial India. Through multiple examples of

corruption and callousness, *Lage Raho*, like Gandhi's own *Hind Swaraj*, foregrounds the 'condition of India' in our own times. It also shows how Gandhian efforts in non-violence and truth-force can still help transform the situation, if applied diligently, sincerely – and with good humour. If nothing else, the film shows how the afterlife of Gandhi still continues to influence and correct our conduct in contemporary India.

Ultimately, *Lage Raho* is as much a celebration of Bollywood as of Gandhi. That is because it is to the former that the credit for most effectively resurrecting the Mahatma should go, certainly much more than to Gandhians or academics. For Bollywood literally revives the spirit of Gandhi by showing how irresistibly he continues to haunt India today. Not just in giving us *Gandhigiri* – a totally new way of *doing* Gandhi in the world – but in its perceptive representation of the threat that modernity poses to Gandhian thought, is *Lage Raho Munna Bhai* remarkable. What is more, it also draws out the distinction between Gandhi as hallucination and the real afterlife of the Mahatma, which is no illusion or pathology at all, but really the repressed conscience of the nation roused once again in the service of the nation. The film's enormous popularity at the box office is not just an index of its commercial success, but also proof of the responsive chord it struck in Indian audiences. But it is not just the genius and inventiveness of Bollywood cinema that is demonstrated in the film as much as the persistence and potency of Gandhi's own ideas, which have the capacity to adapt themselves to unusual circumstances and times. Both Richard Attenborough's Oscar-winning epic, and Rajkumar Hirani's *Lage Raho Munna Bhai* show that Gandhi remains as media-savvy after his death as he was during his life.

To this end, the film deliberately questions the fetishization of Gandhi, and his appropriation by the state. It critiques the Gandhi of statues and portraits and banknotes, and instead recuperates his energy to real-life struggles. By making Gandhi if not its central character, at least its driving force, *Lage Raho* engages with the history of contemporary India going back to colonial times, which we must do in order to trace the roots of the current Indian state. An eloquent critique of the various corruptions and inefficiencies of post-colonial India, the film evokes Gandhi as an alternative and exemplar. The contemporary state of affairs is shown to be deplorable; all three branches of the Government, the executive, the legislature and the judiciary, are either corrupt or hamstrung by bureaucratic and procedural bottlenecks. They are incapable of serving the needs of the common people of India, the *aam aadmi*, or of upholding the rights and dignity of the poorest of the poor. It is in such a scenario of all-pervading inefficiency, lack of accountability and consequent prevalent cynicism in society that we see the space for a 'fixer' like Munna Bhai and an unscrupulous real estate developer like Lucky Singh. The latter wants to occupy and usurp land and properties in Bombay and the former, with his muscle power, obliges by evicting tenants, securing permissions and smoothing irregularities. The strong prey on the weak in such a society, as is evident when Lucky Singh takes over the Second Innings House, forging its lease documents and evicting its senior citizen occupants when they are on a holiday in Goa. It is a world in which pensioners are denied their right to livelihood because some corrupt official is sitting on their files in the hope of a bribe. It is a world in which municipal officers are kidnapped and released only when they agree to bend the rules or look the other way when rich builders and contractors violate the building laws and the zoning regulations. Every man has his price and the rich and the powerful have the ability to pay it.

In a telling scene, Munna's endearingly loyal sidekick Circuit (short for Sarkateshwar – 'Lord of the Beheaded') tells Munna that he knows how to take care of Gandhi's ghost: when Gandhi sees the '*durdasha*' (degeneration) of contemporary India, he will flee right back into the books from which he has emerged to haunt Munna. Gradually the film shows Gandhi on celluloid, not so much addressing the nation as helping its contemporary citizens tackle their civic as well as social problems. Gandhi becomes an antidote, a way of countering some of the worst of the ills that plague us today. He thus becomes the means not just of critiquing postcolonial India but of improving it. Just as Gandhi's *Hind Swaraj* started with a reflection on the condition of colonized India, *Lage Raho* too uses the metaphor of Gandhi to comment on and examine the condition of contemporary, post-colonized India. In choosing a low-life protagonist such as Munna and showing his gradual transformation into a *satyagrahi*, the film becomes a Gandhian text of struggle and hope.

I have been trying to argue that the film, though aimed at popular audiences, does not necessarily trivialize either Gandhi's legacy or his thought. On the contrary it is a serious engagement with the Mahatma in the form of not so much a resurrection, but his afterlife. The very familiar Mahatma becomes more than just a 'familiar', that is the friendly neighbourhood ghost, but an enduring, challenging and even vexing presence in the national consciousness. Literally, he is a ghost that cannot be laid to rest. The film reminds us of Sarojini Naidu's statement on Gandhi's death. Gandhi does not allow us to rest but creates a chemical *locha* (dissonance) in our brains if we are to go by what happens in the film. Bollywood is not known for serious content. Indeed one might despair of the possibility of a profound engagement with any issue of note in a medium that is supposed to cater to the lowest common denominator and whose common currency is cheap and meretricious dolings-out of clichés and trivialities. One central question for us in this film is how authentic its treatment of Gandhi is. Is it a fake and counterfeit sop to the masses, which may be cynically exploited? Is the film just about the marketing of the Mahatma?

My conclusion is that while the film does engage with Gandhian thoughts seriously, it cannot be pigeonholed as a traditionalist or purist exposition either. The film, it seems to me, shows a great deal of ambivalence towards violence in its scheme of things, repeatedly showing the efficacy of violence and the defeat, at least partial, of non-violence. Instead of fetishizing non-violence, Munna Bhai looks at it as a part of a larger arsenal that needs to be employed to combat social evils and corruption. To that extent, the film's take on non-violence is less Gandhian and more in keeping with the traditional Sanatani practices. While the tradition expounds the dictum '*ahimsa paroma dharma*' (non-violence is the highest dharma), it does not rule out righteous violence altogether, especially as a last resort, as in the Mahabharata, when all other recourses have failed. Sanatana dharma, it would seem, espouses the ultimacy of non-violence even if it is somewhat ambivalent as to its immediacy; Gandhi on the other hand upheld both the immediacy and ultimacy of non-violence. Yet Gandhi too supported the use of armed forces to repulse the Pakistani mercenaries' invasion of Kashmir. So there does seem to remain a certain degree of doubt in the movie about Gandhi's non-compromising abhorrence of violence, either at the personal or national level. Munna Bhai, in contrast to Gandhi, seems to adopt a more contemporary, even practical approach, preferring non-violence, endorsing and espousing it, but not ruling out the use of mock-violence to threaten adversaries into submission, as in the climax of the movie. One is reminded of Ramakrishna's advice to the snake that was converted to non-violence and found itself almost battered to death. The sage said to the snake, 'I asked you not to bite, but I did not ask you not to hiss.' In Gandhi's world, both biting and hissing seem to be forbidden. The practice of *ahimsa* does not accommodate either. But as far as Munna is concerned, even if he has given up biting, he still retains the option to hiss rather effectively now and then, especially with the aid of Circuit. While it would be erroneous to conclude that the film merely instrumentalizes non-violence, reducing it from a defining principle in action to a practical ruse, it would still be fair to say that its commitment to non-violence is neither as uncompromising nor as faithful as Gandhi's.

When it comes to the other foundational idea, truth, Munna Bhai shows a much greater consistence and adherence to it, quite in keeping with the Gandhian ideal. In fact if we were to go by the film's idea of what constitutes Gandhism and not just Gandhigiri, then it would be an abiding and enduring commitment to truth, both at the practical (*vyavaharik*) level and the spiritual (*adhayatmik*) level. From Jahnavi's declaration at the beginning of the film, through Munnna's admission that he is not the professor he pretends to be, to Simran's admitting that she is a *manglik* at the end of the film, it is truth that emerges as the highest value. To that extent, the film's understanding of Gandhi is centred more on truth than on non-violence. Thus we even get a contemporary adaptation of Gandhism for our times, where despite the exigencies, contingencies and temptations of a materialist–consumerist ethos, maintaining faith in truth becomes the way out of both the morass of individual inertia and civic dysfunctionality. Gandhian ortho-praxy is observed as an adherence to truth more than to non-violence: this becomes its defining characteristic. The afterlife of the Mahatma, then, is a call not just to non-violent action, but even more so to *satyagraha* in the original sense of the word, as an insistence on truth. The film suggests that we can repay our *rishi rn*, our debt to the Mahatma, by giving up a life lived in bad faith to achieve an existential authenticity which can only derive from the renewal of our commitment, both as individuals and as a nation, to truth. The film, in other words, reminds us that it is only when we walk the path of truth that we will attain Svaraj. When we turn our backs to truth, we will lose much that the founding fathers of our nation achieved through their struggle and sacrifice.

The film is therefore a uniquely creative exposition on neo-Gandhism. To be neo-Gandhian is not to parrot old shibboleths and slogans; it is not to imitate the external appurtenances of the Mahatma's life. Rather it is to become exemplars ourselves at whatever level it is given to us to do so. *Munna Bhai* is an exemplary redefinition of the efficacy of Gandhi in our times. That it made a lot of money only shows that Gandhi still sells; it does not mean that the film has merely and cynically commoditized him or has marketed a stereotypical version of him. For years I harboured the feeling that Gandhi was becoming more and more irrelevant to India, that we were turning our backs on him, that Gandhian institutions were declining, that Gandhians were dying out and the new breed of politicians using Gandhi as a smokescreen for their misdeeds had taken their place. But *Munna Bhai* has demonstrated in unexpected ways that it is not so easy to finish off the Mahatma, that indeed his *afterlife* will continue to inspire if not haunt us for many years to come.

I elaborated on Gandhi's afterlife through *Lage Raho Munna Bhai* because it shows us one way to counter the after-effects of Nathuram's parricide. The mass repression of the murder of Gandhi may be undone by his continuous resurrection through our own form of Gandhigiri. Munna not only makes peace with Gandhi's ghost, but also uses him to change his own life. In the end, the ghost is laid to rest not through an act of exorcism but through absorption, assimilation and emulation. The creative application of Gandhi, the exemplar, in our personal and social life-worlds is the way that Gandhi's haunting of the nation may be turned not just therapeutic, but transformative. The aftershocks of parricide are healed by such life-giving, powerful ideas which hover in the atmosphere of the land, so to speak, till they find fit vehicles, like Munna, to carry them forward. The incessant reapplication of and re-engagement with Gandhi's ideas and life render him an ever-living presence in our midst, thereby negating the logic of his assassination. Killing the Father, then, is not the same as eliminating his influence or presence. If his presence is constantly revitalized, if he is thus remembered, he continues to remain in our midst, not as a spectral presence but as a live source of inspiration. Indeed, the revival of Gandhi that Munna effects is, perhaps, more powerful and significant than his assassination at the hands of a determined zealot.

14 Beyond the monument

Remembering the Mahatma

In his Introduction to *Twilight Memories: Marking Time in a Culture of Amnesia* (1995), Andreas Huyssen remarks, 'Inevitably, every act of memory carries with it a dimension of betrayal, forgetting, and absence'.[1] Early in this exploration, I spoke of the forgetting and absence, if not betrayal, that the monuments dedicated to Gandhi convey. In *Making India: Colonialism, National Culture, and the Afterlife of Indian English Authority* (2012), I offered a semiology of cenotaphs and gravestones as a way to understand the 'Renaissance in India'. There, I argued that the graves of key figures from William Jones to Aurobindo signified a gradual but definite shift from the colonial to the national, from the British contribution to India's modernization to India's own response to it. This response was clearly mixed and ambivalent; India, it would seem, had a complex and multilayered engagement with modernity, welcoming some aspects of it as derived from the West, resisting others even as it asserted its own traditions, modifying the latter in the light of new ideas, and also creating hybrid and altogether new forms.[2] Sometimes what seemed like acceptance was a form of resistance and vice versa; moreover, different religious groups, classes, castes and sections of society reacted differently to the modernizing imperative. To take this argument to its ultimate conclusion, we might read the monuments commemorating Gandhi as themselves representing this rich and complex narrative.

On the one hand, these monuments are supreme embodiments of the newly independent nation's notion of who or what it is. The Gandhi memorial at Raj Ghat is the first major monument of a leader of independent India, the Father of the Nation no less. However, as I showed earlier, it partakes of the dual heritage of older traditions of commemorialization, a tradition in which a community comes into being through the manner in which it remembers. Like the Sufis and the Sikhs whose memorials bring together complex assertions, both secular and sacred, of those communities, Gandhi's memorials are also both political and spiritual, emphasizing his dual legacy as political leader and saintly figure. But the key to understanding these memorials is to unearth what they seek to hide or deny – the killing of the Father of the Nation, which is elided and substituted by the museumization if not mummification of his life. This collective repression, as I have argued, comes from the impossibility of parricide in the Hindu imaginary, a traditional taboo that Nathuram's supremely modern act seems to defy. But the repression is double because it also hides the causal connection between Nathuram's act and the fratricidal Partition of the nation. The implications of this forgetting, the guilt that it induces, and the Mahatma's haunting, which Sarojini Naidu asked for and predicted, have all been touched on in the previous sections. The implication of this whole inquiry, however, is clear: a true reckoning with the issue of the death of Gandhi cannot stop short of the demand for a total transformation of society. Such, indeed, was Gandhi's vision. That the project of Svaraj failed or at least did not materialize as envisaged need not dishearten us. The utopian impulse within it cannot be entirely suppressed.

In her Introduction to *Acts of Memory: Cultural Recall in the Present*, Mieke Bal says that cultural memory is 'Neither remnant, document, nor relic of the past, nor floating in a present cut off from the past,' but it is, 'for better or for worse,' a way of linking the 'past to the present and future'.[3] If I have invoked monumental cultural memory to discuss the killing of the Mahatma, it is, in Bal's words, 'to mediate and modify difficult or tabooed moments' of the birth traumas of a nation because, despite their repression, they 'nonetheless impinge, sometimes fatally, on the present'.[4] Cultural reflection and recall, Bal reminds us, is neither accidental nor fortuitous, even if it is spontaneous or unreflecting; it is, above all, something we 'actually *perform*, even if, in many instances, such acts are not consciously and wilfully contrived'.[5] This recollection of the assassination of Gandhi, then, is one such performance, a re-enactment which has a special purpose.

Of the several kinds of memories, Bal identifies three: 'unreflective habitual, narrative, and traumatic'.[6] It is the latter that have the greatest need to be 'legitimized and narratively integrated'.[7] Such a narrativization is necessary so that these memories 'lose their hold over the subject who suffered the traumatizing event in the past'.[8] But the paradox is that it is precisely such memories that resist easy narrativization or integration. That is because 'Traumatic memories remain present for the subject with particular vividness and/or totally resist integration'.[9] Such memories, which remain 'outside' the subject often result in compulsive repetition of suffering, blind and bewildering, because the sufferer cannot 'master' them. The repression of such memories, in narrative terms, results in two processes according to Bal: in 'ellipsis' and 'omission of important elements' or in 'paralepsis' in which dissociation 'doubles the strand of the narrative series of events by splitting off a sideline'.[10] We have already seen both these features in the ways that two monuments to Gandhi in the nation's capital narrativize Gandhi's life and elide over his murder. At Raj Ghat, the site of his cremation, we see the classical instance of ellipsis, with the details of the assassination of Gandhi practically erased or absent. On the other hand, at Gandhi Smriti, the site of his actual murder, what we see is footprints ending halfway through the lawn, the narrative doubling back as it were to his life, leaving the whole puzzle of his death unresolved. Here, via paralepsis, we are led away from uncomfortable questions about his assassination to the more familiar and comforting story of his life, the heroic saga of a 'Great Soul'.

Bal, a narratologist herself, invokes the work of van der Kolk and van der Hart (1995) to show both the vertical dimensions of repression and the horizontal movement of dissociation:

> Although the concepts of repression and dissociation have been used interchangeably by Freud and others with regard to traumatic memories, there is a fundamental difference between them. Repression reflects a vertically layered model of mind: what is repressed is pushed downward, into the unconscious. The subject no longer has access to it. Only symbolic, indirect indications would point to its assumed existence. Dissociation reflects a horizontally layered model of mind: when a subject does not remember a trauma, its 'memory' is contained in an alternate stream of consciousness, which may be subconscious or dominate consciousness, e.g. during traumatic reenactments.[11]

The trauma of Gandhi's murder is repressed, as I have shown, deep down in the recesses of the Hindu unconscious, with all its horror and prohibition of patricide. But its symbolic indications and symptoms are everywhere present in the way the Mahatma haunts the nation. So too the horizontal dissociations from this trauma are portrayed over and over again in Gandhi's life narratives, reproduced in different parts of India in more or less the same set and chronological arrangement of photographs, with the memory of the murder diverted into an alternate channel of consciousness, irrationally reasserting its dominance from time to time in anti-Gandhian tirades by fanatics, whether Hindu, Muslim, Sikh, or dalit. Similarly, cultural memories of the Partition are repressed or disassociated into triumphal narratives of national independence, usually Indian, but also Pakistani. The Partition itself is re-enacted over and over again not only in communal riots in the subcontinent but also in the never-ending war between Pakistan and India, a war that simmers all along the border, right into the snowy and inhospitable heights of the Himalayas, and down to the beautiful valleys of Kashmir.

We might, however, disagree with Bal that traumatic memory is necessarily solitary, lacking an 'addressee' or 'social component'.[12] Instead, we could argue that there are collective re-enactments of traumatic memory, which might actually help release the pain or give it a narrative form. If it were entirely solitary, 'inflexible and invariable',[13] then the massive monumentalization of trauma would be pointless. To me, remembering Gandhi, even his murder, certainly serves a social function, especially because it is framed in a context in which, as Bal says of normal memory, 'the past makes sense in the present, to others who can understand it, sympathize with it, or respond with astonishment, surprise, even horror; narrative memory offers some form of feedback that ratifies the memory'.[14] It is the narativizing of traumatic events that makes cultural memory an effective way of changing the present and working towards an alternate future. Monuments which cover up the past can be re-read so as to uncover or discover it afresh; they can invite collective witness, moral introspection, penitence, expiation of guilt, and finally positive and remedial action. Such a performance of memorializing 'is potentially healing, as it calls for political and cultural solidarity'.[15] But this is only possible when the trauma of the traumatized party is made 'narratable'.[16] What we have tried to do here is to render 'unspeakable' or 'inexpressible' memories narratable.

Invoking another kind of theoretical practice, Adrian Parr in *Deleuze and Memorial Culture: Desire, Singular Memory and the Politics of Trauma*, distinguishes two ways of reading monuments. The more common approach, such as I have myself adopted in the earlier part of this book, is to look at 'memorials and monuments as texts, arguing that these constitute a language in general, and after examining individual examples . . . demonstrate how these produce meaning'.[17] But following Deleuze, Parr also demonstrates another way of reading them: 'Instead of arguing that the memorial or monument is the effect of a system of signification, libidinal semiotics proposes memorial culture is the effect of an investment of libidinal energies and affects'.[18] What does this mean? It means to liberate the monument from the uses to which the state or any other controlling or 'fascistic' agency seeks to manage its meaning or channel public desire, memory, or mourning. Such a 'schizoid investment . . . in memorial culture,' as Parr clarifies, works 'to extract the poly-vocal movement of social energies and affects at play in the process of public remembrance'.[19] This way of reading monuments saves them from the uses to which they are designed to be subjected.

Monuments, such as Raj Ghat or more specifically Gandhi Smriti, may register 'the social force of collective trauma',[20] especially since there is no other memorial to the hundreds of thousands killed in communal and civil violence during the Partition, yet such a registration, as I have been suggesting, 'operates as an index to prompt the affective dimension of memory to generate future orientated connections'.[21] The memorial no longer allows itself to code the 'labour of memory' to 'fixed use', as desired by the state, or permit the trauma that 'registers throughout the social field . . . as a determinate entity'.[22] Both the monument and the memories that attach themselves to it are liberated from the deathly hallows of the past to accomplish, as Deleuze puts it in *Difference and Repetition*, 'a living connection between the knowledge and the resistance, the representation and the blockage'.[23]

Thus, as Deleuze and Guattari propose in *What is Philosophy?*, 'the monument is not something commemorating a past, it is a bloc of present sensations'[24] or even more forcefully and brilliantly, 'The monument's action is not memory but fabulation'.[25] Later in the same text they add, 'The monument does not actualize the virtual event but incorporates or embodies it: it gives it a body, a life, a universe'.[26] Using the metaphor of music they say 'Monuments are refrains'.[27] Such a 'sensational' reading of monuments helps liberate them from their fixity and limited-use inscriptions and allows them to act in extremely potent ways to energize thought and action. This is what I meant by the 'living' monuments of the Sufi and Sikh saints, as opposed to the dead and decorative tombs of the kings and emperors of Delhi, now only inhabited by bats and pigeons. In the living monuments there are qawallis and sabad kirtans, songs sung to re-energize both the revered dead and the devoted living. The day my class visited Raj Ghat, we saw a group of musicians sitting around Gandhi's Samadhi singing 'Raghu Pati Raghav Raja Rama' in neither inspiring nor mellifluous tones, but still moving *because* they were so amateurish. We too sat on a grassy knoll nearby to sing songs that the Mahatma loved, also songs from the struggle for India's freedom which earlier generations sang, which we repeated spontaneously that day to re-establish our link with them. As Deleuze and Guattari say, 'Sensation itself vibrates because it contracts vibrations. It preserves itself because it preserves vibrations: it is Monument'.[28] By questioning the official narratives, by reusing monuments of the state for our own purposes, we may thus remember and resist, liberate ourselves from past traumas rather than merely disassociating from or repressing them. It is not the casual act of forgetting or ignorance, but the conscious one of remembering and resisting that can effect in healing.

The conflicts, contradictions, and tensions that inhere not only in Gandhi's monuments but also in the narratives around his killing, thus all invite us to work through, if not resolve them – but, as noted earlier, a complete resolution would not be possible without a thorough-going transformation of all of India, a project that we need not abandon just because it is not imminent. Deleuze and Guattari might have implied no less when they declared

> A monument does not commemorate or celebrate something that happened but confides in the ear of the future the persistent sensations that embody the event: the constantly renewed suffering of men and women, their re-created protestations,

their constantly resumed struggle. Will this all be in vain because suffering is eternal and revolutions do not survive their victory? But the success of a revolution resides only in itself, precisely in the vibrations, clinches, and openings it gave to men and women at the moment of its making and that composes in itself a monument that is always in the process of becoming, like those tumuli to which each new traveller adds a stone.[29]

Gandhi's monuments, thus, need not serve merely the interests of the state to offer us fixed ideas of the nation; they need not, likewise, serve to celebrate the saintly life of the Mahatma, the Father of the Nation; moreover, they need also not be just mute testimonials to a forgotten martyrdom; nor, indeed, might they end up as mnemonic symbols of some traumatic experience now repressed from national memory. These monuments, instead, need to be reappropriated as major constituents of a memorial culture whereby a nation not just remembers its past, 'inventing a tradition', giving coherence to its recent, albeit fractured history, but also offering stability and solace to its citizens rather than serving merely as symbols of nationalism to visiting foreign dignitaries. The monuments dedicated to Gandhi must escape from institutional and governmental constraints to act in the present, urging radical intervention and investment towards alternate futures.

While it is crucial to unmask the monumental cover-up and deflection that the nationalized, now globalized, Gandhi memorials enact so as to liberate the living and provocative presence of the Mahatma from beneath them, it is also crucial not to go to the other extreme of fetishizing the trauma that is hidden behind the repression of Gandhi's murder into a sort of hypertrophy of memorialization. We must resist the temptation of consigning the history of the Partition symbolized by Gandhi's murder to what Huyssen calls 'the sign of trauma', functioning in the Indian context, like the Holocaust, as 'the ultimate cipher of traumatic unspeakability or unrepresentability'.[30] But without such a journey of uncovering and recovering our past, no alternative future is possible:

> while the hypertrophy of memory can lead to self-indulgence, melancholy fixations, and a problematic privileging of the traumatic dimension of life with no exit in sight, memory discourses are absolutely essential to imagine the future and to regain a strong temporal and spatial grounding of life and the imagination in a media and consumer society that increasingly voids temporality and collapses space.[31]

We have seen how, to use Huyssen's phrase, 'memory and forgetting pervade real public space'.[32] This essay has been an attempt to offset the forgetting that those very monuments to memory induce by a deliberate and, I hope, liberating act of remembering. It has been a reflection on remembering and forgetting as cultural practices, and how both processes are at play in sites of memorialization, such as Gandhi's monuments. Indeed, it is possible to argue that ours is a culture of forgetting, not of remembering, more so now that the information glut of the postmodern condition assails us with what Frederic Jameson describes as the schizophrenic 'historical deafness'[33] or loss of history. When it comes to overcoming the massive traumas of the Partition and the murder of the Mahatma, neither remembering nor forgetting, by themselves, work. We need a conscious combination of ways of remembering with kinds of forgetting to overcome such traumas; that is how we might come to terms with the mechanisms of trauma but 'forget' the urge to retaliate, to right the wrongs of the past, or to indulge in counter-narratives and revenge histories. At any rate, what we have attempted at the very least is to counterbalance the 'monumental invisibility'[34] of Gandhi's murder and its implications to the psyche of Hindus and the body politic of the nation with a deeply reflective and healing recovery of the traumatic 'truth' of history. In that sense, we have attempted here what the likes of Jan Assmann (1992) and Richard Terdiman (1993) have called the recuperation of cultural memory. It is through cultural memory that societies ensure continuity and self-understanding, passing on collective knowledge, preserved, through social mnemonics. This makes it possible for future generations to assert a collective identity by constructing and participating in a shared past.[35]

15 Gandhi and *Anti-Oedipus*

Whether or not we agree with Basanta Kumar Mallik's assertion that Gandhi's assassination was 'a radical break with past historical patterns',[1] his reading of the outcome of the event bears serious consideration. Mallik believed the assassination had inaugurated an era of 'widespread scepticism that simultaneously neutralized all major traditions' catapulting the world 'into a stage of non-triumphalism, where no traditional scheme could any longer command comprehensive faith and allegiance'.[2] What interests me in Mallik's analysis is not only his evolutionary idea of history, which he shares with other thinkers of his time including Jean Gebser, but his assertion that we would have to search for alternatives in the 'realm of *Non Absolutes*' (italics in original).[3] Perhaps for Gilles Deleuze and Felix Guattari the failed revolution of May 1968 in France also marked a similar break with the past. Certainly, it propelled them to inaugurate a new critical praxis called schizoanalysis, which showed us a way to dismantle the master narrative not only of universal Marxism but also universal Freudism, the latter most aptly symbolized by the straitjacket termed Oedipus. Their attempt too was not to replace one quest for totality by another, but rather to look at splitting and fragmenting both the subject and the object as the means to freedom. It is not in totality that we can find answers, but in fragments.

Jumping from Gandhi's assassination to Deleuze and Guattari may at first seem strange, but serves an important purpose. There is the strange but convincing family resemblance that must be explored. Even if we do not call it a family resemblance, we must certainly not lose out on the immense creative potential of putting (pitting) them in contrapuntal juxtaposition. Both Gandhi and Deleuze and Guattari share a passionate, somewhat anarchic, commitment to freedom. Even if the former is holistic while the latter is fragmentary, what is overriding is the liberative thrust of their work. The kind of freedom that Deleuze and Guattari strove for is surely homologous to Gandhi's own concept of *moksha*. For Gandhi 'Freedom from all bondage is *moksha*'.[4] To quote from Michel Foucault's Preface, Deleuze and Guattari regard freedom as 'living counter to all forms of fascism', finding a way out of 'all unitary and totalizing paranoia'.[5] Both views have in common their commitment to break free from all forms of bondage and damaging authority. Secondly, both Gandhi and Deleuze and Guattari help in our fight against colonialism – not just political, but psychological. After reading Gandhi's murder in Oedipal terms, it would not be proper to leave it at that, without offering a way out. Repression should not be replaced by another form of oppression, this time of psychoanalysis. And it is Deleuze and Guattari who are most enabling in our need to break free from the Oedipal prison house.

In *Anti-Oedipus*, Deleuze and Guattari declare: 'Oedipus is always colonization pursued by other means, it is the interior colony, and we shall see that even here at home, where we Europeans are concerned, it is our intimate colonial education'.[6] We have already seen earlier attempts to dethrone Oedipus. Malinowski, for instance, inaugurates a culturalist questioning of dogmatic Oedipal universalism. That line, followed by other anthropologists, ethnologists, mythographers and folklorists has already led us to India, where we have examined in detail the possibilities of an Indian Oedipus. From within the psychoanalytical tradition, too, it was not just Girindrasekhar Bose, using a culturalist, even anti-colonial reasoning, who questioned Oedipus, but Melanie Klein and others, too, who tried to mitigate its oppressive, reductive and masculinist implications. Indeed, apart from Deleuze and Guattari's ferocious, even delirious dismantling, some other recent attempts to question Oedipus are noteworthy.

In his fascinating overview of some of these attempts, Peter L. Rudnytsky observes:

> Although Freud's notion of the 'Oedipus complex' has had an incalculable impact upon modern culture, a number of recent studies have sought to dislodge the Oedipus myth from the privileged position accorded to it by psychoanalytic theory. This effort, which has come from several directions, represents an important trend in contemporary criticism.[7]

It is, however, somewhat ironic that Rudnytsky's overview stems from his express desire to 'to reassert the centrality of the Oedipus myth'.[8] Apart from the work of Deleuze and Guattari, to which we shall turn to shortly, Rudnytsky identifies two other challenges 'to the psychoanalytic veneration of the Oedipus myth'.[9]

First is the novel thesis of Sandor Goodhart in which he reinterprets the source of the myth, Sophocles's *Oedipus Rex*, to suggest that Oedipus never killed his father Laius. For students of literature and practitioners of criticism, this reading is both exciting and reassuring in its ability to restore to the interpretation of texts a very high order of skill and significance. Goodhart follows and extends Rene Girard's argument that Oedipus was framed for Laius's murder, that the deed could as easily have been done by Creon or Tiresias. Oedipus, in other words, is the scapegoat. Goodhart argues that 'Rather than an illustration of the myth, the play is a critique of mythogenesis, an examination of the process by which one arbitrary fiction comes to assume the value of truth'.[10] Of Laius's 'many murderers' Oedipus is singled out for punishment. Goodhart thus strikes a blow at 'the idolatry of the Oedipal':[11] after all, if the available textual evidence were reassembled or reinterpreted to show that Oedipus was not Laius's murderer, then the entire edifice of Oedipus, based as it is on the twin taboo of patricide and incest, would be severely undermined. If Oedipus never actually killed his father, at least one of the pillars of the Oedipus complex, that of patricide, would come crashing down. So would Freud's theories of civilization, repression, and 'nuclear complex' of all neurosis. Rudnytsky calls Goodhart's exegesis a 'hand-to-hand combat with the received understanding of Oedipus the King'[12] because it problematizes what is generally regarded as the 'truth' of the play, revealing it to be just one of many possible fictions:

> From Freud's perspective of 'demystification', the action of Oedipus the King entails the discovery of a hidden but nonetheless decisive truth; the essence of Goodhart's 'deconstructive' reading is precisely that there is no absolute or final truth to be found.[13]

The paradox of such a reading, however, is that by shifting the blame for Laius's murder to someone else, it is merely shifting the 'truth' of the play, not denying it altogether. If all meaning were indeterminate, we would not be able to make sense of the play, but by offering another explanation for the known facts in the play, Goodhart shows us how someone other than Oedipus could have killed Laius. Of course, such a reading also undermines the impact of the tragedy, the horror of the discovery of Oedipus's unintentional crime, both taking away from the anguish of his mother/wife, Jocasta, and rendering pointless his self-blinding. In a word, with such a reading, the play ceases to be a tragedy. In fact, Rudnytsky uses Goodhart's own strategy to question his (Goodhart's) interpretation: 'But it seems likely that this alternative version of events is included by Sophocles simply to heighten the dramatic irony'.[14] After all, the language in the play is known for its '"double striking" quality'[15] whose express purpose appears to be the highlighting of Oedipus's tragedy. The 'audience knows from the outset that Oedipus is guilty';[16] its 'superior awareness' heightens the effect of watching 'the transformation of Oedipus' hope into despair'.[17]

Apart from destabilizing Oedipus, Goodhart's thesis has little else to offer us, when it comes to Nathuram's slaying of Gandhi. This act, as we have seen, was neither accidental nor unconscious, but deliberately planned and executed. What was perhaps unconscious was that it was patricidal, that it showed the classic Oedipal triangulation in which the same object of desire, Mother India, was the cause of a struggle between a faithful son and an allegedly faithless father. Nathuram's Oedipal intentions might not have been fully conscious to him, nor to the people of India, who had to, perforce, repress the fuller implications of this act. If it were possible that Nathuram had not even killed Gandhi or if he had been wrongfully framed for this murder, then Goodhart's reading would be directly applicable. But, instead, Nathuram waited to be recognized as Gandhi's murderer and used the trial to offer not only an elaborate justification but also his own alternate vision for Hindu India.

The second author that Rudnytsky identifies is Rene Girard, whose justly celebrated *Violence and the Sacred* (1977; 1995) offers an original theory of violence. Girard rescues 'the Oedipal struggle from the familial terrain' but introduces another 'mimetic triangle of the model, the disciple, and the object' in its place.[18] Girard is interested in finding the root of 'the structure of violence itself',[19] which he identifies in mimetic desire. Ignoring that the mother is the object of desire disputed by father and son, Girard argues that all desire is mimetic: 'the subject desires the object because the rival desires it. In desiring an object the rival alerts the subject to the desirability of the object'.[20] Furthermore, this clash of desire leads to violence: 'By making one man's desire into a replica of another man's desire, [mimetism] invariably leads to rivalry; and rivalry in turn transforms desire into violence'.[21]

This conflict between the model and the disciple, the subject and the rival tie them in a cycle of reciprocal violence. That is why 'violence is the great leveller';[22] in violence we become each other's perfect doubles, identical to our rivals in both 'obsession and hatred'.[23]

Girard's theory leads away from Oedipus but into another sort of trap. What is the way out of this cycle of violence? Is it possible to have non-violent or cooperative desire? Instead of violence mimicking itself, can non-violence also be mimicked? At least, as we shall see later, Gandhi thought so. What about sharing or absenting from pressing one's claim? Girard does not fully explain or account for these issues because he is only concerned with cycles of violence. But we can clearly see how profoundly Girard's thesis may apply to the story of the Partition of India. 'Rivalry', Girard says, 'does not arise because of the fortuitous convergence of two desires on a single object; rather, *the subject desires the object because the rival desires it*'.[24] Muslims wanted a nation because Hindus did; it was a mimetic desire that led both to the wholly destructive cycle of reciprocal violence. Further, this mimetic desire continued to reproduce itself, with the Sikhs wanting their own nation, the Kashmiris wanting their own nation, the Nagas wanting their own nation, and so on, each time drawing communities in cycles of fratricidal violence. We can see other instances of conflict, including the one over the disputed Babri Masjid, as arising from such mimetic and competitive desire. As Girard puts it:

> If the model, who is apparently already endowed with superior being, desires some object, that object must surely be capable of conferring an even greater plenitude of being.[25]

This is how two desires converge on the same object; no doubt 'Two desires converging on the same object are bound to clash. Thus, mimesis coupled with desire leads automatically to conflict'.[26] Girard's analysis now reaches its most profound pitch:

> *Mimetic desire* is simply a term more comprehensive than
> *violence* for religious pollution. As the catalyst for the sacrificial
> crisis, it would eventually destroy the entire community if the
> surrogate victim were not at hand to halt the process and the
> ritualized mimesis were not at hand to keep the conflictual
> mimesis from beginning afresh.[27]

If we were to apply Girard to our situation, then Gandhi offered
himself as the surrogate victim for a whole society's crisis. This
was also the crisis of the competing desires for India, for the new
nation that had arisen, free at last, from the shackles of colonialism
and slavery. Girard's idea of such a victim is spelled out in his other
book *Scapegoat*, but it certainly resembles the pagan-Christian
notion of the sacrifice of the priest-king that Frazer elaborated in
The Golden Bough and is so clearly present in the Christian story of
Christ's sacrifice and crucifixion.

Gandhi's great contribution to this crisis of the nation was that
he wanted Indians, especially Hindus, not to be drawn into the
logic of reciprocal violence when faced with the reality of unilateral
violence. Gandhi perceived very clearly that reciprocal violence was
wholly destructive. By offering himself as a scapegoat, he effected
a substitution that turned the unremittingly destructive reciprocal
violence into a ritual violence, at once creative and protective. As he
said in his speech at the prayer meeting on 21 January 1948, nine
days before his assassination: 'The death of a non-violent man will
always have desirable consequences'.[28] By engineering, so to speak,
his own death at the hands of a fellow Hindu rather than a Muslim,
he proved not only that Hindus were not wholly innocent, but
that the logical consequences of Hindu–Muslim violence would
be fratricidal violence between Hindus themselves, as suggested in
his invocation of the destruction of the Yadavas at the end of the
Mahabharata: 'But if we only continue our internecine strife we
shall meet with the same fate as the Yadavas did'.[29] Manubehn also
recalls how Gandhi alluded to the internecine and self-destructive

fighting of the Yadavas when he heard about the altercation between his publisher Navajivan Publishing House and one of his associates, Chandrashankar Shukla: 'Wherever I see, I find internal rifts, like the rifts that existed among the warring Yadavas. Owing to personal differences, we are doing great harm to society'.[30] Yet it is not sufficiently persuasive to see the tussle between Godse and Gandhi over Mother India as a Girardian triangulation wrought by mimetic desire; it is not as if Godse desired India *because* his model, Gandhi, did. Interestingly, Godse was once a follower of Gandhi; to that extent, the model–disciple pattern is evident in their relationship. Yet again, Gandhi's non-retaliation also goes contrary to Girard's notion of reciprocal violence.

That is why it is time to return to *Anti-Oedipus* by Deleuze and Guattari, which even Rudnytsky agrees, is the most defiant repudiation of the Oedipus complex. *Anti-Oedipus* aims at fracturing the 'familialism' of Freud's Oedipus, with its triangulation of the stifling 'tripartite formula' of 'Daddy-Mommy-Me'.[31] It is their way out of this strangulation of what Mark Sheen in his Introduction called the 'holy family'[32] that makes *Anti-Oedipus* so special. Oedipus to Deleuze and Guattari is not just psychological, but supremely social; it is how capitalism controls and rechannels for its own purposes the entire mechanism of desire–production which characterizes the operation of both personal and social libido. What is more, Deleuze and Guattari perform their schizoanalysis through a delirious–delicious prose, bristling with new ideas and coinages. The attempt is to show us how to free ourselves radically – or how free we can be if we wanted.

As Eugene W. Holland explains, *Anti-Oedipus* rejects 'the oedipal axiom of psychoanalysis – that you desire Mommy and envy Daddy, or forego Mommy to identify with Daddy – as a misleading social representation of desire'.[33] Desire as libidinal energy cannot be reduced and subordinated to the 'family triangle' which then becomes its ultimate determinant. Neither is the unconscious structured, as Lacan claimed, like language;

instead it is structured 'like the "word-salad" of schizophrenia, with no center, and no Law'.[34] Oedipus, then, is 'an archaic and reactionary despotism installed at the heart of the nuclear family under capitalism to re-contain the free-flow of desire' and the very 'institution of psychoanalysis' is itself 'the repressive agency of last resort' to 'ensure complete oedipalization' in the face of the deterioration of the nuclear family.[35] The inherent logic of capitalism breaks down, as Marx shows, all barriers to the force of capital; it also recodes desires for its own ends, to generate greater profits. The social effects of such capitalism, which functions as an end in itself, include 'Narcissistic personality-splitting, cynical-defensive disdain for others and for community, and desperate self-absorption': these are not products of the breakdown of the stable or nuclear family, but of 'the libidinal structure of capitalism itself'.[36] *Anti-Oedipus* is about how to resist such recoding in the Name of the Father: 'Schizoanalysis, then, addresses itself primarily to the contradiction between processes of de-coding which free libidinal energy in ongoing social revolution, and processes of re-coding which constrict and limit those energies to the codes of capitalist paranoia'.[37] *Anti-Oedipus* embodies a refusal to be subject to the Oedipal 'castrating mediation', to the programming and conditioning that not just capitalism, but also other master narratives such as Marxism or Freudism engender, all of which are ways of controlling desire and locking individuals into different forms of subjection.[38] Instead of master narratives, Deleuze and Guattari, like Lyotard after them, promote 'minority' discourses that resist totalizing and 'scientific' closure.[39] Summing up a book which resists easy recapitulation, Holland says

> Schizoanalysis thus ends up not only reformulating psychoanalytic doctrine, but also proposing new directions for postmodern revolutionary strategy: provoking struggles on part of all who are engaged in socialized production, against the restrictions imposed by private appropriation and oedipal

despotism on the limitless productive and libidinal forces unleashed in permanent revolution – with the ultimate aim of redistributing wealth and disseminating power for the use and joy of all.[40]

This utopian impulse at the heart of schizoanalysis, along with its uncompromising commitment to truth and freedom, enables us to connect it with Gandhian *satyagraha*.

Rather than lamenting the breakdown of 'whole' individuals, Deleuze and Guattari celebrate the splitting up of the subject. That is what endows the delirium that is desire with 'extraordinary fluidity':

> It might be said that the schizophrenic passes from one code to the other, that he deliberately *scrambles all the codes*, by quickly shifting from one to another, according to the questions asked him, never giving the same explanation from one day to the next, never invoking the same genealogy, never recording the same event in the same way.[41]

Deleuze and Guattari, taking their stand against 'the analytic imperialism of the Oedipus complex',[42] boldly assert:

> Desire does not lack anything; it does not lack its object. It is, rather, the *subject* that is missing in desire, or desire that lacks a fixed subject; there is no fixed subject unless there is repression.[43]

They wish to replace the 'totalizing paranoia' of the Oedipus complex with an 'affirmation that is irreducible to any sort of unity';[44] by shattering the 'iron collar of Oedipus' they hope to 'discover everywhere the force of desiring-production'.[45]

To knock Freud off balance, they take their cue from Melanie Klein's idea of 'partial objects'.

> Partial objects unquestionably have a sufficient charge in and of themselves to blow up all of Oedipus and totally demolish its ridiculous claim to represent the unconscious, to triangulate the unconscious, to encompass the entire production of desire.[46]

Unlike Klein, Deleuze and Guattari regard 'the production of desire' as 'absolutely *anoedipal*':[47]

> Partial objects are not representations of parental figures or of the basic patterns of family relations; they are parts of desiring-machines, having to do with a process and with relations of production that are both irreducible and prior to anything that may be made to conform to the Oedipal figure.[48]

Later, as Rudnytsky points out, they 'expand their discussion of "partial objects"' by showing how they are 'not partial (partiels) in the sense of extensive parts, but rather partial (partiaux) like the intensities under which a unit of matter always fills space in varying degrees';[49] in other words, partial objects are not 'part of' any lost unity, but rather 'intensities' that 'know no lack'.[50] More profoundly, Deleuze and Guattari disagree that the desires of a small child are completely confined to the family or by the 'restricted code of Oedipus'; instead, 'from the very first days of his life, he immediately begins having an amazing nonfamilial experience that psychoanalysis has completely failed to take into account'.[51] What is more, the child is a 'metaphysical being', not just a desiring machine, asking questions such as 'What does it mean to be alive? What does it mean to breathe? What am I? What sort of thing is this breathing-machine on my body without organs?'[52] This leads them to draw the amazingly liberating conclusion: '*the unconscious is an orphan*, and produces itself within the identity of nature and man'.[53] Such 'autoproduction of the unconscious'[54] is unfortunately subjected to the 'bourgeois repression' that is the practice of psychoanalysis.[55] Psychoanalysis, instead of 'participating in an undertaking that will bring about genuine liberation', helps to keep 'European humanity harnessed to the yoke of daddy-mommy and *making no effort to do away with this problem once and for all*'.[56]

Closer to our concerns, Deleuze and Guattari also take on, later in the book, the question of the universal claims made in the name of Oedipus. 'How', they ask 'are we to understand those who claim to have discovered an Indian Oedipus or an African Oedipus?'.[57] They show how though none of the 'mechanisms or attitudes' that constitute the Oedipus complex are to be encountered in other cultures, the advocates of Oedipal universality claim that

> the structure is there, although it has no existence whatever that is 'accessible to clinical practice'; or that the problem, the point of departure, is indeed Oedipal, although the developments and the solutions are completely different from ours.[58]

This to Deleuze and Guattari is not surprising: 'There or here, it's the same thing: Oedipus is always colonization pursued by other means'.[59] Deleuze and Guattari solve the 'well-known and inexhaustible debate between culturalists and orthodox psychoanalysts' over the universality of Oedipus by mocking the idea of Oedipus as 'the great paternal catholic symbol, the meeting place of all the churches';[60] they totally reject 'the postulate common to Oedipal relativism and Oedipal absolutism – i.e., the stubborn maintenance of a familialist perspective, which wreaks havoc everywhere'.[61] They solve the problem by claiming that 'It is colonization that causes Oedipus to exist'.[62] If Oedipus is the 'internal colony' in Europe, elsewhere it is Europe's export, along with alcoholism and disease, of 'familial reproduction' imposed on the 'savages', depriving them 'control over their own social production' and thus Oedipalizing them 'by force'.[63] Or as they say later in the book, 'We are all little colonies and it is Oedipus that colonizes us'.[64] Our own anti-colonialism, then, is another factor, as I already indicated, that links us to Deleuze and Guattari.

Anti-Oedipus extends Freudian repression to the realm of capital, with 'Father, mother, and child' becoming 'the simulacrum of the images of capital ("Mister Capital, Madame Earth", and their child the Worker)'.[65] The ferocious resistance to any form of totalizing thought control thus helps liberate us from our own, somewhat complicit and inauthentic notions of political correctness, which boil down to little more than a ritual genuflection to shibboleths from the left, right and centre. The authoritarian and repressive structure of doctrinaire left parties all the world over is well known, with their intolerance towards any form of dissent. Thus, whether in the social or the personal realms, Deleuze and Guattari wish to destroy the 'familialist reduction' that takes the 'place of the drift of desire'.[66] Invoking D. H. Lawrence, oddly bringing us closer to Gandhi via sexuality as much as chastity, they say: 'Lawrence shows in a profound way that sexuality, including chastity, is a matter of flows, an infinity of different and even contrary flows'.[67] Gandhi's experiments in chastity can thus be read as magnificent attempts to strengthen his desire for non-violence. Chastity, we might argue, sets up a strong current of desire that counters the violence of Partition. Throughout, Deleuze and Guattari never let us forget the revolutionary, utopian drive that informs the desiring machine: 'in delirium the libido is continually re-creating History, continents, kingdoms, races, and cultures'.[68] Gandhi's great desire to transform the world made him, like 'Every loved or desired being . . . a collective agent of enunciation'.[69] His libido did not have to be, 'as Freud believed . . . desexualized and sublimated in order to invest society and its flows'; from the perspective of Deleuze and Guattari, 'on the contrary . . . it is love, desire, and their flows that manifest the directly social character of the non-sublimated libido and its sexual investments'.[70] Gandhi's own experiments with sexuality were thus part of his tremendous investment in personal and social transformation.

What this discussion of *Anti-Oedipus* shows us is that Mohandas or little Mohna, though very attached to his mother and somewhat critical in his autobiography of his father's sensuality, managed through his experiments in celibacy to free himself from the 'iron collar' of Oedipus. He did so even though his biography has been read so obviously in Oedipal terms, especially his enormous guilt over his neglect of his sick father, whom he was nursing on the deathbed, at the very moment of the latter's death, when Gandhi rushed to his own bedroom to have sex with Kasturba, his wife. Then there was a knock on the door to announce his father's demise. Gandhi claimed that the child so conceived was sickly and soon died. Some aver that the incident turned an otherwise sensuous man to revolt against sex, which he associated with dereliction of duty, corruption and death. Gandhi's anti-sexuality, however, was transformed into an enormously productive drive to non-violent social transformation, which we see working even in his last days, when he became a one-man peacekeeping force, not only in Noakhali, Bihar, or Calcutta, but in Delhi itself, which to Gandhi was the symbol of the rest of India. Gandhi managed to liberate himself from the triangulation of the Oedipal family complex to unfurl his desire so that it inundated all of India and the world beyond with its liberative energies. From his 'narrow guilt' restricted to familial desire, Gandhi demonstrated the 'primacy of the libidinal investments of the social field'.[71] Recent work on Gandhi's *brahmacharya*, such as Veena Rani Howard's (2013), attests to such a transformation.

Nathuram, instead, shunned the 'schizoid revolutionary pole' finding himself stuck in the 'paranoiac, reactionary, and fascisizing pole'.[72] Though not restricted to a familial investment, his libidinal energies were nonetheless triangulated in a destructive transference of hatred to the Father of the Nation, whom he murdered ostensibly to protect Mother India, betrayed and defiled by the Muslim Other. However, if reports are to be believed, Godse and Apte's slogan-shouting as they were led to the gallows, 'Akhand

Bharat Amar Rahe' – 'Long Live Undivided India' – lacked both conviction and fervour. How did their act contribute, in any way, to prevent the division of India? How, instead of targeting their rivals, the Pakistanis, as Apte had once boasted he would do, claiming that he planned to blow up their Parliament, did the killing of the old and frail Mahatma help? What did it prove?

Perhaps what is needed is to shift the focus slightly, from Nathuram or Gandhi to the object that they both desired and which Nathuram killed Gandhi for, Mother India, or the nation itself. If we go back to Girard, then we know that the nation is torn between rival suitors, Hindus and Muslims. The Hindutvawadis, unfortunately, deify the nation as mother, which Gandhi refused to do. Instead, he wanted to espouse the nation, not worship her. There is a fundamental difference between the two. Nathuram's deification proved counterproductive. Instead of fighting to overthrow those who held the nation captive, he struck at the very person who strove the hardest to liberate her. That is why, to invoke a totally different but not unrelated duo, Bankim, in a profound and limited sense, is 'wrong' and Tagore is 'right'. We do not need to deify or worship the nation as is shown in *Anandamath*. Instead, we need to find out how best to espouse her. The problem is well defined in Tagore's *Ghare Baire*: who will espouse Bimala, the symbol of Bengal and the nation, not who will worship her as the Mother. Sandip seduces Bimala by exalting her as the Mother, she who is childless and, at that moment, estranged from Nikhil, her husband. Amulya, the young, misguided revolutionary, whom Sandip betrays, does worship her – and dies for it. Nikhil is weak and unassertive, perhaps unable to claim and keep what is his, but, in the end, we must admit it is he who has the right idea. The nation needs to be espoused, not worshipped or pedestalized. We do not need to die and kill for the nation but to live and work for it. This requires concretizing a vision of how the nation should be organized and governed, how all its constituents 'enjoy' her, regardless of how they regard her, whether as Mother and deity or as secular ideal – or as merely a state of flux, a partial object, not a fetishized entity.

The holism and unity that Gandhi championed and aspired to possibly eluded him, but I am not sure that he would therefore endorse Deleuze and Guattari's schizoanalysis, except as a means of personal, individual freedom. Perhaps a new integralism, such as proposed by Aurobindo and the Mother, where nothing short of a change in human consciousness occurs, would equip us to handle such intractable problems. Thus Gandhi's religious politics finds its uncertain foothold somewhere between the schizoanalysis of Deleuze and Guattari and the new integral totality of Aurobindo and the Mother. Gandhi's own evolutionary teleology has been very little explored but he too believed, for instance, that biological reproduction was not the only way to further the human race. A race that had perfected *brahmacharya* would find hitherto unknown heights of potency and creativity, indeed ushering a society of spiritually enhanced, if not perfected beings. Incidentally, celibacy was also the established norm in the Sri Aurobindo Ashram and only later, in Auroville, did the Mother create a space for consensual, though not de-spiritualized sexuality.

Rudnytsky reminds us how Nietzsche in *The Birth of Tragedy* characterizes the grand design of *Oedipus Rex*: 'nothing more nor less than the luminous afterimage which kind nature provides our eyes after a look into the abyss'.[73] For him contemplating the forces of anti-Oedipus is like 'gazing into the abyss' while returning to the Oedipus complex is like the 'luminous afterimage' that Nietzsche spoke of. I find this a clever but utterly unconvincing simile. Whatever affords us a way to free ourselves from the manacles of both oppressive and repressive forces, only that may be considered not just luminous, but empowering. If psychoanalysis gets us there, well and good; but if it creates its own pathologies and repressions, surely we should find a way out. Even Erik Erikson, with whom we started this inquiry, would agree. After all, he likened psychoanalysis to *satyagraha*, in its commitment to discovering the truth. If anti-Oedipus will serve as a way to truth, which destabilizes the repressive regime of Oedipus, then we should not hesitate to embrace it. As to Deleuze and Guattari, there is little chance of their own delirious and disruptive energies becoming an institutionalized straitjacket. Moreover, in their very next book, *A Thousand Plateaus*, they deconstruct much of what they asserted in *Anti-Oedipus*, thereby (re)proving the irreverent philosophy at the heart of the earlier text, adhering somewhat paradoxically to rather than nullifying the arguments of *Anti-Oedipus*.

We cannot leave this topic of Oedipus versus anti-Oedipus without reverting to the problem of the country, scarred at birth by the twin traumas of the Partition and the assassination of the Father of the Nation. The two incidents, I have argued, are inextricably linked, both repressed in the nation's psyche for being so 'unbearable'. For the nation, they pose almost as severe a challenge as Freud's Oedipal complex might to an individual, with the horrific vivisection of the Mother taking the place of incestuous desire and the death of the Father of the Nation soon after as a matter of perpetual guilt and shame. The numerous sexual crimes of the violence of the Partition, of course, leave nothing to the imagination in terms of their violation of ancestral taboos. The real question for all of us, inheritors of this history of trauma, repression and the consequent neurosis is how to heal, how to overcome, how to end this pattern of suffering. For if we do not find the way to do so, we will be condemned to re-enact the Partition over and over again, in a never-ending fratricidal feud with our hostile brother, Pakistan, on our western frontier and in the cynical recurrence of Partition-style riots within our borders. Whether by psycho- or schizo-analysis, is there a collective redemption for us as a people and as a nation divided against itself? This is the crucial question that the second part of this book tries to address.

This probe into the meaning of Gandhi's death started with the manner in which he was memorialized. We found that at both Raj Ghat, where he was cremated, and at Gandhi Smriti, where he was murdered, there was a strange sort of elision of his murder, of its causes and effects. A true engagement with his assassination and its implications was absent at both sites. Instead, an attempt was made to lead back to his life, as the heroic exposition of the career of a Mahatma and the Father of the Nation. The visitors to both memorials, however, subverted this official narrative in their own way, turning these public monuments into parks, recreational grounds, places of picnic, holiday frolic, or just leisure. It was therefore important to go beyond the official channelizing of the force of Gandhi's death, beyond the way in which it was convenient to remember him, to try to find out why it was so difficult to face its full implications.

We found out that there was a massive national project to repress Gandhi's murder because its true meaning would be too disturbing to confront. The impact of the murder was unbearably horrible, almost unspeakable, to the Hindu psyche. That is because Gandhi's assassination was an essentially patricidal act, inconceivable to the Hindu mind, unprecedented in history and myth. Though Nathuram Godse pulled the trigger, pumping the three fateful bullets into the frail, 79-year-old Mahatma, the actual responsibility for the act was vested in a much larger number of actors. These included not only the conspirators or their ideological brethren, but a much wider range of participants and actors, including many of Gandhi's closest associates and followers, not to speak of his erstwhile constituents and supporters. Beyond these, a larger numbers of Hindus, Muslims, Sikhs, Christians, dalits and others who disapproved, disliked, or detested Gandhi and were happy to see him go, might also be considered as partially responsible. And to the extent to which each of us tacitly approved of or participated in hatred and violence against our fellow countrymen and women, we were all complicit in Nathuram's crime.

Such a wide circle of responsibility also binds us all alike in a compact of guilt, which needs expiation. But what is the way? Not merely a process of national reckoning or political psychoanalysis which might reveal some classic Oedipal structure, but something more, something which might actually help undo the logic of Gandhi's murder. We also saw how Gandhi's murder is intimately tied to the Partition of India, how, in fact, the two were inextricably linked even in his killer's mind. Furthermore, that Gandhi's death did not remove him from the national consciousness, but instead produced a sort of haunting, which one of his closest disciples, Sarojini Naidu, actually wished for the nation. In other words, in seeking for a more powerful and extensive afterlife for the Mahatma, she actually wanted his continued, if somewhat spectral, presence in our midst. As if to prove how this was possible, Bollywood offered us an alternative to Attenborough's moving biopic, which was a worldwide success. Hirani, however, left the life of Gandhi to Attenborough, unpacking instead the Mahatma's hallucinatory, if not haunting, reappearance. Bollywood thus showed us 'Gandhigiri', a novel way of doing Gandhi in the world. Basanta Kumar Mallik's thesis of Gandhi's death causing a rupture in the historical process, ushering a new era of non-absolutes offered us a way to turn to Deleuze and Guattari, whose *Anti-Oedipus* inaugurates a novel libertarian praxis called schizoanalysis. After all, it would not do to recolonize India under the sign of Oedipus after Gandhi's hard work in liberating us from British imperialism. Nevertheless, following Gandhi, we may have to embark upon our own individual and collective truth-finding and truth-telling to discover how to expiate for the crimes of the Partition and the slaying of the Mahatma, how to heal ourselves and the nation from the traumas of our traumatic birth as the children of a fractured midnight.

Part II

'My death is my message'
Mahatma, the last 133 days

16   Arrival in Delhi

A few days before leaving Calcutta, Gandhi was asked by the newly constituted Shanti Sena Dal (Peace Force Corps) for a message. Peace had returned to Calcutta, thanks to his efforts; now the Dal, made up of volunteers from all communities, had pledged to maintain it. They would patrol sensitive areas to inspire confidence and prevent the eruption of violence. In a way, the feuding communities had come to an understanding, brokered and presided over by a fasting Gandhi, that they would not shed each other's blood. Almost miraculously this covenant has still persisted in Calcutta, underwritten and renewed from time to time by the changing power structures and governments. Now that he was leaving, the Shanti Sena Dal wanted a message from him. Blessing the 'soldiers of peace', he told them 'My life is my message'.[1] This simple five-word sentence was written in Bangla and given to Devtosh Das Gupta, Secretary of the Dal, when he called on Gandhi.[2] That Gandhi really meant it is evident in his repeating the same words in his letter of 29 November 1947 to Anasuyaben Sarabhai.[3]

In a sense, this whole book has been an attempt to understand the fuller significance of this message. What we have tried to do is to understand and articulate the coherence of an exemplary life. Given how he regarded himself – 'My life is my message', as we just saw – Gandhi invites the possibility of being read in terms of a consistency in *anubhav* (original experience), *vichār* (thought and ideas) and *āchār* (conduct and action). The best place to examine these in action was the end of his life, where Gandhi's beliefs, principles and basis for living were sorely tested. He was forced to admit that he had been wrong on a number of issues, including non-violence, which had been the cornerstone of his whole public career and had come to be identified so closely with his praxis. While he believed that Indians were trying out non-violence against the British, they were actually only offering passive resistance, the weapon of the weak. Gandhi struggled the hardest to bring about Hindu–Muslim unity, which now seemed almost impossible after Partition. Finally, he gave up his life in persisting against all odds to live on his own terms and for what he thought was right.

In all, despite the odds stacked against him, his ideals betrayed by his followers and associates, and the freedom he fought for itself turning out to be a bitter harvest, Gandhi persisted. We have therefore to try to understand what made him do so. Even after his death, Gandhi persists. By persistence is meant not just continuation, but also an insistence, an ability to persevere in the face of odds. This book is an attempt to examine why and how Gandhi and his ideas continue to matter. It tries to capture what it is that makes the Mahatma challenge, puzzle and exasperate us, to discover how he continues to be relevant, even contemporary, and to define what saves him from simply fading into oblivion. The last days of his life offer us an unparalleled vantage point from which to examine this issue. In fact, during these days, with growing premonitions of his death, we could turn the phrase around to read it as meaning 'My death is my message'. Thus, paradoxically, it is not just his life but his death which is his message. It is from this edge of the abyss, as it were, that we may re-examine key facets of his life in an integral rather than fragmentary fashion, showing what he has to say not only to his own times but to ours. This is why these last 133 days of his life, from his arrival in Delhi on 9 September 1947 to his murder on 30 January 1948, bear closer examination.[4] Indeed, the second part of this book tries to bring to life the meaning of his death so as to show how Gandhi substituted 'death' for 'life' in his famous statement, 'My life is my message'. He thus proved that in death as in life, the message was the 'same'. By dying the way he lived, he demonstrated the efficacy of the message. The message of truth and non-violence was, in other words, as much worth dying, as living for. But by dying for it, he gave life to what otherwise might have died, the new nation that he had fought so hard to create, and an old civilization based on friendship between two communities that seemed all but dead with the Partition of India.

At first, what we see resembles almost the enactment of a black comedy or theatre of the absurd played out in macabre colours on the blood-soaked plains of north India. On the one hand – two new nations, India and Pakistan, embroiled in civil strife, in compulsive and retaliatory cycles of murderous violence, rape and unprecedented exchanges of population characterized by endless caravans of refugees snaking across borders incarnadine, newly etched in blood and fire. On the other hand – an old, frail Mahatma, captive within the walls of nationalist India's richest tycoon, a Father of the Nation, whom no one was listening to, still scolding his errant children in his feeble voice, trying in prayer meeting after prayer meeting to bring his truant flock to order. Anyone disinclined to be charitable to Gandhi might thus view him and his last mission impossible in Delhi. While Gandhi preached non-violence and mutual empathy, much of northern India and Pakistan were in flames all about him. A lone, old man, shrunken and gaunt, his voice hoarse with shrieking the same admonitions to homicidal mobs – urging them to refrain from butchery, rape and internecine bloodshed – might indeed resemble a prophet in the wilderness.

But the very persistence of the lonely Mahatma acquires epic proportions in his last days. He *never* gives up – regardless of the odds. He continues, day after day, repeating, insisting on the same message. Until, miraculously, the tide begins to turn, slowly but surely, and peace is restored. What at first may seem like the almost ludicrous contrast between the continuing, even escalating conflagration of violence across the land and this image of an old man simply sitting at prayer meetings and *scolding* his children comes, on closer examination, to reveal the extraordinary triumph of the one true man over the misguided and mad mob. It is not just a matter of words of wisdom versus images of violence, but of the power of love over the self-forgetfulness of hatred. The cloistered old Mahatma, who at first seems ineffectually sermonizing while the world falls to pieces, slowly reassembles, restores and makes whole these very shards and broken bits of the nation, paying with his very breath and life-blood to do so. The force of *ahimsa*, animated by the spirit of the fragile Mahatma, becomes a mighty praxis in the blood-soaked streets and back alleys of north India and Pakistan.

17 'Do or die'

An old formula in the capital of new India

As soon as he reached Delhi, Gandhi issued a press statement that was later published in his own paper, *Harijan*:

> I knew nothing about the sad state of things in Delhi when I left Calcutta on Sunday last. On reaching Delhi, I have been listening the whole day long to the tale of woe that is Delhi today. I saw several Muslim friends who recited their pathetic story. I must do my little bit to calm the heated atmosphere. I must apply the old formula 'Do or Die' to the capital of India.[1]

Gandhi had spent nearly a month in Calcutta, dousing the flames of communal hatred there. Earlier, in both Noakhali and Bihar, he had brought back peace and stopped the murderous strife between Hindus and Muslims. In Noakhali, the Hindu minority had been terrorized and targeted; in the retaliatory violence in Bihar, it was the Muslims who were the worse sufferers. In Calcutta, where he reached thereafter, angry mobs were targeting Muslims, attacking mosques, rioting, looting, and killing. H. S. Suhrawardy, the Premier of pre-Partition Bengal, had requested Gandhi to remain in this strife-torn city till peace had been restored. Gandhi invited

Suhrawardy to stay with him to show Hindu–Muslim solidarity to the divided populace. They moved into Hyderi Mansion in Beliaghata on 13 August 1947, just two days before independence. On 15 August 1947, the day India became independent, Gandhi was fasting, spinning and praying to atone for the sin of Partition. From 1 to 4 September Gandhi fasted for the end of communal hatred, triggering the miracle of Calcutta. The feuding parties signed a pledge to end violence, and normalcy returned to the city.

Gandhi had originally planned to go to Punjab from Bengal because it was the site of the worst atrocities of the Partition – killing, rape, loot and displacement – but the situation in Delhi had quickly deteriorated so much that he went there instead. Delhi was the capital of India and to Gandhi the testing ground of the new nation. In Delhi, the influx of hordes of refugees from Pakistan had turned the city almost into a tinderbox. These immigrants not only needed to be settled, but they were seething with anger over what they had suffered – loss of home and property, forced displacement, not to speak of rape, killing, destruction of families, separation from loved ones. Their entire lives had been uprooted and pulverized. They sought revenge. There was a real danger that, in retaliation, the Muslims of Delhi would be driven out. This would also be to the financial advantage of the Hindu and Sikh residents and refugees. They would be able to take over the properties and businesses of the Muslims who had left or been driven out. Gandhi became the one-man peacekeeping force of the new republic. To him Delhi was the symbol of all of India. If peace returned to Delhi, if the life and property of its Muslim residents were protected, he believed it would send a powerful signal not just to the rest of the country but also to Pakistan. Perhaps the two recently parted neighbours might be able to live in peace afterwards.

When he assessed the situation, Gandhi's fundamental contention, which he repeated over and over again, was that retaliatory violence was both ethically wrong and impractical. Mimicking one's enemy, as Girard showed, would only lead to a cycle of never-ending violence; Gandhi concurred:

I am prepared to understand the anger of the refugees whom
fate has driven from West Punjab. But anger is short madness.
It can only make matters worse in every way. Retaliation is no
remedy. It makes the original disease much worse. I, therefore,
ask all those who are engaged in the senseless murders, arson
and loot to stay their hands.[2]

'Retaliation is no remedy'; in fact, it only debases one to the same
brutal level as one's enemy – this became the theme of his last days
on earth; this was the keynote of his Delhi initiative. As he said
to P. C. Joshi, the General Secretary of the Communist Party of
India when the latter came calling, 'We must not degrade ourselves
by following the ways of Pakistan'.[3]

It is true, however, that Gandhi felt lonely and frustrated. As
he told Joshi, 'Somehow or other I have never felt so resourceless
as I am doing today . . . I feel like a General without an army. To
whom am I to give orders?'.[4] But he was not bereft of hope. He
had the miracle of Calcutta to go by. 'You do not know the story
of Calcutta', he told Joshi. 'There it looked literally like overnight
conversion'.[5] Shrewd politician and strategist that he was, he
was aware that the miracle of Calcutta was not merely because
of his moral force. On the very day that he had moved into
Hyderi mansion an angry mob had attacked him. Later, when he
addressed a meeting of Muslim businessmen at the Grand Hotel,
he again faced a violent demonstration. In both instances, Gandhi
not only faced up to the protesters rather than escaping from
them, but told them that they could kill him if they liked but he
would not stop working for peace between the two communities.
In addition to Gandhi's own actions, which 'turned the wave' of
Hindu sentiment, he acknowledged that 'The Muslim mind was
ready', as were the businessmen, who were 'tired of strife'.[6] Many
years ago, something similar had happened in South Africa,
where there was an 'overnight conversion of the European mind'
after Gandhi was attacked and beaten: 'When the whole thing

including my interview appeared in the press the next morning, the Europeans felt ashamed and the atmosphere changed'.[7] Gandhi was hoping to pull off a similar transformation in Delhi, but he also wondered if that would be possible: 'If some such thing happened here, my mission would succeed. But I am afraid it will not happen'.[8]

The very evening of his arrival on 9 September 1947, Gandhi addressed his first prayer meeting during this final phase of his life in Delhi. In it, in his own intimate, inimitable way, he describes his feelings on reaching Shahadara railway station after crossing the Yamuna to enter Delhi:

> When I reached Shahadara Sardar Patel, Rajkumari Amrit Kaur and others were there to welcome me. But I did not find the usual smile on the Sardar's lips. Gone too was his jocular temperament. After alighting from the train I found some police personnel and others also equally sad. Has the city of Delhi which always appeared gay turned into a city of the dead?[9]

He quickly saw the seething violence, the hatred between communities, the huge influx of refugees, the crippling shortages of food and clothing and the early onset of a cold winter. The two countries, India and Pakistan, on suddenly becoming free of British imperialism, had also given in to lawlessness and partial anarchy. The old authority of the Raj had ended and in its place the two new states had yet to get a firm hand on the reins of power. Indians and Pakistanis, Gandhi observed,

> are not forced to do anything against their will under the crushing burden of Imperialism. Today they can do anything they choose. But if they wish to face the world with honesty, freedom should not mean that there need be no rule of law in both the Dominions.[10]

Just as he repeatedly opposed retaliatory violence, he also encouraged respect for the rule of law. Those who had genuine grievances had to appeal to the authorities rather than resorting to lawlessness or direct action.

It may be argued that Gandhi was bound to fail because he demanded exceptional conduct from the common people of the subcontinent. He did not take into account the way average men and women felt; he did not accept the general weaknesses of ordinary people. However, it would not be entirely correct to assume this. Actually, Gandhi was quite aware of the workings of ordinary human nature, but he refused to believe that people could not rise above it. He was willing to allow for mistakes, which had to be admitted and repented for, but he refused to let people deliberately do harm to others without telling them that they did so.

As always, Gandhi gambled on the heights to which his otherwise gentle, loyal and spiritually alive countrymen might be roused to ascend, not the barbarous and murderous depths to which they could and had descended. He did not think that Indians were especially lacking in humanity just because they did not turn brutal and homicidal with the organized precision and orderly discipline of Europeans. On the contrary, the very primitivism of subcontinental violence suggested that it was amenable to the kind of appeal to sentiment and moral force that he had developed a special skill and expertise in nurturing.

18   The final *yajna*

Before his first week in Delhi ended, Gandhi gave notice to the residents of Delhi and to the citizens of the two new states of India and Pakistan of what he intended to do. He also tried to spell out why and how he planned to carry out his mission. His words were broadcast to a very wide audience through All India Radio, which transmitted the speeches he gave at the daily prayer meetings he presided over at the Birla House. India was independent; for the first time in his life, the official medium of the state was available to him. He became, literally, the voice of the nation. He called his plan of action a *yajna*; a sacred sacrifice, invoking as was wont of him an ancient word, pregnant with meaning and symbolism.

A *yajna*, at its most basic, is a Vedic ritual in which offerings are made to Agni or a specially prepared and invoked sacred fire to the accompaniment of mantras or chants. The recitation, for the ritual to be effective, must be performed correctly, with the right intent and form, according to prescribed rules. The chants themselves are sacred formulae through which the ends of the ritual are accomplished. They actually describe what is being done, offered, or performed while the ritual is in progress. Each *yajna* thus has a specific meaning and a purpose, but the general aim is to worship and make offerings to deities, re-establish cosmic unity, and to pray for the good of the whole society. Whatever is offered into the sacrificial fire is believed to be consecrated and to reach the Divine.

Gandhi's *yajna* was to stop Hindus and Muslims from murdering, raping, looting and displacing each other in the subcontinent. He also wanted the two new countries, India and Pakistan, to live in peace and amity with one another. He wished to put a halt not just to the violence but also to the transfer of populations between these countries; Hindus and Sikhs being driven out of Pakistan into India and Muslims from India to Pakistan. He was totally against such ethnic cleansing. In fact, he wanted those who had left their homes in either country, either involuntarily or of their own accord, to return. He especially wished that the women from both sides, who had been abducted, raped and held hostage, be restored to their homes and families. Finally, he wanted the two communities to live in peace within each country. The first and crucial step in accomplishing these ends was the restoration of peace and normalcy in Delhi, which Gandhi believed to be the symbol of the whole country. Peace in Delhi, of course, meant several things: not just safeguarding the life and properties of the Muslim residents of the city, but assuring those who felt forced to leave for Pakistan that it was safe for them to stay; in addition it meant resettling and becalming the hundreds of thousands of Hindu and Sikh refugees who had poured into the city after being driven out of Pakistan, many of whom were baying for the life and properties of the Muslims residents of the city; finally, it meant coping with enormous shortages in food, clothing and housing in the new capital. Gandhi wanted his *yajna* to tackle, if not solve, all these seemingly insurmountable problems.

If so, what were the offerings and oblations that Gandhi had to pour into his symbolic sacrificial fire? First of all, he wanted a cleansing of heart, followed by a cleansing of hands – rage replaced by compassion, revenge by fellow-feeling, hatred by brotherhood. He wanted Hindus and Sikhs to renounce retaliatory violence and take positive steps to safeguard the life and properties of Muslims in Delhi. He wanted Muslims who remained in India to avow their loyalty to India over Pakistan. He also wanted Muslims who had hoarded arms in the city in order to defend themselves to surrender their caches of weapons and take refuge in the good offices of the newly formed Government of India. He also wanted the controls over food, grains and cloth to be lifted so that supplies could be improved. On a more sombre note, he also expected several Indians, both Hindus and Muslims, to lay down, if necessary, their very lives for one another, rather than succumb to violence. He often used the expression that he would 'dance with joy' if he heard of such martyrdoms. Eventually, of course, Gandhi offered his own life as oblation in his *yajna*. Not by accident, he had been preparing for such a finale for several months, regarding it as a true test and validation of his life's work. Before he was murdered, he went on a fast for five days, from 13 to 18 January 1948, thus literally cleansing and purifying himself so that when he was actually killed, his offering was fit to be accepted by the supreme heavens. In that sense, he was in the highest state of purity when he departed from this earth.

The nature of his agenda and the basis for his action in these last days of his life were laid out in a series of early prayer meeting speeches. Speaking on 12 September 1947, he admitted:

> It is natural to feel, 'why not kill the Muslims because our brothers have been killed.' But I for one cannot kill even the actual murderers of my brothers. Should I then prepare myself to kill other innocent people? I do not believe in meeting evil with evil . . . I would like to request you not to regard the Muslims as your enemies.[1]

Gandhi did not wish to minimize or underestimate the enormity of Partition, but he was clear that to carry its illogic any further would only be to destroy one another and the hard-won freedom that both countries had just earned: 'Just because the country has been divided into India and Pakistan, it does not befit us to slaughter the Muslims who have stayed behind'.[2]

Gandhi's speech at this prayer meeting is one of his most important, not only because it sets out the entire basis of his thought and action during the last phase of his life, but because it also shows how mistaken his critics were in alleging that he was partial to the Muslims or incapable of facing the reality of what was happening in Pakistan. Gandhi's remarks at this prayer meeting clearly show that he was not turning a blind eye, as his critics claimed, to the plight of the Hindus and Sikhs left behind in Pakistan: 'I have seen the terrible plight of the Hindus and Sikhs of Pakistan ... I claim that my pain is no less than that of any Punjabi'.[3] But how could that be? What was the proof that Gandhi felt their pain when none of his near and dear ones had suffered in the same manner? Gandhi's answer is stunning in its assertion of his empathy for all sufferers:

> If any Hindu or Sikh from the Punjab comes and tells me that his anguish is greater than mine because he has lost his brother or daughter or father, I would say that his brother is my brother, his mother is my mother, and I have the same anguish in my heart as he has.[4]

Gandhi's assertion of identity with all sufferers gives him the right to exhort and cajole them. It was both an ethical and an existential assertion of non-separation from them. Moreover, it was a direct outcome of his renunciation of a private self or identity. Without a trace of that sort of selfishness, how can there be any difference between 'mine' and 'yours'?

Gandhi admits that he also feels anger and outrage like anyone else, but not yielding to them gives him strength: 'I am also a human being and feel enraged but I swallow my anger. That gives me strength'.[5] Gandhi repeats his earlier admonition that returning barbarism with barbarism is no solution: 'Should I say that the Hindus and Sikhs of Delhi and those who have come from outside should become barbarians because Muslims are becoming barbarians?'.[6] Moreover, Gandhi strikes at the very heart of any assertion of moral superiority on the part of Hindus and Sikhs just because they did not initiate but merely retaliated against the Pakistanis: 'The people of Pakistan resorted to ways of barbarism, and so did the Hindus and Sikhs. And so, how could one barbarian find fault with another barbarian?'[7] Only he or she who has not sinned has the right to cast the first stone. In this case, Hindus and Sikhs could not claim that high moral ground. Instead, Gandhi pleads,

> That is why I would like to appeal to all of you to save Hinduism and Sikhism, save India and Pakistan and thus save the whole country. If we remain good to the end, the Muslims of Pakistan would have to be good too. That is the law of the world. No one can change it.[8]

The law that Gandhi refers to is the principle that one party cannot indefinitely go on hurting the other if the other refuses to retaliate. Unilateral violence is very soon spent, but there is no stopping reciprocal violence.

How does Gandhi 'know' this? It is his own experience that serves as a guide: 'I have had enough experience in my 78–79 years'.[9] Gandhi believes that vengeance belongs to the Lord, not to human beings: 'I can say in the light of my own experience that it is not for us to avenge anybody's wrongs'.[10] A few days later, Gandhi repeats this much more forcefully: 'Who are you to punish the wicked for their wrong deeds? They are going to be punished themselves. I have no doubt about it. This is the essence I have drawn from all religions'.[11] Moreover, to return good with good is like a business transaction: 'He who does good to one who has been good to him is a mere Bania and a pseudo-Bania at that'.[12] Banias were a trading caste, known for their astuteness in business; from time to time Gandhi referred to himself as one, being born in such a community. To him a 'true Bania' is one who made profit, who ensured that he got a better return than just his investment.

To return good with good, to Gandhi, was thus not the mark of a true Bania, but only of a pseudo-Bania. A true Bania would return evil with good so as to get a higher return, the good of his adversary, on his investment: 'I say that I am a Bania myself; and I am a true Bania. May you not become pseudo-Banias. True human being is he who does a good turn for evil'.[13] Gandhi asserts that he learnt this lesson early in his life and that he still believes in it: 'I learnt this in my childhood. I still believe in the rightness of this'.[14] Now Gandhi comes to the essence of his teaching in a time of great conflict: 'I would like you to return evil with good'.[15] This he considers to be the sum and substance of dharma:

> Let us know our own dharma. In the light of our dharma I would tell the people that our greatest duty is to see that the Hindus do not act in frenzy, nor the Sikhs indulge in acts of madness.[16]

When questions were repeatedly being raised about the loyalty of the Muslims who remained behind in India, Gandhi did not leave them out: 'I appeal to the Muslims that they should open-heartedly declare that they belong to India and are loyal to the Union'.[17] Next he turns his appeal to the Muslims in Pakistan, but he wishes the Muslims in India to carry his message to the former: 'And I want the Muslims here to tell the Muslims in Pakistan who have become the enemies of the Hindus, not to go mad'.[18] He wants such Muslims not only to 'remain faithful to the Union, and salute the tricolour' but also to exhort their co-religionists in India to 'surrender all their arms': 'I would like the Muslims to surrender all the arms in their possession to the Government. The Hindus too should surrender all their arms'.[19] The result would be clear for the world to see: 'We should tell them that whatever happens outside, we in Delhi would live like brothers'.[20] He gives them the example of Calcutta and Bihar: 'The same thing happened in Calcutta and the Hindus and the Muslims have started living like brothers. The Hindus in Bihar have adopted the same attitude'.[21]

If Delhi can be saved, then Gandhi can carry its positive results to Punjab which is the worst affected part of the country: 'You must soon create such a situation in Delhi that I can immediately go to the Punjab and tell the people there that the Muslims of Delhi are living in peace. I would ask for its reward there'.[22] To Gandhi peace is the reward of peace. The big flaw in Godse's argument was that he considered being peaceful the same as being weak.

Gandhi, it is clear, is peaceable but not weak. Nor is he unaware of Pakistan's intentions:

> The Muslims wanted Pakistan and they have got it. Why are they fighting now and with whom are they fighting? Because they have taken Pakistan, do they want the whole of India too? That will never happen.[23]

What makes him so sure? Given the hundreds of years of Muslim domination in the region, how can Gandhi categorically declare that Pakistan can never take over India? It is because Gandhi has a better sense of the strength of awakened India, and of the Hindus who played a great role in it. He strikes at the cowardice of the Pakistanis in targeting the minorities: 'Why are they killing the weak Hindus and the Sikhs?'.[24] What will further ethnic cleansing accomplish? By the very logic of violence, once you have eliminated the Other in your midst, you will start fighting among yourselves, as indeed the recent history of Pakistan has borne out. Destroying or driving out minorities does not end violence; it only gives rise to further violence when the majority turns on itself. The image of Gandhi as partial to Muslims that the Hindu right sought to project is ill-founded: 'If there is any Muslim who has gone mad and who secretly keeps machine-guns in his house, we would punish him. But no one can touch the Muslims who are loyal to the country'.[25] It is a convenient lie to try to justify his killing or to hide anti-Muslim policies.

The lie that Gandhi favoured the Muslims or wished to appease them was created and became an excuse to kill the old man who spoke inconvenient truths. It is true that some of his remarks may be construed as favouring Muslims or weakening Hindus by enjoining them to non-violence and leaving them unarmed against their aggressive adversaries. Yet when the need arose, as we shall see later, he even approved of the army being sent to Kashmir to push back the invaders and protect the defenceless civilians. It is thus a canard to think that he wanted Hindus or Indians to be weak. But it is equally wrong to argue that Hindu fundamentalists are the sole or greater enemy; all fundamentalists are enemies; it is communalism to selectively condemn Hindus to appease Muslims. It is not as if the right wing alone has misunderstood Gandhi; so have the Congressmen. Gandhi was not interested in appeasing anyone, nor did he wish to favour one group over the other. His sympathies were naturally with the underdog; he wanted the stronger groups to show graciousness, not out of weakness but out of magnanimity.

From an insistence on non-retaliation, which he repeats over and over again, Gandhi goes on to derive a new meaning not only of *sanatanism* but also of inter-religious harmony. In his prayer meeting on 13 September 1947, continuing from the previous day, Gandhi said, 'I claim to be a true Hindu and a *sanatani* Hindu at that', he says, but adds in the very next breath, 'That is exactly why I am also a Muslim, a Parsi, a Christian and a Jew',[26] thus giving an entirely new definition of what it is to be a traditional Hindu. Only a true Hindu, he implies, can have the breadth of vision to see all the different religions of the world as 'the branches of the same tree'.[27] How then can one branch be superior or inferior to another, truer to the tree or more authentic than the others?

> Which of these branches should I keep and which should I discard? From which branch should I pick the leaves and which should I ignore? For me all are the same. That is how I am made. How can I help it? There would be absolute peace if everybody starts thinking like me.[28]

However, to carry the metaphor forward, he does imply that some branches, of their own accord, do weaken, rot, or even drop off. It is this process of self-destruction that he wants to avoid in India and Pakistan. Great traditions fall not so much by external aggression, Gandhi suggests, but by their own inner weaknesses and wrongdoings. Gandhi's criticism, however, is very different from Iqbal's who, in *Shikwa aur Jawab* (Complaint and Answer) engages in deep soul-searching on the fall of Muslims from their heights of power and glory. Iqbal's answer is that the decline of Islam was because Muslims were not obedient and zealous servants of the Lord. Like Moses's admonitions to the deviant Jews, Iqbal wants Muslims to return to their uncompromising fidelity to Allah so that they might regain their former glory. Gandhi, on the other hand, addresses all – Hindus, Sikhs, Muslims, Christians, and others – only to remind them that it is not because of their lack of zeal or loyalty that they will decline, but because of their wrongdoing, folly and persistence in the path of evil. Hindu cultural nationalists, on the other hand, saw the Partition as an opportunity to establish Hindu dominance, an idea that Gandhi found abhorrent.

Gandhi, like the Buddha, believed that human beings rose or declined by their deeds: 'If we wish we can turn either into heaven or by our own deeds into hell'.[29] Furthermore, he was quite alive to the very real possibilities of both countries resembling the latter:

> And if both the countries become hell, an independent man has no place there. After that we are only doomed to slavery. This thought is gnawing at my heart. My heart trembles and I wonder how I will make any Hindu, Sikh or Muslim understand all this.[30]

To imagine that freedom would be lost, and that Indians would be enslaved again, filled Gandhi with anguish.

Gandhi also wished to abolish violence from the private domain. As individuals, he believed that we should also be courteous and non-violent. Violence, if unavoidable, must be left to states, which to him were inherently violent in any case. He constantly urged people not to take the law into their own hands, but to rely on the Government to redress their wrongs. Today, few would repose as much confidence in the government machinery, but perhaps in those days, Gandhi was much more optimistic:

> I tell you that if we become good and behave well the Government will see that justice is done to us. Let the Governments fight each other; but we would not quarrel among ourselves. We would remain friends.[31]

Gandhi's related contention was that the power over life and death vested only in God or a higher order, not in any individual or human agency. To him, even an aggressor such as Hitler could not kill us unless our time had come. The real power over life and death only belongs to God, therefore none should be afraid regardless of how powerful or well-armed the adversary is: 'However powerful the person who wants to kill us is, he cannot kill us so long as God protects us'.[32] Human beings must therefore never deviate from righteous conduct, leaving the punishment of wrongdoers either in the hands of the Government or to an even higher authority. They must not take the law into their own hands or fear death.

Gandhi is aware that Pakistan has double standards. He does not hesitate to indict it. As he had said earlier, 'The Government of Pakistan has forgotten its duty',[33] a charge that he repeats a couple of days later in his prayer meeting of 14 September 1947: 'It is failure of the Government of Pakistan that the minorities have to run away from there'.[34] Jinnah's double standards are also not hidden from him; Jinnah, Gandhi knows, only complains about the plight of the Muslims, not the sufferings of the Hindus:

> I did not like the statement made by the Qaid-e-Azam . . .
> why does he not mention what happened to the Hindus in
> West Punjab? If Bihar indulged in evil acts they repented it.
> In Calcutta the Hindus came to me and repented before me. It
> would be a noble thing if the Muslims do the same and admit
> that they have done wrong things.[35]

But just because he is aware of Jinnah's duplicity, he cannot be
partial himself:

> I have seen the things and how can I close my eyes to them?
> Nor can I cover up the crimes committed by the Hindus. I
> want to be faithful to all religions. I can betray neither God
> nor men. I wish to be loyal to all.[36]

The failures of the Government of Pakistan are all too evident to
him. Lahore, a historic city to whose greatness Hindus and Sikhs
also contributed, is now denuded of them:

> Lahore is almost empty. It is the city built up by the Hindus where
> I saw the big mansions of the Hindus and so many educational
> institutions – where else do you find so many colleges? . . . Today
> who is in possession of those colleges? All this hurts me. And I
> feel ashamed that the Government of Pakistan can be so mean.[37]

Clearly the charge against Gandhi, that he turned a blind eye to the
sufferings of the Hindus or that he never spoke against Pakistani
misdeeds, is wrong.

In addition, Gandhi is also acutely aware of how sorry a figure
the two recently independent but now feuding countries present
to the world:

> the European powers, be it Russia, France or Britain, as well
> as America will laugh at us and say that we are not capable of
> preserving our freedom. We are only capable of being slaves.[38]

This would ironically only prove colonial claims that Indians were incapable of self-rule. As Winston Churchill, who persisted in believing that granting independence to India was a mistake, famously remarked:

> Power will go to the hands of rascals, rogues, freebooters . . . all Indian leaders will be of low calibre and men of straw. They will have sweet tongues and silly hearts. They will fight amongst themselves for power and India will be lost in political squabbles.[39]

In contrast, again and again, Gandhi also makes a different point in the context of the battle between Muslims and Hindus: if they (the Muslims) are brutes, should we (the Hindus) also follow suit? Yet he also knows that such an argument cannot hold good if the violence in Pakistan continues:

> I also want to tell the Muslims that if the Muslims in West Punjab, the Frontier Province, Baluchistan and Sind go crazy and the Hindus and the Sikhs cannot live in peace there, then the situation becomes difficult for us here. After all, we are all human beings. So let them understand humanity. How long can we go on persuading?[40]

But Gandhi's ethical idealism is not naive. He knows full well what the Pakistani ambitions might have been, but either because he is aware of his own strength or of the impracticality of such ambitions, he is not afraid and wishes that other Hindus and Sikhs should also not be. Without mincing words he says:

> let the Muslims admit their mistakes. Let them say that they had wished to conquer Delhi and turn the whole of India into Pakistan but now they have realized that it is not possible to turn India into Pakistan. They must be content that they are already having Pakistan.[41]

Such a realization might result in a resolve in both communities and nations to save and serve one another: 'Then it would so happen that both India and Pakistan would compete with each other in being good and more sincere in their humanity'.[42] Religion, in that case, would not matter: 'Whether we look towards Mecca or towards the East, truthfulness lies in our own hearts, and what matters is that our hearts should be clean'.[43] On the other hand, if Hindus and Sikhs also pay back Muslims in the same coin of violence and retribution, Gandhi would rather die than stand mute witness to it:

> I told you that since I had come here I would also wish to die here. If we go on indulging in acts of frenzy and become overcome by rage and kill the Muslims, I can have nothing to do with it. I do not wish to be a witness to such a thing. . . . That is why I would say that whatever wrong the Muslims may do, you have got to be good. If you really want to avenge the evil deeds it can only be through the deeds of goodness.[44]

But of course, returning cruelty with kindness, evil with good, violence with non-violence is not revenge at all; it is the highest form of religion. Again, Gandhi wishes, like a good Bania, to derive greater profit from others' misdeeds than to lose whatever little virtue one possesses in senseless retaliation. Godse vs. Gandhi is thus, ultimately, also about profit and loss of virtue; Godse's way leads to moral bankruptcy, Gandhi's to good fortune. But this is impossible to understand from a commonsensical point of view. It can only become evident from a foundational belief that the purpose of human life is ethical progress and spiritual realization. It is only when the 'higher' good of winning the soul is clearly perceived that an apparent 'loss' at the human, material level is seen as the basis of spiritual profit.

On the night of 14 September, it rained. But instead of enjoying the autumn showers in a violence-ravaged city, Gandhi's heart weeps for the refugees exposed to the elements:

During the night as I heard what should have been the soothing sound of gentle life-giving rain, my mind went out to the thousands of refugees lying about in the open camps at Delhi. I was sleeping snugly in a verandah protecting me on all sides. But for the cruel hand of man against his brother, these thousands of men, women and children would not be shelterless and in many cases foodless. In some places they could not but be in knee-deep water. They have no other choice. Was it all inevitable? The answer from within was an emphatic 'No.' Was this the first fruit of freedom, just a month-old baby? These thoughts have haunted me throughout these last twenty hours.[45]

Gandhi's identification with the sufferers, his penetrating grasp of the real causes of their discomforts, and his cure to their woes is all too evident in his remarks during the prayer meeting on the evening of 15 September 1947. It was a Monday, Gandhi's day of silence, so his speech was read out by someone else. 'Have the citizens of Delhi gone mad?' he asked. 'Have they no humanity left in them? Have love of the country and its freedom no appeal for them?'.[46] He knows that he is blaming Hindus and Sikhs first, because the city belongs to them. But he continues, 'Could they not be men enough to stem the tide of hatred?'.[47] Gandhi is, however, aware that both sides have made mistakes, but his advice is 'precise and firm. Its soundness is manifest':

Trust your Government to defend every citizen against wrongdoers, however well-armed they may be. Further trust it to demand and get damages for every member of the minority wrongfully dispossessed.[48]

What the successive governments in independent India have done, however, is to show that they are incapable of being trusted. Each has played havoc with the nation, offering a deadly cocktail of politics and religion. Pakistan has possibly fared even worse. The citizens of neither country can trust their governments, so perhaps this exhortation of Gandhi would not work in times of unrest and insecurity. The India of that time was, of course, different, with leaders like Nehru and Patel at the helm. But when governments are weak or the rule of law suspended, non-governmental actors fill the vacuum not just to settle scores but to grab their own advantage. This does not mean that Gandhi is utopian or unrealistic. For example, in a disciplined society such as Japan, we saw after the 2010 tsunami how there was no looting or rioting. In the US, on the other hand, the experience of the hurricane in New Orleans was quite different.

The options, as Gandhi states them, are as follows: 'Either the minority rely upon God and His creature man to do the right thing or rely upon their fire-arms to defend themselves against those whom they must not trust'.[49] It is obvious that Gandhi opts for the former, but can the latter option be ruled out entirely? It would seem that our natural propensity is not to rely on God or others, but on our own strength or capacity for self-preservation. At least that way we can be responsible for both our victories and defeats, but if we surrender agency altogether, whom can we blame when things go wrong? Gandhi's politics during this last phase is to shift the populace from the latter to the former, it is to create trust not only in God, but in man too. After all, what option do we have other than to trust one another? Indefinite distrust either of God's laws or of fellow human beings, sole reliance on the strength of arms, uncompromising self-reliance in one's own capacity to save oneself – all these will only lead, according to Gandhi, to mutually assured destruction.

Reading through this speech, one is suddenly confronted with this remarkable statement: 'Those who seek justice must do justice, must have clean hands'.[50] Personally, I was struck by it because Gandhi uses the exact same words in the first half of this sentence as he did in his first book, *Hind Swaraj* (1909), where he admonished his reader not to be so harsh on all Englishmen just because he was fighting for India's freedom from the British: 'We who seek justice will have to do justice to others'.[51] To give one's adversary his due is a great Gandhian principle. Rather than distorting or demonizing the Other in order to justify one's violence, it is our duty according to Gandhi to see the Other in the best possible light so that one's own behaviour may be according to the highest possible standards. Again, Gandhi clearly sees one's moral profit, even if not always immediate worldly gain, in this. The second half of the statement made on 15 September 1947, however, shows how much more sanguine the situation now is: our own hands are not clean, Gandhi reminds us; they are blood-soaked too. Then how can we merely blame the Pakistanis or the Muslims?

The culmination of Gandhi's *yajna* was of course his fast from 13 January to 18 January 1948. This fifteenth fast of his life also proved to be his last. On the eve of the fast in his prayer meeting on 12 January 1948, he said, 'Fasting is his last resort in the place of the sword.... My impotence has been gnawing at me of late. It will go immediately the fast is undertaken'.[52] All his near and dear ones were alarmed by his sudden decision, though they should not have been. Gandhi had had to fast in Calcutta too, before the violence could end. Now in Delhi, he again lay down similar conditions: his fast would end 'when and if I am satisfied that there is a reunion of hearts of all communities brought about without any outside pressure, but from an awakened sense of duty'.[53] Perhaps it was a tall order, but Gandhi was not fasting purely for an external goal or result: 'A pure fast, like duty, is its own reward'.[54]

That he took this fast seriously is clear in his letter of 16 January 1948 to Mirabehn in which he called it his 'greatest fast'.[55] He added, though, 'Whether it will ultimately prove so or not is neither your concern nor mine'.[56] Unlike the repeated allegation against him that he was appeasing the Muslims, Gandhi clarified in his prayer meeting on the day of the fast, 'I do not say this in order to appease the Muslims or anyone else. I want to appease myself which means that I want to appease God'.[57] Indeed, one specific target of the fast were the people of Pakistan:

> I must say to all those who reside in Pakistan and mould its fortunes that they will fail to make Pakistan permanent if their conscience is not quickened and if they do not admit the wrongs for which Pakistan is responsible.[58]

It is incorrect, if not mischievous, to contend that Gandhi was fasting against the Hindus and the Sikhs of Delhi. Even in the last days of his life Gandhi maintained, 'if I am able to achieve success here I shall go to Pakistan and try to make Muslims understand their folly'.[59] That is why, when Gandhi said

> Since I have undertaken the fast in the cause of the Muslims, a great responsibility has come to devolve on them. They must understand that if they are to live with the Hindus as brothers they must be loyal to the Indian Union, not to Pakistan.[60]

It would be a mistake to consider only the first half of this paragraph and to quote it out of context. Gandhi was calling upon the conscience of the Muslims to live in harmony with Hindus both in India and Pakistan when he said that he was fasting for them. Nathuram's defence, before a careful examination of Gandhi's last days, is therefore revealed to be an elaborate tissue of lies, a deliberate fabrication of half-truths and allegations whose sole purpose seems to be to justify the unjustifiable.

Three days into the fast, on 16 January, when his health was weakening alarmingly and when the doctors attending on him began to worry for his life, he said, 'I may say that I am in no hurry at all. Hurry will not help our work. I feel ineffable peace'.[61] Even the day before he ended his fast, he said 'I shall fast for as many days as I can and if it is the will of God that I should die then I shall die'.[62] Earlier, he had insisted that no one should do anything just to please him, nor should there be any hurry because of the threat to his life:

I do not want that anyone should do anything incompletely and tell me that everything is all right. When there is perfect peace in Delhi there will be peace all over India. I have no wish to live if I cannot see peace established all round me, in India as well as in Pakistan. This is the meaning of this *yajna*.[63]

It was, literally, do or die for Gandhi. On the fifth day, already very weak, with alarming signs of deterioration, he said,

I shall terminate the fast only when peace has returned to Delhi. If peace is restored to Delhi it will have effect not only on the whole of India but also on Pakistan. . . . So long as things do not return to normal in Delhi, they will not be normal either in India or in Pakistan.[64]

He had staked his life on peace in Delhi. When he ended his fast on 18 January 1949, representatives of the feuding parties had given written pledges to end the violence and retaliation. Gandhi said, 'I shall break my fast. Let God's will prevail. You all be witness today'.[65] That he was to lose his life to gain peace in Delhi just a few days later would not have been a matter of regret to him. Indeed, his soul, to use one of his favourite expressions, would have 'danced in joy' for having won such a death, though what he really wanted was to see, on the very 'verge of death', his childhood dream that 'Hindus, Sikhs, Parsis, Christians and Muslims could live in amity not only in Rajkot but in the whole of India'; if they could do so, they 'would all have a very happy life'.[66] Then though he was an old man, his 'heart would dance. Children would then frolic in joy to see that there is no strife any more. I urge all of you to help me in this task'.[67] Today, in many parts of India, the children of independent India do frolic around Gandhi's statues, but his dream of seeing all communities of India living together in peace and friendship is still unrealized.

19   Partitioning women

One of the repeated charges against Gandhi is that he enfeebled Hindus, making them incapable of defending themselves against the more belligerent and martial Muslims. Hindu nationalism still appeals to many because it calls for the renewal of '*Kshatriyahood*', of strong and militant Hindus who are able to retaliate against aggressive and warlike Muslims. Memories of Hindu defeats at the hands of Muslim invaders and fears of a repetition of those horrors also trigger anti-Gandhian diatribes. Perhaps the most traumatic and disturbing issue in such narratives is the plight of Hindu women, captured, abducted, defiled and eventually lost by weak Hindu men, who could not protect them. These women were not only dishonoured themselves, but brought shame to the community from which they came; even worse, they now belonged to the Muslim enemies, bearing and rearing the latter's children, thus increasing the strength of the Hindu-killers. During the terrors of the Partition, as is now quite well documented, the women from both sides of the religious and national divide suffered the worst.[1] As Urvashi Butalia puts it: 'The story of partition, the uprooting and dislocation of people, was accompanied by the story of the rape, abduction and widowhood of thousands of women on both sides of the newly formed borders'.[2] National histories are uniformly silent about this shameful but real aspect of the Partition. Literally hundreds of thousands of women were forcibly 'exchanged', not once but sometimes multiple times, during this process. Many of these were then tracked down by Government agencies from both sides and persuaded or coerced to return to their 'original', but now displaced families. The latter did not always welcome back these 'soiled' women, many of whom ended up in camps, shelters and other state-supported institutions. Several thousands who had lost their husbands were pensioned off by Government of India. But many who settled with their abductors, rapists, or with families of the other religious community became mothers of children who grew up in two hostile countries, suspecting and hating their own step-siblings and cousins on the other side of the border. The Partition thus not only divided the two communities but also made them re-mingle with one another in sordid and traumatic ways.

The women who were reported missing on both sides were designated 'abducted'. This, as Butalia explains, was 'a catchall description that has come to be used for all women (and some men) who disappeared during the confusion of partition'.[3] Though most of the missing women might have actually been abducted, some would have stayed back willingly. This was never officially acknowledged. As to the numbers, estimates vary and are not entirely trustworthy, but as Butalia, relying on Government records and secondary sources, reckons

> the number of Hindu and Sikh women abducted in Pakistan was roughly 33,000 – although some estimates put this figure at 50,000 – (this did not include women from Kashmir and it was felt that if these were added the figure could well have reached 50,000). Lists received from Pakistan showed the figure of Muslim women abducted in India to be around 21,000.[4]

What was Gandhi's attitude to these women, who constituted an inflammatory and unresolved area of friction between the two communities?

Soon after his arrival in Delhi on 9 September 1947, Gandhi starts receiving reports about missing Hindu and Sikh women. Three days later, he refers to this problem in his prayer meeting of 12 September 1947. He starts by mentioning reports from the North-West Frontier Province of Pakistan, where Hindus and Sikhs are being driven out. He says that the Government of Pakistan is responsible; in fact, he names Jinnah himself: 'The Government of Pakistan has forgotten its duty. I shall appeal to the Qaid-e-Azam Jinnah who is the Governor-General of Pakistan to desist from such policies'.[5] Why, he asks, are Hindus and Sikhs fleeing from Pakistan? 'Because', he continues, 'they are afraid that they and their wives would have to die and that their wives would be abducted. They are in danger and so they are fleeing'.[6] While beseeching Hindus and Sikhs not to retaliate because it would be 'barbaric' and not to punish innocent Muslims in India for what their co-religionists were doing in Pakistan because it would be against all norms of natural justice,[7] Gandhi squarely blames the state of Pakistan for not doing its duty.

In his speech at a Daryaganj mosque on 18 September 1947, Gandhi tells the Muslims of Delhi assembled there that he will work for their safety and security, but he also wants them to condemn the happenings in Pakistan. He urges his audience to exert pressure on the Pakistani state and on their co-religionists across the border so that the lives and properties of Hindus and Sikhs there can be guaranteed. He specifically speaks against the abduction of women and forcible conversions:

> Abducted women had to be returned, forcible conversions considered null and void. The Hindus and Sikhs of Pakistan and the Muslims of East Punjab had to be reinstalled in their own homes. In Pakistan and the Union they should produce conditions that not even a little girl, whatever her religion, should feel insecure.[8]

This is the stance Gandhi takes, though in retrospect it seems somewhat unrealistic. He wants the transfer of populations to stop and all abducted women to be restored to their homes and families, thus reversing the wrongs that were going on instead of accepting them as fait accompli.

The ethnic cleansing in NWFP was repeated in other parts of Pakistan. In his discussion with Gandhi on 25 September 1947, J. B. Kripalani, the prominent Congress leader and then president of the party, who was from Sind, apprised Gandhi of the deteriorating situation there. When Kripalani had met Jinnah in Karachi, the latter had absolved himself and the state of all responsibility, saying that Pakistan was merely a victim of the propaganda of the Indian press. As reported in Gandhi's *Collected Works*:

> Towards the close of September, Acharya Kripalani, the Congress President, had met Jinnah at Karachi and drawn his attention to the rapidly deteriorating position of the minority community in Sind. In reply, he got only a long tirade against the Indian Government. The minority community in Sind, Jinnah maintained, had nothing to complain of. . . . The Pakistan Government, he said, had nothing to answer for; on the contrary, it was the innocent victim of wanton and malicious exaggeration by the Indian Press.[9]

While Kripalani urged an orderly exodus of Hindus and Sikhs from Sindh, with special trains and armed protection, rather than a distressed and disorderly scramble after they had been squeezed to destitution and desperation, Gandhi maintained that all Sindh leaders had to go to Pakistan to resist the atrocities even unto their own deaths. So incensed was Gandhi by the happenings in Sind that he even said India should go war, if necessary:

> I totally disapprove of the exchange of populations. Let us
> declare war. We shall fight and die fighting if we are destined
> to. They have abducted and molested 12-year-old girls.[10]

Of course, Gandhi was proved wrong; the exchange of populations
did happen. Perhaps his refusal to accept what was unfolding
before his eyes is an instance of the stubbornness characteristic of
Gandhi that some of his critics have harped on.[11] Yet to Gandhi,
to accept that Pakistan was only for Muslims and India only for
Hindus would be tantamount to both countries signing their own
death warrants.

In a significant development, during his prayer meeting of 26
November 1947, Gandhi shifts his focus to the consequences of
the abductions rather than dwelling only on the causes. He now
deals with the human problem of the acceptance of these women.
In a culture where even Sita, Rama's wife and veritable paragon of
virtue, had to undergo a trial by fire to prove that she was chaste
and where she was banished to the forest anyway because of a
washerman's gossip, what chance would ordinary women, raped
and abused by Muslims, have to be welcomed back to their
husbands and families? But Gandhi, the votary of Rama and
saintly Father of the Nation, takes a clearly pro-woman and most
humane position on such sexually exploited and violated women:

> Many of our women are in Pakistan. They are being molested.
> Those unfortunate women are made to feel ashamed. In my
> view, they have no reason to feel ashamed. It would be gross
> injustice if any woman is considered worthless by society and
> abandoned by her brothers, parents, and husband because she
> had been abducted by the Muslims.[12]

But Gandhi also adds that no woman who is really pure can be
raped. How does he arrive at this conclusion? He says that a really
chaste woman would die before she is molested. How true such

a statement is can only be guessed at. It implies a belief that is religious, like Gandhi's advocacy of the almost miraculous powers of *brahmacharya*, or sexual self-control. No feminist would agree with Gandhi, but it is interesting to see how, speaking of Sita, in her controversial novel *The Rape of Sita*, Lindsay Collen's eponymous protagonist actually consents to be raped by Rowan because she does not want to be beaten up and broken in addition to being raped.

Not submitting but withholding consent, on the other hand, was a major part of the Gandhian praxis; would it work in situations of extreme violence when gangs of men held, abused and passed around abducted women? Gandhi maintains, almost as an article of faith, 'It is my belief that any woman who has the purity of Sita cannot be touched by anyone'.[13] However, rather than expecting such high standards of his contemporaries, he quickly adds, 'But where can we find women like Sita these days? And not all women can be like Sita'.[14] Therefore, he asks:

> Should we show contempt for the woman who had been forcibly abducted and tyrannized? She is not a woman of loose character. My daughter or wife too could be abducted and raped. But I would not hate her for that reason.[15]

Once again, Gandhi collapses the difference between himself and others. Their daughters and wives are like his own kith and kin. Indeed, in an incident which several biographers have found callous and shocking, Gandhi endangered the life of little Manu when he asked her to walk back in the evening along a deserted path in riot-affected Noakhali to retrieve a pumice stone which she had dropped and which was used to massage his feet. When she returned unharmed, he said that there was no point singing '*Ekla chalo re*' – Tagore's famous song, 'Walk on alone' – if his own companion were too afraid to do so.[16] Gandhi did not hide behind his Mahatmahood but subjected himself and his kin to the same kind of dangers that the ordinary people whom he was trying to transform had also undergone. Was this a way to make Manu a fellow-participant in his hardest experiments with truth and non-violence?

A few days later, Gandhi, quite matter of fact, returns to the issue of abducted women:

> Muslims in Pakistan have abducted our young girls. Attempts are being made and must be made to rescue them. Let us try to get back every abducted girl who is still alive there. If these girls have been raped, have they lost everything by it? At least, I do not think so.[17]

He acknowledges that Hindu and Sikh girls have been abducted; he announces the steps taken to rescue them; finally, he urges their families to accept them honourably. The sin is not upon the victim but upon the perpetrators of the evil, Gandhi reminds us. But when it comes to women, how many would have the courage to live up to such a precept? Women's honour was equated with their sexuality remaining under patriarchal control; and a family or even a nation's honour was equated with the honour of its women. Thus innocent girls were made to bear the brunt of the pathologies and insecurities of a whole society.

In his prayer meeting of 29 November 1947 Gandhi alludes to the attempts to extort money from the families of missing girls in order to release them. Such ransom-seeking was utterly obnoxious to him:

> I had said yesterday that we should not give even a cowrie to get back the abducted girls. Those who have committed the crime of abducting our girls should restore them to us, and also do penance at the same time. It would not do to give any money to claim the girls back.[18]

But what are the means of prevailing upon the culprits to give up the girls they have held in custody? That Gandhi does not spell out. No vigilantism or non-state action is endorsed. Retaliation is of course out of the question:

> But there is a very alarming report. It is reported that in the East Punjab we are ill-treating the Muslim girls, whom we have forcibly kept. I just cannot understand how we could have stooped so low. I must admit that I cannot bear to see this. We should regard those girls as our mothers or daughters.[19]

It is not clear if an exchange of abducted women on both sides occurred because Hindus and Sikhs had also resorted to the same measure. Was this the bargaining tool that ensured the cooperation of the Pakistan authorities who, otherwise, would have simply washed their hands off any responsibility? Trading in one another's daughters, however, to Gandhi was most abhorrent: 'Those Muslim girls are like my own daughters. How can I indulge in pleasures, be alive and eat and drink while somebody ill-treats my daughters?'[20] Instead he insists on collective, even universal responsibility:

> But when someone commits a crime anywhere I feel I am the culprit. You too should feel the same. If I were to commit any crime you should also think that you too were guilty of it. Let us all merge in each other like drops of ocean. If the drops of ocean remain apart they would dry up. But when they mingle together in the ocean they can carry huge ships across their expanse. As with the ocean so with us. After all we also are an ocean of human beings. If one person commits a crime, it amounts to all of us committing it.[21]

This lofty doctrine, however, fails to assuage the wounds of the afflicted. These wounds they will not regard as collective but as individual, uniquely their own, in which others cannot share nor mitigate their trauma. Thus, locked into their own private hells, the outraged victims seethe with hatred and thirst for revenge. In the fragment of a letter written on 30 November 1947, Gandhi again lays down the proper way of treating abducted girls: 'Girls forcibly abducted are not to be treated as defiled. And does defilement only apply to women and not to men?',[22] but he also despairs of others understanding him: 'How long must I go on writing? What can I write? My heart is crying'.[23]

What is important, however, is Gandhi's consistency. If he tells Hindus and Sikhs not to retaliate, he also tells the same thing to the Muslims. It is the charge that he was partial to the latter and against the former that is untrue. It is this canard of chicanery and favouritism that Hindu fanatics levelled against Gandhi to justify his murder that is repeatedly revealed to be untrue. As Gandhi said to a Muslim delegation at Panipat, which he visited on 2 December 1947:

> In Pakistan many Hindu girls have been forcibly converted and subjected to extreme barbarities. Hindus too have done similar things. But I am telling you how you should behave like true Muslims. You should seek help from the Pakistan Government and persuade your brethren there to console the young women who have been abducted. You should tell them: 'Sisters, you have been cruelly treated. We forgot that we were human. From now on you are our mothers, our sisters, our daughters.' If you work in this spirit you can make Pakistan really *pak* – really pure.[24]

It is not only Hindus and Sikhs who ought not to retaliate; Gandhi also urges Muslims to behave as true Muslims, by honouring the daughters and sisters of Hindus and Sikhs. That, to Gandhi, is the only way to make Pakistan pure or holy. But it begs the question of whether that was the real reason for the Partition, to create a pure state where citizens could practise the highest form of Islam?

In the same address, it is interesting to see the gradual shift in his position about the transfer of populations. He tells the Muslims, 'If, of course, you want to go of your own will, no one can stop you',[25] but he would never ask them to do so: 'you will never hear Gandhi utter the words that you should leave India. Gandhi can only tell you that you should stay, for India is your home'.[26] What if their lives are threatened in India? Gandhi doesn't hesitate to add, 'And if your brethren should kill you, you should bravely meet death. That is the way I am made. That is the way I would have people behave'.[27] Hearing such impossible advice, should the Muslims of that period have accused Gandhi of being partial to Hindus for asking them to stay back in a hostile India to die, if necessary? Gandhi asks Muslims to behave in an exemplary way, safeguarding only their dignity and, careless of their lives and property, devoting themselves 'wholly to service'.[28] If they did so, Gandhi assures them, 'Hindus will worship you and you will be able to serve not only Pakistan but also the Muslims living in India'.[29] Such impossibly high standards for the common Hindus and Muslims of his time are not at all unreasonable as far as Gandhi is concerned. In fact, that is the only way to prevent the 'undoing of the country' and to save 'the independence . . . gained without shedding a drop of blood'.[30] Otherwise, he tells his audience, 'You are cutting off your own feet'.[31] Even so, despite all the harm done, it is not too late: 'If even now you take up the work of service without asking where and by whom the present tide of violence was started, you can still taste the nectar of freedom'.[32] Gandhi comes back to his fundamental premise to justify his argument: 'If my brother has become mad and wants to kill me, does it mean that I should also go mad? To return evil for evil makes for the fall of both parties'.[33] But suppose the one who has gone mad is not my brother, but my enemy? Wouldn't I be justified in killing him? Gandhi would say that all men are brothers; there are no enemies, therefore none deserves to be killed, least of all Hindus or Muslims, who have lived together in the same country for centuries.

In the prayer meeting of 7 December 1947, Gandhi returns to the question of the abducted women, actually offering numbers: 'Some say that about 12,000 women had been abducted by Hindus and Sikhs and twice that number had been abducted by Muslims in Pakistan'.[34] These figures do not include the women abducted from Kashmir by the Pakistani raiders who had crossed over. Gandhi will come to them later. At this time he is concerned with how to restore them to their families. He admits that many of the women themselves do not wish to come back:

> It is said that the women concerned do not now want to return, but still they have to be brought back. Muslim women similarly have to be taken back to Pakistan. It is also said that the Sikh and Hindu women concerned have embraced Islam and married their Muslim abductors. It could be true. But I do not admit that they are not willing to return. Similar is the case of Muslim women in India.[35]

I do not believe that Gandhi wanted the women to be abducted twice over, forced to cross over into India or Pakistan against their wishes. Instead, what he implies is that if they were to be welcomed back with true love and warmth, why would they, who were taken against their will, raped and brutalized, not wish to join their own families? That is why he insists that those who have lost the women should be ready to take them back with kindness and love. If not, they would be as barbaric as those who abducted and assaulted the women in the first place:

> It would be a barbarian husband or a barbarian parent who would say that he would not take back his wife or daughter. I do not think the women concerned had done anything wrong. They had been subjected to violence. To put a blot on them and to say that they are no longer fit to be accepted in society is unjust.[36]

Once again, Gandhi places the burden of rehabilitating the women upon the governments of the two new nations: 'The Governments should trace all these women. They should be traced and restored to their families'.[37] While blaming Pakistan for starting the madness, 'In my view Pakistan is responsible for spreading this poison', he also wonders, 'what good can come from apportioning responsibility?'[38] when both sides have been barbaric, regardless of who started it or which side abducted more women than the other?

On 26 December 1947, Gandhi again appeals to the men whose female relatives have been abducted: 'If my daughter has been violated by a rascal and made pregnant, must I cast her and her child away?'.[39] He does not insist any more that a pure woman cannot be raped against her will, he is rather more practical, willing even to extend his support to the children born of such violation: 'Nor can I take the position that the child so born is Muslim by faith. Its faith can only be the faith of the mother who bore it'.[40] Here Gandhi again departs from the patriarchal norm which insists that a child takes on the religion of its father. He wants to empower the women, who, though raped, have every right to raise their children as they deem fit. He adds the rider, 'After the child grows up he or she will be free to take up any religion',[41] thus totally undoing the competitive politics of the warring faiths, each trying to increase its numbers by stealing and impregnating women from the other side not just to insult them but to increase its own power. He also admits that it is very difficult to convince the abducted girls to come back: 'Today we are in such an unfortunate situation that some girls say that they do not want to come back, for they know that if they return they will only face disgrace and humiliation'.[42] Again we see Gandhi's idealism tempered, albeit reluctantly, by realism. Faced with an uncomfortable or disagreeable truth, Gandhi does not back off but faces it without accepting the defeat of the ideal that he wishes to cherish and uphold.

The following month, January 1948, Gandhi addressed the Pakistan-sponsored invaders who had tried to take the state by storm. By precipitating a crisis, they impelled Hari Singh, the Dogra ruler of Jammu and Kashmir, to accede to the Indian union. Thereafter, the protection of the territory and its people became the responsibility of the Government of India. Eventually, troops were airlifted to the valley and the tide of invasion stemmed before it engulfed the whole state. It was the first military action of the newly formed nation of India, and against its own neighbour, Pakistan, an erstwhile part of the same state. In his prayer meeting on 27 January 1948, just three days before he was killed, Gandhi directly addressed the raiders in Mirpur, Kashmir:

> I must ask the raiders and the Government of Pakistan, for the sake of humanity and for the sake of God, to return all the abducted women with due respect and without waiting to be asked. It is their duty. I have enough knowledge of Islam about which I have read a good deal. Nowhere does Islam bid people to carry away women and keep them in such a disreputable condition. It is irreligion, not religion. It is worship of Satan, not of God.[43]

That most of these women were also Muslims only proved Gandhi's point that these acts against women were totally irreligious and barbarous. No matter in the name of which religion, they could not be condoned.

Along with other leaders, so insistent is he that the abducted women from both sides be restored, that both governments form official agencies to recover and repatriate such women. But not to take such measures would have meant that the two sides simply left these women to their fate, rendering them not just abducted but abandoned too. Again, the principle that Gandhi adopts is to force the two new states to be accountable for the life and safety of their citizens even as he exhorts private citizens to abjure violence and desist from taking the law into their own hands. Gandhi's key strategy is to restore the rule of law in a state of chaos and lawlessness. Much of the violence and disorder had erupted in the interregnum when the colonial state had been summarily dismantled with minimum regard to how its erstwhile subjects might suffer such a sudden removal of authority. The two new nations would take a while to insert their own state machinery into this vacuum and to take charge of the situation.

In all of this confusion and uncertainty, however, women suffered very badly, as did the old, the infirm and the children. The plight of women was far worse because they were not only abducted and sexually abused, but were also fought over by both communities and the two newly independent states. It would seem that no one cared or was able to attend to what they themselves wanted. Their sufferings were too gruesome to be spoken of or acknowledged and their voices were silenced in the national histories. Gandhi helped greatly to shape the state policy towards these victims. As Butalia concludes,

> Clearly, while the State instituted what was a major humanitarian operation, and one which, with all its faults, was also beneficial to large numbers of women, it none the less constructed women differentially from men. Not citizens in their own right – and this at a time when citizenship and the question of rights were key questions being debated – but mothers, sisters, wives who had both to be rehabilitated, and protected, who had to be brought into the mainstream economically, but retained within the family, whether 'real' or simulated, and whose sexuality had to be kept in check. Not surprisingly, no such concern was reflected for men.[44]

The abduction, rape and degradation of women was a shameful and disgusting part of the Partition violence. Again, during the struggle for Bangladesh, the Pakistani army carried out large-scale atrocities on the East Bengalis, which included genocide and rape. This form of deliberate sexual terror shows the deeply misogynistic streak in the campaign for religious self-assertion in the subcontinent. The aim is not merely to dominate over the other community but to brutalize and terrorize them into utter subjection and humiliation. The fruits of such actions, however, sow the seeds of deep-seated hatred, as Gandhi warned, that lead to repeated cycles of counter-violence and retribution. Gandhi bore witness to this terribly traumatic aspect of the Partition, but he did not remain silent. He spoke out loud and clear not only against retributive sexual violence and rape, but also for the honour and safety of the women. He was one of the few who said again and again that the women who were raped were not defiled or tainted but only victims of the brutality of men. He repeatedly urged their families to treat them kindly and take them back honourably. In many respects, Gandhi also goes counter to patriarchal values in these pronouncements, a fact often overlooked by his critics.

20   Gandhi at an RSS rally

Gandhi's praxis of absolving the other and assuming responsibility for one's own ill deeds was tested on 16 September 1947 when he addressed a rally of the Rashtriya Swayamsevak Sangh (RSS).[1] The venue was the Bhangi (Sweepers) Colony, where Gandhi himself used to stay. A report of this visit was carried in the *Harijan* of 28 September 1947.[2] RSS, a Hindu right-wing organization, was active at that time in the protection of the Hindus and, some say, in retaliating against the Muslims. Earlier, Gandhi and Dr Dinshaw Mehta had met M. S. Golwalkar, the chief of the RSS. Gandhi had heard that the RSS had been responsible for killings and violence. Golwalkar, however, had 'assured him that this was untrue. Their organization was enemy to no man. It did not stand for the killing of Muslims. All it wanted to do was to protect Hindustan to the best of its ability'.[3] Gandhi went to the RSS rally, perhaps to find out the facts for himself.

Gandhi began his talk by recalling his visit to an RSS camp several years back at Wardha, where he had been taken by his associate and prominent businessman, Jamnalal Bajaj.[4] He said he had been 'impressed by their discipline, complete absence of untouchability and rigorous simplicity'.[5] He was also 'convinced that any organization which was inspired by the ideal of service and self-sacrifice was bound to grow in strength'.[6] But now came the characteristic Gandhian turn,

215

at once moral and pragmatic: he said that 'in order to be truly useful, self-sacrifice had to be combined with purity of motive and true knowledge'.[7] Note that he said 'useful', not 'successful'. Success might come through other means, but of what ultimate use could it be? Did the RSS have these qualities, self-sacrifice combined with purity of motive and true knowledge? Certainly, it did not when it came to one of their co-ideologists, Nathuram, whose purity of motive was at best doubtful and true knowledge almost certainly absent. The result, as Gandhi said, was 'known to prove ruinous to society'.[8]

A crucial admission on Gandhi's part during this speech was that his methods might not be applicable to the newly formed state of India: 'If he had his way, he would have no military; not even police. But all this was tall talk. He was not the Government'.[9] This is a crucial distinction between his own views and those of the Government. Gandhi admits that the kind of state that he wanted had not been realized. It is also a prelude to Gandhi's later confession of the failure of his ideal of *ahimsa*, or non-violence. When Gandhi says 'All this was tall talk' he is, in effect, conceding that his sort of state and polity had not been realized anywhere else in the world; even India, despite all his experiments in *satyagraha*, is not really a state based on higher spiritual principles. But within the bounds of what was practical and feasible, Gandhi would always push for adherence to the highest possible moral principles rather than a cynical disregard for them in the interests of expediency or selfish gain. Furthermore, by distancing himself from the Government, he was trying to carve out a space where the sort of 'saintliness' that he wished to practise could also work in the public sphere. In effect, it was also an admission that the two could not automatically go hand in hand; politics and saintliness had to be bifurcated after all. They might have gone well together during the struggle for independence but now their split was all too evident once again.

Gandhi tells the RSS that Hinduism, which they were striving so hard to protect, would die if it did not eradicate untouchability: 'One thing was certain, and he had been proclaiming it from housetops, that if untouchability lived, Hinduism must die'.[10] However, this the RSS had already accepted, even if most of their top functionaries were upper-caste and Brahmin, their official ideology was for Hindu, not caste, identities. Similarly, Gandhi told them that if 'Hindus felt that in India there was no place for anyone else except the Hindus and if non-Hindus, especially Muslims, wished to live here, they had to live as the slaves of the Hindus, they would kill Hinduism'.[11] The allusion here was to the RSS ideology of Hindutva, derived from V. D. Savarkar's pamphlet of the same name first published in 1923. In it Savarkar had asserted that India could only belong to those who regarded India as their *pitribhumi* and *punyabhumi* – fatherland and a holy land – i.e., the Hindus; those who did not accept India as both their fatherland and holy land could only live in it as second-class citizens. Golwalkar in *We or Our Nationhood Defined* (1938) goes even further:

> in Hindusthan exists and must needs exist the ancient Hindu nation and nought else but the Hindu Nation. All those not belonging to the national i.e. Hindu Race, Religion, Culture and Language, naturally fall out of the pale of real 'National' life.[12]

Gandhi warns against the harm that such a doctrine might produce, even to the destruction of the very religion that the RSS was professedly safeguarding. Gandhi is also quick to point out, in the very next sentence, that the same logic held true for Pakistan: 'Similarly if Pakistan believed that in Pakistan only the Muslims had a rightful place and the non-Muslims had to live there on sufferance and as their slaves, it would be the death-knell of Islam in India'.[13] This even-handedness of Gandhi was always suppressed and denied by Godse and right-wing Hindus who claimed that Gandhi was partial to Muslims. Actually, Gandhi was partial to truth, something that none of his opponents could quite stomach.

Gandhi once again referred to his meeting with Guruji Golwalkar. He repeated what he had said at the end of his prayer meeting on 12 September 1947, though there is a crucial difference between the two reports. There Gandhi reported Golwalkar as saying that the RSS 'stood for peace',[14] but here Gandhi clearly says, the RSS 'did not believe in ahimsa'.[15] However, Golwalkar had assured Gandhi that the RSS 'did not believe in aggression. . . . It taught the art of self-defence. It never taught retaliation'.[16] Gandhi reminds his audience of this conversation of just a few days ago with their chief. When Gandhi had told Golwalkar that he had received 'various complaints about the Sangh' both in Calcutta and Delhi,

> The Guruji had assured him that though he could not vouchsafe for the correct behaviour of every member of the Sangh, the policy of the Sangh was purely service of the Hindus and Hinduism and that too not at the cost of anyone else.[17]

Gandhi clarified his stance to the members of the RSS, repeating once again that though he was a friend of the Muslims, he was no enemy of the Hindus and Sikhs: 'It was true that he was a friend of the Muslims', as he was of the 'Parsis and others', that too 'since the age of twelve'.[18] But this did not mean that he was not a friend of the Hindus and Sikhs: 'those who called him the enemy of the Hindus and the Sikhs did not know him. He could be enemy of none, much less of the Hindus and Sikhs'.[19] The instrumental phrase is that those who called him so 'did not know him'. This was Nathuram's tragedy; he did not know the man he killed. This, indeed, is our tragedy too – we do not know the man we either adore or hate. When Gandhi said 'much less' in the above sentence it actually meant that though he was everyone's friend and the enemy of none, his investment and involvement in the moral well-being of Hindus and Sikhs was perhaps the greater given that he was not only born unto them but that he also espoused and considered himself a practitioner of Sanantana Dharma.

The RSS is often fond of considering this visit of Gandhi as giving them a 'clean chit', a certificate endorsing their innocence and absolving them of any wrongdoing in fomenting communal violence. Actually Gandhi had said something different: 'He did not know whether there was any truth in the allegations made against the Sangh. It was for the Sangh to show by their uniform behaviour that the allegations were baseless'.[20] As Gandhi does not wish to judge others, he is also withholding his verdict on the RSS. This does not mean that he endorses their stance or pronounces them innocent of charges of carrying out attacks against the Muslims. What he said is that they would have to counter such charges by their 'uniform behaviour' to the contrary; only then would such 'allegations' against them be proven as 'baseless'.

This exchange with the Sangh was not a one-way street; Gandhi invited questions at the end of his speech. Didn't Hinduism permit the 'killing of an evil-doer', asked a member of the audience, citing the Gita. Didn't Krishna urge Arjuna to kill the Kaurvas? Gandhi replied that 'One had to be an infallible judge as to who was the evil-doer before the question of killing could arise'.[21] It was almost as if he was adding Christ's injunction to Krishna's: 'one had to be completely faultless before such a right could accrue to one. How could a sinner claim the right to judge or execute another sinner?'.[22] As to whether the 'right to punish the evil-doer was recognized by the Gita', Gandhi parried the question by suggesting that such a right could 'be exercised by the properly constituted Government only'.[23] He urged the RSS to have faith in Government, not to 'become judge and executioner in one'.[24] Mentioning Nehru and Patel by name, he said 'They are tried servants of the nation. Give them a chance to serve you. Do not sabotage their efforts by taking the law into your own hands'.[25]

Gandhi did not want India to imitate Pakistan, especially when the latter was deviating from its stated principles and also from the tenets of Islam:

> Has not the Qaid-e-Azam proclaimed that Pakistan is not a theocratic State and religion would not be imposed by law? But, unfortunately, it is true that this claim is not always

put into practice. Would India become a theocratic State and would the principles of Hinduism be imposed on non-Hindus? I hope not. If that happens India would cease to be land of hope and promise. Then it would not be a country to which not only all the races of Asia and Africa but the whole world would look with hope. The world does not expect from Hindustan whether as Indian Union or Pakistan meanness and fanaticism. It expects greatness, goodness and generosity from Hindustan so that the whole world can learn a lesson and find light in the midst of the prevailing darkness.[26]

Gandhi considers 'Hindustan' the larger entity of which both the Indian Union and Pakistan are members. Both nations, therefore, would no longer serve as examples to the rest of Asia if they became theocratic or authoritarian. Imposing one's beliefs on others just because one has the power to do so was not the right way, according to Gandhi. Thus, the majoritarianism of the Hindu right held no appeal to him.

Gandhi had made his views clear to the leaders of the ruling Congress Party in a speech to the All India Congress Committee (AICC) on 15 November 1947:

I have always held that if Pakistan belongs to Muslims alone, then it is a sin which will destroy Islam. You may blame the Muslim League for what has happened and say that the two-nation theory is at the root of all this evil and that it was the Muslim League that sowed the seed of this poison; nevertheless I say that we would be betraying the Hindu religion if we did evil because others had done it. Ever since my childhood I have known that Hinduism teaches us to return good for evil. The wicked sink under the weight of their own evil. Must we also sink with them?[27]

That the wicked will be brought down by their own misdeeds is a doctrine that requires immense faith in the justness of the cosmic order. Members of the Hindu right, as indeed many of their counterparts in the Congress, lacked such conviction. Instead, they thought that the more pragmatic alternative was to pay back in the same coin, something Gandhi rescinded, especially when it meant descending to the barbarism of one's adversaries.

But going back to Gandhi's assassination, it is not only a fact that Godse belonged to the Mahasabha and edited a Hindu extremist newspaper whose masthead had Savarkar's photo in the inset, but that the two organizations, the RSS and the Mahasabha, then shared a common ideology. When Gandhi ended his fast on 18 January 1948, both the RSS and the Hindu Mahasabha had signed the Declaration pledging communal harmony and the end of sectarian strife. One representative, Ganesh Datt, had signed on behalf of both the RSS and the Mahasabha.[28] That Nathuram went on to murder Gandhi indicates that either he did not consider himself bound by this pledge or that the pledge itself was not sincere in the first place. What seems likely is that while Delhi was deeply touched, even transformed by Gandhi's presence, speeches, and, finally, his fast, hard-line members of the Hindu right elsewhere were unmoved and unaffected.

Gandhi, however, was not unaware of this mistrust and hatred. Godse, Apte and their team of assassins exploded a bomb on 20 January 1948 on the premises of Birla House. Gandhi was unhurt. In his prayer meeting the following evening, he addressed what had happened. Quoting his favourite scripture, he asked, 'Is it not said in chapter IV of the Gita that whenever the wicked become too powerful and harm dharma God sends someone to destroy them?'.[29] This was a telling allusion because Nathuram would also use the same scripture to justify his action. But Gandhi had already anticipated, and, the trained lawyer that he was, refuted such an appeal:

The man who exploded the bomb obviously thinks that he has been sent by God to destroy me. I have not seen him. But I am told that is what he said when questioned by the police. When he says he was doing the bidding of God he is only making God an accomplice in a wicked deed. But it cannot be so.[30]

Gandhi minces no words here: killing anyone in the name of religion or as a religious duty is wicked, especially killing a man like him. God cannot be an accomplice to murder; we humans alone will have to answer for it.

Moreover, the claim that killing Gandhi would save Hinduism, he points out, is so specious, so self-delusive, so mistaken, so ultimately false:

Therefore those who are behind him or whose tool he is, should know that this sort of thing will not save Hinduism. If Hinduism has to be saved it will be saved through such work as I am doing. I have been imbibing Hindu dharma right from my childhood. . . . Therefore having passed all the tests I am as staunch a Hindu today as intuitively I was at the age of five or six. If God deems it fit to make anyone the instrument for saving Hindu dharma, it could be none but me. Do you want to annihilate Hindu dharma by killing a devout Hindu like me?[31]

Gandhi lays claim to being a 'staunch' and 'devout' Hindu, much more so, in fact, than those who want to represent Hindus. Hindu dharma can only be saved by him – 'none but me', he asserts. This is indeed a very tall claim. Gandhi deliberately puts himself at the very centre of what Hinduism in our times is. This is his way of challenging us all, Hindus and non-Hindus alike, to choose between him and his opponents. Choose we must; we cannot be on both sides at once. No wonder earlier in his prayer meeting of 14 January 1947, the day of Makarsankranti that is sacred to most Hindus, Gandhi had rejected the other common allegation, that he wanted to make Hindus weak: 'I want everyone to become strong',[32] which is a totally different model to becoming strong at the expense of someone else. He thus puts himself and his version of Hinduism on trial, not shying away from the contest that had been thrust upon him.

In his prayer meeting on 27 September 1947 Gandhi openly rejected his adversaries' accusation that he was 'ruining Hinduism':

> I tell them that what they call my mistake is not a mistake. The real thing is that we are all possessed by a madness today and talk all sorts of things. When we get over that madness, we shall talk sense. That is why I say that what I am saying cannot be a mistake. Those who think I am making a mistake are themselves mistaken. . . . Because Pakistan is not following its religion should I start teaching the Hindus that they should also give up their religion? I have never learnt such a thing. If we protect our Muslim brethren and remain pure ourselves, it would have its own effect on Pakistan.[33]

The greatness of Hinduism would lie not in imitating Islam, especially when it was being most un-Islamic as in Pakistan after the Partition, but in maintaining the fundamental humanistic principles of Hinduism even in the face of severe odds. That would be its true test. If it became a mirror image of a distorted version of Islam, how would it remain itself, remain Hindu, remain worthy of its own name?

No doubt, Gandhi's idea of Hinduism was also quite different from that of the RSS or the Hindu Mahasabha. Very modestly, this is how Gandhi advanced his own definition:

> Once a friend who was an eminent advocate asked me to define Hinduism. I told him I was neither a lawyer like him nor a religious leader and was really unable to define Hinduism, but I would suggest that a Hindu was one who had equal respect for all religions.[34]

But while Gandhi is tentative in his definition, he is categorical in asserting that killing a devout Hindu like himself would only lead to the annihilation of Hinduism. The radical and far-reaching import of Gandhi's assertion should not be lost on us: those who claimed to save Hinduism were actually destroying it. That religious zealots and fanatics are usually the destroyers of religion has now come home to us in the most unsavoury and costly ways. It is as if the very enemies of religion champion religion to achieve their ends. If they declared themselves to be brutal, barbaric, bloodthirsty and power-hungry killers, who would support them? But if they described themselves as true defenders of the faith then they will have many adherents. If Nathuram was not saving Hinduism what was he doing? He, like many other Hindu nationalists, was actually misled by a heady and powerful ideology that promised a better version of the nation, one in which the Muslim 'problem' would be solved once and for all. Such a vision continues to appeal to many Hindus despite the adverse results of the policy to purge Pakistan of Hindus and other religious minorities, including Christians and Ahmediyas. Ethnic purging and genocides in other parts of the world, too, have usually had disastrous repercussions on those nations. Removing or subduing ethnic minorities or adherents of other religions does not help the majority. The violence does not end with the removal of the Other. The so-called self now splits to create other Others. The violence directed at Others returns directed at the self. This we see being played out in Pakistan, where the Taliban, a creature of the Pakistani Government, army and intelligence agencies, is now killing, threatening and destroying Pakistanis themselves.

The blame for Gandhi's murder continues to be laid at the doorstep of the RSS, while the RSS has consistently denied any involvement. Since Nathuram had once been a member of the RSS, the organization came under a cloud. Many prominent leaders were arrested and the Government banned the RSS on 4 February 1948. The ban was only lifted in July 1949, after protracted negotiations on a new constitution for the organization, which Golwalkar framed in March 1949 and submitted to the Home Ministry for its approval. Later, when the Kapur Commission conducted an inquiry into Gandhi's murder, it found no material evidence to show the involvement of the RSS in the conspiracy:

> RSS as such were not responsible for the murder of Mahatma Gandhi, meaning thereby that one could not name the organization as such as being responsible for that most diabolical crime, the murder of the apostle of peace. It has not been proved that they (the accused) were members of the RSS.[35]

However, with unfailing regularity the Sangh continues to be charged with killing Gandhi for reasons which may best be described as political.

The accusers, for the most part avowed leftists, secularists, or supporters of the Congress, are by no means entirely innocent themselves. The Hindu Mahasabha, whose involvement was more direct, was itself after all once a part of the Congress, acquiring a separate identity only after Savarkar took over its reins in the late 1930s.[36] The RSS, though sympathetic to the Mahasabha, refused to support its political ambitions,[37] and would float its own party, the Bharatiya Jana Sangh, in 1951. What Gandhi's visit to the RSS rally makes perfectly clear is that though the two had different views on what the Indian nation should be like, the latter was not interested in annihilating the former. As for Savarkar, the leading Hindu nationalist ideologue and author of *Hindutva*, he and Gandhi were old adversaries, having faced off with each other as early as 1909. Gandhi's *Hind Swaraj* was a response to the Savarkarite ideology of using violence instrumentally to achieve political ends, including the independence of India and later a Hindu state. Gandhi's murder was a direct outcome of this clash between two versions of Indian nationalism or, to put it even more specifically, two versions of Hinduism. In using violence to achieve political ends Nathuram was true to his brand of Hindu nationalism. What he didn't realize, perhaps, was that at the precise moment that he succeeded in murdering Gandhi, he had also shown the inferiority of his brand of both nationalism and Hinduism. Gandhi's murder put paid to any ambition that the Mahasabha and its followers may have had of using Indian independence as a pretext to turn India into a Hindu nation. When another Hindu nationalist party, the Bharatiya Janata Party (BJP), the successor to the Bharatiya Jana Sangh, and thus a grandchild, so to speak, of the RSS, did get the opportunity to come to power in Delhi, it could only do so in 1998, 50 years after Gandhi's murder, and then as the leading member of a coalition of a wide range of parties, many of whom were not supporters of Hindutva or Hindu nationalism. Unlike the RSS, which is still deeply ambivalent about Gandhi, the BJP has no qualms in officially embracing him. Several of its leaders are self-professed Gandhians or admirers of Gandhi, the most recent example being the on–off BJP ideologue Sudheendra Kulkarni, who authored a massive tome called *Music of the Spinning Wheel: Mahatma Gandhi's Manifesto for the Internet Age* (2012). Savarkar's and Nathuram's politics, let alone their brand of Hinduism, have had few takers. It is only when Hindu nationalists started treating Gandhi as less of an untouchable that they found favour with the Indian masses.

The Hindu right is still uncertain and ambivalent about Gandhi's Hinduism, as they are about his politics. Hindu nationalists, in so far as they still strive to create a Hindu nation, are totally at odds with Gandhi's politics and his notion of the nation. As to Gandhi's Hinduism, it would appear that Hindu nationalists are unable to digest it, if they understand it in the first place. Like the Ambedkarites, they don't quite know what to do with the Mahatma; to reject him totally is not only politically inexpedient but also morally untenable, but to accept him fully is also terribly difficult, if not impossible. The attraction–repulsion thus continues, turning into a continuous, contentious and unresolved ambivalence.

21 Saving India

The prayer meeting of 16 September 1947 had to be discontinued. One of the members of the audience had objected to the verses of the Koran that had just begun to be recited. The man who created the disturbance shouted, 'To the recitation of these verses, our mothers and sisters were dishonoured, our dear ones killed. We will not let you recite these verses here.' Others in the audience raised anti-Gandhi slogans, 'Gandhi *murdabad*' (death to Gandhi).[1] Order could not be restored; the meeting ended. On the following day, 17 September 1947, Gandhi was back with a response in a brief but very important speech:

> I have decided not to hold the prayers till every man present in the audience is ready for it. I have never imposed anything on anybody, then how can I impose a highly spiritual thing like prayer?[2]

Gandhi was persuasive, even peremptory in his loving commands, but never coercive, never dictatorial.

Carrying on, Gandhi repeats that he understands the anger and the anguish of Hindu and Sikh victims of the Partition, especially those driven out of their homes and villages in West Punjab. He understands, in other words, why they are objecting

227

to the recitation of the Koran. But he does not want to abandon a prayer that he believes in, or change its format just because some people object to it. 'It appears', Gandhi observes 'that millions of people have been benefited' from his prayer meetings.[3] But 'Either the prayer should be heartily accepted as a whole or it should be rejected ... the recitation from the Koran is that part of the prayer which cannot be discontinued'.[4]

Gandhi comes back to this problem the following week, in his prayer meeting on 23 September 1947, after some semblance of order and normalcy have been restored. His argument is that the Koran itself needs to be separated from what the Muslims of that time were doing:

> because the Muslims are harassing the Hindus and Sikhs and killing them, should we get angry over the Koran? What the Muslims have done is not good, but what harm has the Koran done?[5]

Gandhi then asks if we should stop praying simply because one believer has done wrong: 'If one devotee of God commits a sin, shall we stop repeating His name?'.[6] If the practitioner of one religion is the wrongdoer, should the text of that religion be rejected? 'If the devotees of God say that what the Hindus have done is bad, does it also mean that the Gita is bad?'.[7] Similarly, 'If the Sikhs have done bad things, should we stop reading the Granth Saheb? What harm has the Granth Saheb done?'.[8] By the same logic, the wrongdoing of some Muslims cannot be used to ban recitations from the Koran in the prayer meeting.

Allowed to continue, Gandhi offers a radical departure from his usual line of promoting non-violence: 'I am not proposing to you my method of non-violence, much as I would like to, for I know that today no one is going to listen to my talk about non-violence'.[9] What, then, is an alternative to non-violence? It is, according to Gandhi, faith in the Government, in democracy, and the rule of law. As opposed to this, if 'every man takes the law into his own hands' there would be anarchy; it would mean the end of social order; the state itself would not be able to function. 'That', warns Gandhi, 'is the way to lose our independence'.[10]

To drive out the Muslims just because the Hindus and Sikhs were driven out is also against any notions of justice: 'You cannot secure justice by doing injustice to the Muslims'.[11] Moreover, if wrongs were done to Hindus and Sikhs in West Punjab, wrongs were also inflicted on Muslims in East Punjab. So no side is entirely innocent. What had to be worked out, at the earliest, was a settlement between the two feuding parties. If a settlement were not possible, Gandhi, good lawyer that he is, suggests arbitration, with both parties agreeing to the verdict of an impartial adjudicator.[12] If even this did not work, Gandhi warns, what would ensue is war, which is of course loathsome not just to him but perhaps to his listeners too.[13] The undesirability of war taken as self-evident, Gandhi says that the only way left is for people to 'give up their madness and come to their senses',[14] a phrase that he repeats a few moments later.[15]

Seeing disaster staring him in the face, Gandhi gives his viewers a final ultimatum: 'I have decided not to live to witness the country being ruined by fratricide'.[16] He is 'constantly praying to God' that 'He should take me away before any calamity befalls this sacred and beautiful land of ours'.[17] Gandhi would prefer to die rather than witness the destruction of India and Pakistan in a communal conflagration. Here he introduces a new theme, that of his own death, into his daily discourse. It is a theme that never quite leaves him; indeed, he reiterates it to almost his dying day.

The very next day, Gandhi, as mentioned in an earlier section, gave a speech to Muslims in a Daryaganj mosque. He asked them to 'issue a public statement that all Hindu women abducted by the Muslims in Pakistan should be restored to their families'.[18] So that no one in the Indian Union should doubt their loyalty, he also urged them to unequivocally condemn the Pakistan Government where it had departed from the civilized conduct and demand that all those Hindus and Sikhs who had to leave their homes in Pakistan should be invited to return with full guarantee of their safety and self-respect.[19]

So that it did not remain confined to a small live audience, Gandhi also published his speech in the *Harijan* of 28 September 1947. Why, it bears asking, didn't the Hindu nationalists read these statements? Why did they refuse to see Gandhi's impartiality, his equal love for all communities? Why did they spread lies and hatred against Gandhi by calling him a partisan of the Muslims, set on weakening the Hindus?

In the prayer meeting that evening, Gandhi, for the third time, repeats the phrase, 'Today we have all lost our senses'.[20] Is that how he explains the violence, the hatred and the bloodshed of the Partition, as a temporary stupidity, a madness? Is his whole effort directed at bringing two nations back to their senses? Is violence itself a sort of bout of senselessness, like a frenzy? Is that his theory of violence, as a form of derangement of the normal state of order? In any case, what he insists on is breaking the cycle of reciprocal violence and replacing it with one of reciprocal peace. If the Indians declare a unilateral and unambiguous cessation of hostilities, Gandhi believes that the other side is bound to follow suit. In making his argument, again, Gandhi admits: 'I am told that the whole thing was started by the Muslims. It is true. I think there is no doubt that the trouble started from their side'.[21] 'But', he adds in the very next breath, 'what is the point in harping on it all the time?'.[22] To harp on others' wrongdoing repeatedly foments hatred and counter-violence. Instead, Gandhi says, 'I have to see what needs to be done today'.[23] He admits that he is almost helpless: 'I am just skin and bones. What can such a man do? Whom can he convince?'.[24] But if Gandhi is weak, God is not: 'God can do everything'.[25]

Throwing himself at the mercy of the almighty, Gandhi invokes the story of Gajendra Moksha, which he had alluded to in the prayers recited earlier. The reference is to a famous bhajan by Meerabai, rendered so movingly by M. S. Subbulakshmi:

doobte gajraaj rakhyo
kiyo baahar neer

(You saved the drowning elephant king,
Removed him from the waters.)[26]

The story is found in the eighth Canto of Srimad Bhagawatam, the most important text in the cult of Krishna. The king of elephants, Gajendra, goes to cool off in a lake, only to have his leg caught in the jaws of a crocodile. No matter how hard he tries, the elephant cannot free himself. Finally, he begins to tire and despairs of ever escaping the clutches of the crocodile. In sheer desperation and abjectness, he surrenders to the Lord, calling out to Him to save him, pleading that he has no other recourse.

Iconographically, this is often represented as the beautiful white elephant, dragged down into the lake by the crocodile beneath the murky waters, offering a lotus flower in his truck to Vishnu, the saviour Lord. Considered a powerful allegory for man's inability to escape sin by his own efforts, this story is very important in Vaishnavism. It certainly illustrates God's mercy, for Vishnu, heeding to the call of his devotee, descends from the heavens and beheads the crocodile with his *sudarshan chakra* (divine discus), thus saving the elephant. But it also shows that sincere and utter surrender to divine mercy is the only way human beings can be free. Otherwise, the urge to err is so strong that none can turn their mind to the divine. Certainly, by man's own efforts he cannot resist the draw of depravity; only the Lord can free him, making him sinless. The crocodile stands for the pull of sensuality, all that is alluring, all that binds and enslaves us. We are trapped in carnality; no amount of effort on our part can free us. But if God helps us, then we will be saved.

This is the purport of Meera's bhajan. Gandhi, rather cryptically, turns it into a metaphor for the condition of India, so afflicted by the crocodile of communal hatred and the frenzy of retaliatory violence. The great nation of India, with its hard-fought and precious independence, is now prey to all the lower passions and baser drives. Without God's help, how would India, the elephant king, be saved? Describing the plight of India, Gandhi says: 'Hence, night and day, I turn to Him. I say: "O God, come. Gajaraja is sinking – India is sinking – save her"'.[27] Gandhi continues to have high expectations from India and Indians, as he did from the days prior to *Hind Swaraj*. Somehow, he feels Indians understand his message, that spiritual force is greater than military might, that we must forswear violence in order to save our souls. 'What', he asks, 'if everybody in Pakistan is depraved? I would say, let our India be the sea in which all the inflowing dirt may be washed away. We cannot do bad things because others do them'.[28] He is sure that if Delhi is won, Pakistan will also turn. He tells his audience, 'When I go to Pakistan I will not spare them. I shall die for the Hindus and the Sikhs there. I shall be really glad to die there'.[29] Hindu nationalists do not usually quote these words. Some persist in the canard that Gandhi favoured the Muslims and turned a blind eye to the sufferings of Hindus. They claim that Gandhi wished to pacify and weaken the Hindus by asking them to be non-violent so as to make the Hindus an easy target of the violent Muslims. But it is clear that Gandhi did not wish to weaken the Hindus; it was simply that the kind of strength he wished to awaken in them was not the strength of arms.

Once again, Gandhi reiterates his resolve to die rather than see India and Pakistan destroy each other: 'I shall be glad to die here too. If I cannot do what I want to do here, I have got to die'.[30] Gandhi is trying his utmost to save India and Pakistan. In his prayer meeting of 21 September 1947 he says: 'Hindus, Sikhs and Muslims cannot continue to live the way they are living now'.[31] The situation is intolerable to him: 'It pains me very much and I shall do everything humanly possible to remedy the situation'.[32] But if he cannot make a difference he would prefer to die than to be a helpless witness to the destruction of India: 'Let me tell you that if I cannot do what my heart desires, I shall not feel happy to remain alive'.[33]

As he repeats in his prayer meeting a month later, saving India – and Pakistan too – is his top priority:

> if for some reason or other we are unable to forge friendship between Hindus and Muslims, not only here but also in Pakistan and in the whole world, we shall not be able to keep India for long. It will pass into the hands of others and become a slave country again. Pakistan too will become a slave country and the freedom we have gained will be lost again.[34]

The erosion of the sovereignty of Pakistan has been all too evident over time. First, it suffered under a series of military dictatorships, then it became almost a satellite state of the US, funded to fight the latter's war against communism in Afghanistan, and now it is torn by sectarian strife between Islamic extremists and the state. The roots of both the authoritarianism and loss of Svaraj, if Gandhi is to be believed, go way back to the very genesis of that nation. India, on the other hand, has gone towards a different kind of communal politics, where vote banks and identity politics hold the nation to ransom. That much of this politics is cynical, exploitative and divisive is all too evident.

On the following day, 22 September 1947, Gandhi returns to the theme of what might happen if India is lost. It is a matter of grave concern and anguish to him. To Gandhi, India has always been a symbol of the higher aspirations of colonized people; she has risen not just for herself or her own selfish interests, but for all the nations of the world. India's independence is not at the expense of others. That is why he says,

If India fails, Asia dies. It has been aptly called the nursery of many blended cultures and civilizations. Let India be and remain the hope of all the exploited races of the earth, whether in Asia, Africa or in any part of the world.[35]

That is why India's adherence to decency, good conduct and non-violence, even in the face of provocation and adversity, is so crucial. Saving India, to Gandhi, is also a way to safeguard the interests of the other subaltern and downtrodden nations of the world. It is to show them that one can win and secure one's freedom through the proper means, without attacking and destroying other nations and peoples in the process. This would demonstrate the viability of international relations on a different footing, not just self-interest or the domination of others. A few days before his death, Gandhi repeated what the loss of India might mean to the rest of the world. Saving India would mean 'the regaining of India's dwindling prestige and her fast-fading sovereignty over the heart of Asia and therethrough the world', but if India were lost, 'the loss of her soul by India will mean the loss of the hope of the aching, storm-tossed and hungry world'.[36]

Gandhi was preoccupied with how grave the threat to the country was. In his speech at the prayer meeting on 24 September 1947, he referred to India, following one of the bhajans recited, as a 'wrecked boat':

We can all describe ourselves today as 'wrecked boats'. And then we pray to God that He may bring us to the shore; that is, without His grace our boat cannot reach the shore. This is the condition of our country today and I see it everyday.[37]

The very next day, he likened India to an infant nation faced with 'a sudden calamity': 'Our freedom is not even one-and-a-half months old. What can a child of a month and 10 days do?'.[38] Then he returned to the theme of the leaking boat:

I told you yesterday, and I am telling you today, that ours is a wrecked boat. It is quite true that God alone can bring it to the shore. But we also must make efforts. If the boat has a hole somewhere we must try to stop water coming in with whatever may be available to us. But I have seen that if water starts flowing into the boat, they throw it out with the same speed. The boat then continues to sail in spite of the leak. But this can happen only if God helps. With God's grace it moves and reaches the shore, but if God does not help it sinks. That is why I would say that man should make effort and seek the help of God.[39]

The two metaphors of the dying elephant king and the wrecked boat show the seriousness of the threat, as Gandhi perceived it, not just to India's sovereignty but to her very existence. The nation could not survive without God's help, but each citizen had to do his or her best too. Like a great helmsman, Gandhi wishes to steer this precarious ship of state, that has sprung so many leaks on its maiden voyage, to the safety of the shore. Then he can afford to lay his oars to rest.

Partition, as he acknowledged in a letter two months later, was a big mistake: 'I realize what a blunder we have committed in partitioning the country' but as if that was not enough, 'we continue to make more and more blunders'.[40] What was the way out? He points out the way in a letter to an unnamed correspondent, 'If heart unity is not restored in Delhi, I can see flames raging all over India'.[41] Restoration of peace in Delhi was the first step; neighbourly relations with Pakistan the next. That was the only way to save both countries:

What happens in Delhi will happen in the whole of India. And what happens in India will happen in Pakistan. . . . When that happens India and Pakistan will unitedly be able to serve the world and make the world nobler. I do not wish to live for any other purpose. A man lives only to raise humanity. The only duty of man is to move towards God. . . . Let us uphold another's religion as we uphold our own.[42]

It was crucial to be both brave and wise, not only good.[43] He takes pains to explain what being wise and brave might mean, especially in the context of those times. It gave him a chance to expound his theory of non-violence, trying to show his audience why it would still work, despite being so severely tested. This, perhaps, was one of the most important projects of his last days and saving India was its cornerstone.

22 Ahimsa:

'Softer than a flower and harder than a stone'?[1]

Gandhi's lifelong experiment with Ahimsa or non-injury to others was sorely tested during the last days of his life. As he put it in the fragment of a letter dated 2 January 1948, 'Why is it that the freedom achieved through non-violence is sought to be sustained by violence?'[2] That he agonized over this question is certain: 'Maybe it was the will of God that I should witness this day. Now I have to do or die'.[3] Used so effectively against the British, *ahimsa* seemed to fail when two Indian communities, the Hindus and the Muslims, were battling one another in the aftermath of the Partition. It is another matter that the British only protected their own and when Indians were killing one another, they did not or could not interfere. What if Subhas Chandra Bose's Indian National Army had actually marched to and taken Delhi instead of being defeated and repulsed by Indian soldiers in the colonial army? It would certainly have changed the self-perception of Indians, from having won their freedom non-violently to having repossessed their nation after throwing out their foreign rulers. For most, non-violence was the second best, if more practicable option. Gandhi knew that the superiority of non-violence was for the truly brave; those who were not afraid to die, who could continuously absolve their adversaries of wrongdoing, and who could suffer for the crimes of others, waiting patiently for a change of heart. While he was convinced that it could work against any adversary under any circumstances, many of his followers might not have been as convinced. Could non-violence work against the Taliban, Hitler, Stalin, or, to offer an example from an earlier time, Taimur or Nadir Shah? Many, not only in his time but also today, do not believe it would.

Whatever be the answer to such a question, Gandhi demonstrated again and again that it did work even in the worst cases of rioting and bloodshed between Hindus and Muslims. Gandhi brought peace to Noakhali, Bihar, Calcutta and Delhi. This is a proven historical fact. What the army, the police, and the rest of the political leadership could not do, Gandhi accomplished practically single-handedly. This was the miracle of non-violence or of its only true votary in our times, Gandhi. What Gandhi achieved was so astonishing that it bears closer study.

The terrible bloodletting of the Partition, undoubtedly, brought the frail and ageing Mahatma to the brink of despair, even making him admit that most of the people of India never really believed in *ahimsa* or practised it. To them, it was merely an expedient, the only available weapon of the weak; what they had practised was not the non-violence of the brave that Gandhi advocated, but the passive resistance of the feeble, which erupted into barbarism when colonial authority was absent. The violence that he saw all about him, Gandhi termed cowardice. What bravery was there, he asked, in looting, killing and raping those who could not defend themselves? Marauding mobs of rioters were to him a sign of barbarism. When anyone resisted such aggression, Gandhi applauded, even if that meant the death of the resister. When the Pakistani mercenaries and raiders invaded Kashmir, unleashing a reign of terror and pillage on the hapless populace, he reluctantly endorsed the Government's plan to airlift troops to protect them. He justified this by admitting that states and governments could not be entirely non-violent, at least in present times. He also made a distinction between the violence of the brave, which to him was akin to non-violence, and the cowardice of naked aggression and instrumental violence, which he never condoned. Gandhi's doctrine of non-violence was thus considerably modified in the process, but he never gave up on it. For all disputes between non-state actors, he continued to insist on the efficacy, even necessity, of non-violence. Whatever the odds, Gandhi persisted and, in the end, the tide turned. Most Muslims stayed back not only in Delhi, but in the rest of India too. Whatever might have happened in Pakistan, India remained the plural society that Gandhi had insisted upon.

Gandhi explained the 'law' of non-violence to his audience during the prayer meeting on 21 September 1947. Non-violence meant non-retaliation; if you do not react, he said, you disarm your enemy:

> Suppose there is a friend whom I abuse and he abuses me still more in turn. It is all right. But if I hear his abuses in silence, how long will he go on abusing? If he beats me, I submit to that too. I do not raise my fist against his fist. Do you know what would happen in that case? I have seen that if a man swings his fist in the air, he injures his own hand. Even a boxer boxes against a big stiff cushion. He enjoys the game only when he strikes against some tangible object. But if the boxer does not keep something in front of him he becomes helpless and is able to do nothing.[4]

In any game, however adversarial, if one of the two players refuses to participate, the game comes to an end. Gandhi continues:

> What I have told you is an eternal truth. I am the only one steadfastly clinging to it. People are not following that path these days. God alone knows if I will be able to stand by that truth till the end. I am making a simple point today.[5]

As the example given above shows, non-retaliation works between friends and members of the same family whose enmity is only temporary. That is how Gandhi responded to the violence of the Partition. He saw it as a fight not between enemies but between feuding brothers.

Perhaps Gandhi perceived that few agreed with him that non-retaliation was the best way to counter the violence unleashed by the Partition. Gandhi, continuing his soul-searching in his speech to the AICC on 15 November 1947, even goes to the extent of giving the argument in favour of violent retaliation its due. What if it is true that hitting your opponent back harder than he hits you sends out a strong message?

> It is held by some that if we perpetrate worse atrocities on Muslims here than what have been perpetrated on Hindus and Sikhs in Pakistan, it will teach the Muslims in Pakistan a salutary lesson.[6]

But even if that were true, what, asks Gandhi, does that do to the Hindus and Sikhs – 'They will indeed be taught a lesson, but what will happen to you in the meanwhile?'.[7] Would it not mean that we would also lose our humanity? So Gandhi says, 'You must be humane and civilized, irrespective of what Pakistan does. If you do what is right Pakistan will sooner or later be obliged to follow suit'.[8] Indeed, 'we have been obliged to copy Pakistan in its misdeeds and have thereby justified its ways'.[9] In other words, we must emulate only good, never evil, because if we imitate evil that would not be a way to counter but only to strengthen it. If that is what we really wish, why say that we want to counter evil in the first place; we should instead say that we are only looking for an excuse to become evil ourselves. To argue that we will temporarily resort to evil only to overthrow evil is thus a dangerous argument. Instead, non-retaliation actually strengthens, not weakens us:

We will not return blow for blow but will meet it with silence and restraint. Restraint will add to your strength. But if you copy what happens in Pakistan, then on what moral basis will you take your stand? What becomes of your non-violence? . . . if you maintain the civilized way, whatever Pakistan may do now, sooner or later, she will be obliged by the pressure of world opinion to conform.[10]

Even if retaliation might be effective, Gandhi wants India to refrain from doing so. As he said in his prayer meeting on the first day of his fast, 13 January 1948, 'No one should find fault with the Muslims whatever they may do';[11] likewise, he told the Muslims, 'Let them not take offence at whatever Hindus and Sikhs may do'.[12] Absolving the other of wrongdoing and not imitating the wrong oneself was the only way to lasting peace. Unfortunately, the world did not recognize the moral superiority of India's position, but rather accepted self-interest as the principle of state policy and treated both Pakistan and India as moral equals for ever so long. This perception has changed only recently with proof of the complicity of the Pakistani state in acts of international terrorism.

During his last days in Delhi, Gandhi gradually but definitely moves from this position of absolute non-retaliation to one of qualified, partial and conditional self-defence, even if not retaliation. That is why he said that neither party should be offensive or retaliatory; but this does not mean that one should succumb meekly to the other. As he told his audience in his prayer meeting on 26 September 1947, 'Let us arrive at a mutual and friendly settlement. Why can we not do so? We Hindus and Muslims were friends till yesterday. Have we become such enemies today that we cannot trust one another?'.[13] But he also warned them of the possibility of war if this was not possible: 'If you say that you are never going to trust them, then the two sides would have to fight'.[14] Gandhi was not a naive idealist; he knew what the logical outcome of retributive violence was: 'If they decide to kill two persons for every person killed in Pakistan, who would care for whom?'.[15] His basic position was 'We should not take the offensive. But we must be ready to fight, because when war comes it does not come after giving a warning'.[16] Speaking on 27 September 1947, and as reported in the 5 October 1947 issue of *Harijan*, Gandhi once again warned of the possibility of war and urged Indians to be ready for it: 'In the event of a war between the Union and Pakistan, the Muslims of the Indian Union should be prepared to fight against Pakistan'.[17] The accusation that Gandhi would have passively allowed the wholesale slaughter of Hindus and Sikhs because of his unreasonable insistence on non-violence is quite mistaken.

Gandhi repeatedly insisted that his was not the way of the weak, cowardly and helpless. Instead, he asserted, 'I have been a fighter for many many years, more than 60 years'.[18] But Gandhi's 'weapons' were unorthodox: 'But I fight not with the sword, but with the weapons of truth and non-violence'.[19] The real answer, therefore, to the charge that Gandhi was trying to weaken Hindus is that it was not true; he was only trying to teach them how to fight with another set of weapons. The only way to counter that is to allege that he was lying or that he was mistaken, which is to say that we cannot use truth and non-violence to fight, but only swords and guns. Gandhi never said that if you can't fight with truth and non-violence, you mustn't fight at all, but surrender or die. Instead, he taught unarmed men and women to face superior adversaries without being afraid. What is more, Gandhi would say that without truth, if not some degree of non-violence, no army could function. To keep one's morale, every soldier had to live by a code of conduct, which involved restraint as much as indulgence in violence. It might be fair to say that the people who thought they were fighting non-violently were cowards, in which case, why should Gandhi be blamed? If Hindus were a defeated people, how could Gandhi be blamed for it? Moreover, killing unarmed and outnumbered targets, raping women and terrorizing ordinary civilians could by no stretch of the imagination be considered acts of bravery. Gandhi, we must not forget, recruited soldiers for World War I and raised ambulance corps for the Boer War and the Zulu Rebellion. If the safety of Indian citizens was to be threatened by a warlike neighbour, and the people were unable to defend themselves non-violently, Gandhi would not have hesitated to support or strengthen the Indian armed forces. It is only that non-violence was his preferred weapon and he would not accept, in the face of his own experiments over decades, that it did not work. It did work, but it required a high level of training, aptitude, dedication and hard work. But then to be a good soldier in the conventional sense also required similar qualities. Without truth, discipline and self-restraint, neither could function effectively. No wonder Gandhi had called *ahimsa* 'a universal principle' whose 'operation is not limited by a hostile environment'.[20]

Gandhi's *ahimsa* did not, as he often said, depend on favourable circumstances, nor did he expect its adherents to buckle under pressure: 'we would stand firm even if the whole world was against us'.[21] It was not the weapon of the weak, but of the fearless, of those who were not afraid to die. Furthermore, it required faith that 'No one can kill us. No one can destroy Hinduism. If it is destroyed, it would be at our own hands'.[22] Gandhi did not believe that others had the power to destroy or dominate us; they could do so only if we allowed them to do so. Power over life and death, in all circumstances, was vested only in God, not in human beings. So no one need fear dying before his or her time. What Gandhi preached to his Hindu and Sikh audiences was not meant exclusively for them; equally it applied to their adversaries, the Muslims. He said, 'Similarly if Islam is destroyed in India, it would be at the hands of the Muslims living in Pakistan. It cannot be destroyed by the Hindus'.[23] Giving people the complete right to their lives and to their faiths, Gandhi enjoined on them supreme responsibility too. By this logic, we had only ourselves to blame for our own downfall, not the wickedness of our enemies, or circumstances. If the Muslims or the British conquered India, it was only because Hindus were weak; we could not blame the latter for our weaknesses; Gandhi famously said in *Hind Swaraj*, 'The English have not taken India; we have given it to them. They are not in India because of their strength, but because we keep them'.[24] By the same token, we could take it back from them too. It was a matter of withholding our consent. Similarly, none could harm the Hindus and Sikhs if they did not permit them to. On the contrary, resisting, even through arms if necessary, a large army of invaders would actually be a form of non-violence. In his prayer meeting on 5 November 1947 Gandhi offered this novel interpretation, seemingly going against much of what he had written on the subject, when he spoke at length on the invasion of Kashmir:

> Supposing an army of a lakh of armed Afridis invaded the place and a handful of people offered armed resistance in order to protect the innocent children and women and died fighting, then they could be called non-violent in spite of their using arms.[25]

This is one of the rare occasions when he justified armed and violent resistance. He was changing the meaning of non-violence by positing that even armed self-defence against the raiders was a form of non-violence. Yet such self-defence could never turn into retaliation, revenge, or the use of force against the weak and defenceless, or any other instrumental use of violence.

At the same time, Gandhi was also acknowledging that most Indians had not understood his idea of non-violent struggle. He observed on 6 November 1947 in a letter to two American friends,

> If we grant that such liberty as India has gained was a tribute to non-violence as I have repeatedly said, non-violence of India's struggle was only in name, in reality it was passive resistance of the weak. The truth of the statement we see demonstrated by the happenings in India.[26]

If Indians had been truly non-violent, Gandhi argued, they would never have descended to the barbarism of the Partition. Their non-violence was mere convenience and expediency. They did not wish to fight; they were demoralized and disarmed, so passive resistance suited them. They found it easier to be beaten up than to beat others up; this didn't mean that they were really brave or unafraid. Gandhi, pushing this line of thought further, admits in his exchange with his American correspondent, Richard B. Gregg,

> What has, however, clearly happened in my case is the discovery that in all probability there is a vital defect in my technique of the working of non-violence. There was no real appreciation of non-violence in the thirty years' struggle against British Raj. Therefore, the peace the masses maintained during that struggle of a generation with exemplary patience, had not come from within.[27]

Gandhi had in fact called off civil disobedience when violence broke out in Chauri Chauri. Does this mean that despite the delay of so many years, the masses had still not learnt what non-violent resistance was really about? Instead, it was merely repression. Gandhi continues:

> The pent-up fury found an outlet when British Raj was gone. It naturally vented itself in communal violence which was never fully absent and which was kept under suppression by the British bayonet. This explanation seems to me to be all-sufficing and convincing.[28]

Speaking in his prayer meeting on Christmas Eve, 24 December 1947, Gandhi lamented:

> The fruit of independence has been that today Hindus, Muslims and Sikhs have become one another's enemies. As I

have admitted earlier I had been under the delusion that our struggle was truly non-violent. God had rendered me blind and I was misled. . . . What we offered during the struggle was passive resistance which simply meant that we would not kill the British though in our hearts we wanted to kill them. But we had not the power. When the millions took up passive resistance it did bring about our freedom. The freedom we have obtained is crippled freedom. It is only partial.[29]

This is as severe an indictment of India's freedom struggle and its much-vaunted claims to non-violence as any we might find. It was a flawed non-violence, a flawed satyagraha which resulted in a flawed freedom; Partition was the result, all too palpable and horrible, of this flaw.

Similarly, in the middle of his fast, too weak to go to the prayer ground, in a speech that was broadcast to the audience from his room on 15 January 1948, again, Gandhi admitted: 'I have made the discovery that what I and the people with me had termed non-violence was not the genuine article but a weak copy known as passive resistance'.[30] Then he went on to say something extraordinary: 'Naturally, passive resistance can avail nothing to a ruler'.[31] In other words, no state can be seen as cowardly and ineffective, even if some individuals might be permitted to be so. Since we have not found a way for a state to be non-violent, then it must also not practise passive resistance: 'Imagine a weak ruler being able to represent any people. He would only degrade his masters who, for the time being, had placed themselves under his trust'.[32] Gandhi was saying this in defence of Sardar Patel, who was perceived to be a tough Home Minister. For the state to be weak, said Gandhi, would be only to send the wrong message.

This admission, however, does not shake his own faith in non-violence. If others did not understand or follow it, the 'law' of non-violence was not therefore disproved. On the contrary, here, in the worst conflagration of domestic violence, was the opportunity to test its efficacy again. As he said in his letter to Karl Struve, written on the first day of 1948, and later published in *Harijan* as 'Ahimsa Never Fails':

> In any case, whatever I have said does not refer in any way to the failure of ahimsa, but it refers to my failure to recognize, until it was too late, that what I had mistaken for ahimsa was not ahimsa, but passive resistance of the weak, which can never be called ahimsa even in the remotest sense. The internecine feud that is going on today in India is the direct outcome of the energy that was set free during the thirty years' action of the weak. Hence, the proper way to view the present outburst of violence throughout the world is to recognize that the technique of unconquerable non-violence of the strong has not been discovered as yet. Not an ounce of non-violent strength is ever wasted.[33]

But while Gandhi was 'mistaken', what happened to the masses and to the country? Wouldn't they have been better off if they had a violent outlet, as Franz Fanon argues in the *Wretched of the Earth*, for their pent-up frustration: 'At the level of the individuals, violence is a cleansing force. It frees the native from his inferiority complex and from his despair and inaction; it makes him fearless and restores his self-respect'.[34] Violence can be therapeutic, restoring as Fanon thought, the wholeness of a traumatized and fractured psyche of the colonized, allowing the sufferer to feel empowered and enabled by an outburst against the oppressor. But who is to say that the violence of the weak is necessarily better than the non-violence or passive resistance of the weak? It is strength, whether violent or non-violent, as Nietzsche would say, that is desirable, but even so, isn't non-violent action and strength necessarily superior to violent action and strength? If non-violence could achieve similar results as violence, with much less loss of life, would it not be better? In India's case, however, it is not the colonizers that had to bear the brunt of the counter-violence, but Hindu and Muslim subjects themselves, who erupted into a civil war that has still not ended. But Gandhi, obviously, clung to his belief in non-violence, telling General Cariappa, the new Chief of the Indian Armed forces on 3 December 1947, even in the face of the invasion of Kashmir, 'Violence can only be overcome through non-violence. This is as clear to me as the proposition that two and two make four. But for this one must have faith'.[35]

In his interview with Kingsley Martin on 27 January 1948, just three days before he was shot, Gandhi once again reflected on the 'failure' of non-violence in India:

> Gandhiji explained how the freedom movement had not been a non-violent movement in the highest sense of the term. If it had been the non-violence of the strong no butchery such as had taken place recently could have come about. He discovered this while he was on his pilgrimage in Noakhali and ever since this discovery he had been impressing the fact on everyone. He felt that non-violence during the struggle for independence was an expedient, i.e., resistance to the white man was undertaken in a non-violent manner simply because we had no military strength with which to offer battle.[36]

The upshot of all this is that Gandhi's non-violence was spectacularly successful in stopping the violence between Hindus and Muslims, not just in Noakhali, Bihar and Calcutta, but also in Delhi. However, he admitted that states as they are constituted at present could not practise it. Therefore, limited violence, with the army and the police using it only as the last resort and only in self-defence, was justified. Gandhi's last experiments with *ahimsa* convinced him that a change of heart was a better guarantee for lasting peace than armed might. But the question that he could not, perhaps, answer fully was how to ensure that kindness, non-violence, non-retaliation and self-restraint were not mistaken for weakness or cowardice. That is why during his last days Gandhi gradually became drawn into an arrangement in which a strong defence establishment would be inevitable for the Indian union, though it would remain under civilian control and a part of the democratic state. But with the reins of organized violence firmly in the hands of the state, Gandhi still wanted non-violence to remain the operating principle in the personal spheres of Indians. Let the states battle between themselves; at least the citizens should learn to live in peace with one another. As he acknowledged in January 1948, 'They praise my ahimsa but say that it cannot be effective in politics, that it should be confined only to spiritual matters'.[37]

No wonder, towards the end of his life, in his prayer meeting on 23 January 1948, Gandhi found time to appreciate one of his 'Others', Subhas Chandra Bose, who had raised an army to fight the British and wrest India's independence, in contrast to the non-violent struggle of the Congress Party which he had led:

> Someone reminded me of Subhas Babu's birthday. Subhas Babu was a votary of violence while I am a devotee of ahimsa. But what does it matter? I know that the most important thing is that we should learn from other people's virtues. . . . We should emulate him in his virtues and forget his deficiencies. Subhas was a great patriot. He laid down his life for the country. He was not by nature a fighter but he became commander of an army and took up arms against a great empire.[38]

There was no meanness and smallness in Gandhi. He was not petty or vindictive, as his opponents alleged. A brave man himself, he respected other brave men, even if they disagreed with him. That even extended to one who was the champion of a violent overthrow of the empire.

23   Hindu–Muslim amity

During his last four-and-a-half months in Delhi, almost the entire
focus of Gandhi's deliberations on *ahimsa* was Hindu–Muslim
relations. He had started his political career with making unity a
plank, then very reluctantly lowered his expectations to amity, but
in the end, he was willing to settle for peaceful coexistence or civil
tolerance – anything but the murderous violence and unremitting
enmity that he was witnessing all about him.

Yet this did not make Gandhi blind to political realities; the
entire basis of the Muslim League and its call for Pakistan being
little more than a clever misuse of religion for political ends. The
Muslim League was not averse to invoking the martial history of
the Muslim conquerors of India to justify the use of violence to
achieve its goals. In his prayer meeting on 24 September 1947,
Gandhi spoke out against the League and its brand of violent
politics:

> I am a witness to the propaganda of the Muslim League
> that the Muslims would *take* Pakistan by force, not by
> negotiating for it, not by pleading their case with the
> Hindus and other non-Muslims. It was our misfortune that
> for years they went on clamouring that they would take
> Pakistan by force.[1]

But the scope for misunderstanding was always there; if one party gets what it wants by threats and violence while the other party claims that they gave it willingly, who is to be believed? The confrontation that Gandhi wanted to avoid at all costs was, it would appear, inevitable. As Gandhi continued,

> But that will never do. What is the point in having it by force? In a way we can say that they have not taken Pakistan by force. Rather we have granted it, the Congress has granted it. There would have been no Pakistan without the British agreeing to the demand. However much the Congress might have agreed to it, the ultimate power was in the hands of the British.[2]

Gandhi is forced to admit that the demand for Pakistan could not have been ignored; Hindus and Muslims could not work out a compromise to live together in one country; the British, who were the rulers of India, granted the League's demand for Partition. A tragedy of colossal proportions, which he had tried so hard to avert, became a reality.

Perhaps the roots of this conflict lay buried deep in the history of the subcontinent. Muslim invaders had eventually conquered the land, but not entirely subdued or vanquished the people. When the Mughal power weakened, Hindus and Sikhs had started reasserting themselves. But before the latter could defeat the former comprehensively, the British had established themselves as the rulers of India. With the exit of the British, the older, unfinished business between Hindus and Muslims once against came to the fore. Perhaps the only reason the British could win India is because of the rivalry between Hindus and Muslims in the first place. Even after 800 years of living in close proximity, the two communities had still not found the formula to live with each other. It was only when a superior imperial power intervened that they stayed within their colonially apportioned or allocated spaces. With the creation of Pakistan, a militaristic and hostile country, the problem had become many times more intense.

Gandhi knew this as he did the source of the violence during the Partition. How to contain the aggression of an armed and violent adversary was his problem too, perhaps as much as that of the more militant of the Hindus and Sikhs. He gave his detailed analysis of this problem in his prayer meeting of 24 September 1947. In fact, before the meeting started, a slip of paper was passed on to him in which the questioner asked that when Pakistan was driving out Hindus and Sikhs from East Punjab, if Gandhi continued to advise the Indian Government to keep Muslims in India and to treat them as equal citizens, 'How could the Union Government bear this double burden?'[3] This is how Gandhi responded:

> I know everything that has happened there. The Muslims went berserk. They thought that since they were now free they could kill and slaughter. It all started from there. And once it started, there were the Sikhs who are also warriors. How could they take it lying down? They also started killing and slaughtering. That is the story which is not yet over.[4]

Whereas the Hindus and Sikhs thought that retaliation was the only language that Pakistan would understand, Gandhi thought otherwise, as we have already seen. But Gandhi's point was that the solution to the problem of Pakistan could not be effected through force. He considered the Hindu nationalist idea of Hindu dominion over the whole subcontinent also to be a pipe dream:

> Now suppose the Muslim League does something crazy because something got into its head. And then we think that if they can behave like that let us also behave in the same manner. You may want to rule the whole of India and destroy Pakistan. But I tell you that we have agreed to the formation of Pakistan. Where then is the question of destroying it? We

cannot destroy it. We cannot destroy it with our physical strength or with the help of the sword. If we try to destroy Pakistan, both the countries are going to sink.[5]

It is such thinking, leading to mutually assured destruction, which led him to say, 'Ours is a wrecked ship'.[6] If Muslims could not destroy Hindus and rule over India and if Hindus could not defeat the Muslims and rule over all of India, the only way forward was for both sides to give up thoughts of dominating over the other and to find a way to live together peacefully.

With the skill of the trained lawyer that he was, Gandhi tries to convince his listeners of the futility of a violent solution. For Muslims to kill all the Hindus would be impossible; similarly for Hindus to get rid of all the Muslims would also be impossible. Therefore, the only way was to accept one another and one another's differences:

> After all, there are only 4½ crores Muslims in the country. Why should we be scared of them? Suppose you kill 4½ crores Muslims, what would you do after that? And there are so many Muslims in Pakistan. Whom would you kill there? The Pakistanis would like to settle accounts with you for those 4½ crores Muslims here. You would not be able to accept that challenge, because they would have the support of the whole world. That is why I say that we should remain pure. Let us keep our accounts clear. Let us not be in the position of debtors.[7]

But does this mean that the Hindus and Sikhs should remain passive victims? No, Gandhi assures them that if they listen to him and take the moral high ground, the Indian Government will take up their cause: 'If we are in the position of creditors, I tell you that your Government will have to give ultimatum to Pakistan',[8] but under no circumstances should the people take the law into their own hands: 'do not take the law into your hands, do not use your guns and do not kill anyone'.[9] Gandhi is convinced that those who are pure and good will ultimately triumph because there is a divine force that controls our destinies:

> If you do this much, victory will be ours, and our ship which is beginning to sink will be saved. God is always on the side of truth. God can never abandon us but if we give up God, if we forget Him and abandon the right path, what can God do?[10]

Gandhi speaks with the certainty of one who knows the laws and the workings of the universe, but he also speaks as one God-fearing man to an audience of Indians who also intrinsically share his views.

Gandhi continued with this theme in the prayer meeting of the next day, 25 September 1947, asking his audience, 'What is your duty?',[11] then going on to answer his own question: 'It is to live together in amity and not to regard the Muslims as your enemies'.[12] But what about the aggressors and the wrongdoers? They, according to Gandhi, 'would automatically meet their own end'.[13] Attacking, killing and regarding others as our enemies was 'cowardice on our part, and it has a weakening effect on us'.[14] The strong and courageous, according to Gandhi, ought not to 'quarrel with others':[15]

> Every place is burning. It is our duty to extinguish that fire, pour water over it, without which it cannot be put out. Our first task is to make the people understand [the situation]. I try to convince them as well as you in the same terms. I shall repeat the same thing to the whole world till my last breath. The glorious land that was India has become a cremation-ground today. It has become that barbarous.[16]

We cannot forget how Gandhi extolled the traditional civilization of India in *Hind Swaraj*, preferring it to Western-style modernity.

But the Partition showed how much brutality and violence lay hidden beneath the surface in this troubled land. Instead of caving in under the enormity of the situation, Gandhi faced up to it with extraordinary heroism and courage.

His message was to hammer home to his audience that the fighting between the communities had nothing to with religion; it was instead an aberration, a departure from the real meaning of religion. Gandhi spoke as a religious man, as one who had not only read but practised many faiths. He also predicted the following day in his prayer meeting of 26 September 1947 that religions which commit or permit such crimes would themselves not last: 'What is going on is not Sikhism, nor Islam nor Hinduism. We are somewhat familiar with each of these. Can any religion which indulges in unworthy things survive?'.[17] A month later, in his prayer meeting of 24 November 1947, he stressed once again that without rapprochement between the warring communities, there could be no future for India or Pakistan. The imperative of the hour was therefore obvious: 'The first and foremost today is communal harmony'.[18]

The separation of religion from nationalism was therefore imperative. As he said on 28 November 1947, 'No man who values his religion as also his nationalism can barter away the one for the other. Both are equally dear to him. He renders unto Caesar that which is Caesar's and unto God that which is God's'.[19] The allusion is, of course, to the Bible, to Jesus's words, but Gandhi, applying them to the current context, stresses that faith and politics are best kept in two separate compartments because allowed to mix, they become a deadly and explosive cocktail.

He insisted that India not imitate Pakistan, but treat its Muslims with respect and courtesy, something he repeated over and over again:

Pakistan has to bear the burden of its sins, which I know are terrible enough.... What is of moment is that we of the Union copied the sins and thus became fellow-sinners. Odds became even. Shall we now awake from the trance, repent and change or must we fall?[20]

Thus he was also compelled to admit that Hindus and Sikhs were not too far behind in the scale and score of atrocities either. Narrating incidents against Muslims in Kathiawar, his own native place, he concluded: 'This is my sad tale, rather, the sad tale of the whole of India, that I have placed before you'.[21] In his prayer meeting on 30 November 1947, he once again regretted the actions of his own co-religionists: 'I have great respect for the Sikhs in my heart but today, everybody, whether Hindu or Sikh, is going astray and India is being destroyed'.[22] The calamity was so great that everything that India had stood for was about to be destroyed: 'Are we going to drag India into dust after raising her high? Are we going to destroy our religion, our achievements and our country? May God save us from all this'.[23] What was more, as we have already seen, Delhi was the key: 'I see my battle has to be fought and won in Delhi itself '.[24] As he repeated on 20 January 1948: 'Delhi after all is an ancient city and what is achieved in Delhi is bound to have an impact on the whole of India and Pakistan'.[25]

To the displaced Hindus and Sikhs, furious and thirsty for revenge, Gandhi said, 'good should be returned for evil. We must not copy the wrong-doer, we must emulate the man who does good'.[26] How should those wronged by members of one community regard the other community? Gandhi said, for his part, 'I shall continue to trust the Muslim friends till it is proved that they cannot be trusted. Trust begets trust. It gives one the strength to face treachery'.[27] Gandhi was firm in his belief that those who persisted in good even though they were betrayed would, in the end, prevail. Hindus and Muslims, in any case, were not enemies. Especially, those Muslims who had stayed back in India, Gandhi said, must not be treated as enemies. As he said in his prayer meeting of 18 December 1947: 'If you want to safeguard Hinduism you cannot do so by treating as enemies the Muslims who have stayed on in India'.[28] Furthermore, Gandhi was convinced that Islam too would be weakened by its intolerance: 'The same rule applies to Muslims. Islam will be dead if Muslims can tolerate only Muslims. The same goes for Christians and Christianity'.[29] So sure was he that he said, 'My days in this world are numbered. Soon I shall be gone. You will then realize that what I said was right'.[30] He repeated the same warning in his prayer meeting of 20 December 1947: 'Likewise it will be the doom of Islam if Pakistan decides that no Hindus and Sikhs may live there'.[31] Five days later, in his prayer meeting of Christmas Day, 1947, Gandhi again repeated:

> I want to say to the Government of Pakistan in all humility that if their claim to being the greatest Islamic power in the world is true, they should make sure that every Hindu and every Sikh in Pakistan is justly treated.[32]

Again, in his prayer meeting on 2 January 1948, he said, 'If there is a war both countries are going to bleed. I do not wish to be alive to see that. I do not wish to be a witness to that carnage'.[33] He added this warning for good measure: 'There are now perhaps thirty or thirty-five millions of Muslims in India. If we harass them we shall not survive as a nation nor can our Hinduism'.[34] Likewise, he warned a few days later in his prayer meeting of 7 January 1948, 'If the Pakistan Government allows the people to be murdered in this way, the Government will not last long'.[35] At least in partial measure, Gandhi's prediction has come true, especially in the case of Pakistan, where both the state and the state religion are wobbly. The policy of eradicating or converting minorities has indirectly resulted in ruining Pakistan itself whereas India's pluralism is now so much more vibrant, attractive and viable. The continuous state of hostility between India and Pakistan has, however, proved costly and debilitating for both states. Gandhi seems almost to have prophesied this in his prayer meeting of 18 December 1947:

'It should not be our fate to be eternal enemies of each other. It will only end in our ruin'.[36]

But Gandhi was not blind to the fanatical streak in Islam, though it pained him greatly:

> I saw a couplet in an Urdu magazine today. It hurt me. I do not remember the words but the substance is this: 'Today Somnath is on the tongue of everyone. If the temple is renovated it will have to be avenged. A new Ghazni must come from Ghazni to avenge what happened in Junagadh.' It is painful to think that such a thing can issue from the pen of a Muslim.[37]

It is clear that Gandhi would not have regarded Mahmud Ghazni, who raided India 17 times, sacking the famous Somnath temple among many others more than once, a great or good Muslim. But did that help the victims of Ghazni or change the hearts of those who espoused his brand of Islam? To this sort of question, Gandhi had only one answer: 'I have said that I must do or die; which means that I shall either bring about Hindu–Muslim amity or lay down my life'.[38] The rabid anti-Hindu sentiments of some Muslims was not going to change Gandhi: 'This sort of thing cannot affect my resolve. I cannot return evil for evil. I can only return good for evil'.[39] To those who might react with anger or hostility to such sentiments, he added, 'I tell you all this so that you may not be taken in by such things. You must not remember the wrong that Ghaznavi did'.[40] But almost as if to make sure that Hindu fanatics might not use such statements to condemn him for weakening Hindus, Gandhi added, 'Muslims should realize and admit the wrongs perpetrated under the Islamic rule'.[41] Nothing of the sort has, of course, ever happened. There is no Indian equivalent of the Truth and Reconciliation Commission of South Africa, which helped to heal the wounds of apartheid after the collapse of the latter. Such a process has never happened between Hindus and Muslims in India. Instead, there is denial and appeasement in India, while in Pakistan there is unashamed and continued aggression and the promotion of militarist Islam.

No surprise that Gandhi, from time to time, admonished Indian Muslims too, asking them to be more patriotic or responsible. On 14 January 1947, he told a Maulana who wanted the Government to send him to England if they could not protect him in India, and who felt that British colonialism was better than independence:

> Do you not feel ashamed of asking to be sent to England? And then you said that slavery under the British rule was better than independence under the Union of India. How dare you, who claim to be patriots and nationalists, utter such words? You have to cleanse your hearts and learn to be cent per cent truthful. Otherwise India will not tolerate you for long and even I shall not be able to help you.[42]

The charge of appeasement and favouritism is thus misplaced. Gandhi was clear that the Muslims who remained in India should be patriotic, even willing to defend the country or fight with fellow-Muslim Pakistanis, in case of a war. In the prayer meeting on the same day, Gandhi stated that it was wrong to say that he wanted to weaken Hindus: 'I want everyone to become strong'.[43] As he said in his prayer meeting the day before he died, 'Why do you presume that I do not understand the sufferings of the refugees? Why do you presume that because I am a friend of Muslims I am an enemy of Hindus and Sikhs?'[44] This, indeed, is the false binary that Gandhi wished to undo: to be a friend of Muslims meant automatically to be the enemy of Hindus and Sikhs, and vice versa. He wanted to reassert the possibility that one could be well disposed towards both. But such a position was unacceptable either to Godse or to the League.

On 13 January 1948, the day Gandhi started his fast, a train carrying Hindus and Sikhs from Bannu was ambushed by tribesmen at the Gujarat, in West Punjab. The assigned escort of troops could not defend the train. Hundreds were killed and maimed; many women and girls were abducted. In anguish, Gandhi said in his prayer meeting that afternoon:

> What has happened in Karachi? Innocent Sikhs were murdered and their properties looted. Now I understand the same thing has happened in Gujrat. There was a caravan coming from Bannu or somewhere. They were all refugees running away to save their lives. They were waylaid and cut down. I do not want to relate this grim tale. I ask the Muslims if in their name this kind of thing continues in Pakistan, how long will the people in India tolerate it [?].[45]

There was after all, he was telling the Muslims, a limit to the tolerance of Hindus and Sikhs. He was urging the Muslims to act, to do something to stop such attacks. He warned, 'Even if a hundred men like me fasted they would not be able to stop the tragedy that may follow'.[46] 'It is impossible', he added, 'to save the Muslims in the Union if the Muslim majority in Pakistan do not behave as decent men and women'.[47] Towards the end of his life, speaking at the Urs of Khwaja Qutubudin Bakhtiyar Kaki in Mehrauli, which he himself had intervened in to save from protesting Hindus, Gandhi said, 'Only today I have read that Hindus have been killed in the Frontier. The Muslims here should be ashamed of it'.[48] He did not hesitate to scold Muslims, just as he criticized Hindus and Sikhs.

Gandhi was not unaware that Hindus and Sikhs were upset with him for his insistence on their 'making up' with the Muslims. He even acknowledged, as in his prayer meeting of 28 December 1947, that he was called 'mad' for saying so:

> I say we should not treat Muslims as enemies. But people turn away from me. They say I am mad. I must say that if the masses do not listen to me they will be doing harm to their dharma.

I say nothing improper. Tulsidas says that compassion is the essence of religion. You may say that Tulsidas was mad but no other book is as popular in the country as his *Ramayana*. It is not only in Bihar or in Delhi where it is popular, it is read everywhere. I only repeated what Tulsidas said. Why then do they say that I am mad?[49]

Gandhi's 'madness' was of course quite different, quite the opposite of the madness of the mobs of feuding Hindus and Muslims. As Gandhi put it in his prayer meeting on New Year's Eve, 1947:

After all madness seized us only after it had seized people in Pakistan. I shall not go into the various stages and degrees of madness. If sanity does not return we shall lose both India and Pakistan. There will be a war.[50]

He pleaded with the Hindus and Sikhs, 'To you, brothers, I shall only say, do not let yourselves become mad'.[51] It was almost as if he was positing his own kind of loving, compassionate, non-violent madness against the murderous madness of the communities in conflict. Kartar Singh, who came with a Sikh delegation, said: 'Afflicted men cannot be balanced men. Everybody cannot be a Mahatma Gandhi',[52] but could everyone also descend to levels of barbarism? Which madness was 'easier'?

Gandhi even wanted the people who had left their homes and migrated to the other side to come back. He believed that there could be no peace if the transfer of populations was not stopped and reversed:

They point out that transfer of populations of such magnitude cannot be reversed. I do not hold this view. Even if I am the only one to say it I shall still say that so long as people do not go back to their homes there will be no peace in the two countries.[53]

Gandhi's hopes were belied, even his fears have come true. The displaced people never came back; it is true that India and Pakistan are still not at peace. It is here that Gandhi's notion of the Partition as a never-healing wound has been proven correct by history:

> All the comforts you can provide to the Sikh and Hindu refugees are not going to heal the wounds they have suffered. It will be a matter of perpetual distress to them that they have lost their hearths and homes and if there is a war in fifty years' time or a hundred years' time, they are going to remember this. Such things are not forgotten.[54]

How right Gandhi was. Neither side has forgotten; indeed, so many years after, there is still an outpouring of writing on the subject, in addition to a serious scholarly interest in it. In his letter of 2 January 1948 to Jaisukhlal Gandhi, Gandhi liked the situation to a 'fiery pit' where anything could happen; he was sure, though, that he would have to 'do or die. There is no third way'.[55] He appealed to his listeners, 'How can I go to Pakistan so long as we are behaving here as they do in Pakistan? I can only go to Pakistan after India has cleansed herself'.[56]

Gandhi also spelled out his vision of a pluralistic India in which all communities would be entitled to equality and dignity, regardless of their religious affiliations. Writing in the Gujarati *Harijanbandhu* of 18 January 1948, he said:

> All Hindus, Muslims, Sikhs, Parsis, Christians and Jews who people this country from Kanyakumari to Kashmir and from Karachi to Dibrugarh in Assam and who have lovingly and in a spirit of service adopted it as their dear motherland, have an equal right to it. No one can say that it has place only for the majority and the minority should be dishonoured.[57]

It is interesting how he still includes Karachi in his idea of India. The Partition, obviously, was neither a settled fact, nor the new borders of India and Pakistan uncrossable.

On 16 January 1948, three days into Gandhi's fast, the Government of India reversed a Cabinet decision to withhold the 55 crores owed to Pakistan as a part of its share of the finances of undivided India. The Indian Government had withheld the money after Pakistan-backed raiders invaded Kashmir. It was a way of putting pressure on Pakistan to desist from its acts of aggression. However, taking its cue from Gandhi's pleas to show generosity and goodwill, the Government issued a communiqué explaining its change on the earlier position enunciated by Vallabhbhai Patel in his statement to the press on 12 January 1948.[58] Gandhi welcomed this gesture as 'large hearted' but hastened to add, 'This is no policy of appeasement of the Muslims'.[59] He argued, instead, that 'This is a policy, if you like, of self-appeasement'.[60] Gandhi elaborated that 'No Cabinet worthy of being representative of a large mass of mankind can afford to take any step merely because it is likely to win the hasty applause of an unthinking public'.[61] This unusual and far-reaching step, according to Gandhi, was an assertion of 'sanity' in 'the midst of insanity':

> In the midst of insanity, should not our best representatives retain sanity and bravely prevent a wreck of the ship of State under their management? What then was the actuating motive? It was my fast. It changed the whole outlook. Without the fast they could not go beyond what the law permitted and required them to do. But the present gesture on the part of the Government of India is one of unmixed goodwill. It has put the Pakistan Government on its honour. It ought to lead to an honourable settlement not only of the Kashmir question, but of all the differences between the two Dominions. Friendship should replace the present enmity.[62]

This, was the last straw, so to speak, as far as the Hindu right was concerned. The conspirators' bomb attack on Gandhi took place four days later, on 20 January 1948. But surely their plot was already in process, since they had been planning the assassination for several months. To pin the blame on the release of 55 crores to Pakistan, as Gopal Godse claimed, is dishonest and misleading.[63] Rather, it added one more excuse to do away with the Mahatma. Gandhi, on the other hand, persisted in his belief that trusting even one's adversary was a mark of the brave: 'we should trust even those whom we may suspect as our enemies. Brave people disdain distrust'.[64] Gandhi's ideal, even in the face of such bitter and bloody clashes, was as uncompromisingly utopian as ever: 'The letter of my vow will be satisfied if the Hindus, Muslims and Sikhs of Delhi bring about a union, which not even a conflagration around them in all the other parts of India or Pakistan will be strong enough to break'.[65] In the process, he set a high standard on the success of his *yajna* in Delhi. To his credit, there has been no communal riot in Delhi, even in the worst of times, between Muslims and Hindus. The pogrom against the Sikhs in the wake of Indira Gandhi's assassination in 1984 was a different matter, with organized mobs led by leaders of a political party, but there was no outbreak of Hindu–Muslim violence. It would seem that the truce brokered by Gandhi between the two communities has still endured.

On his part, like a true Bania, Gandhi wondered how the Pakistanis would reciprocate India's generosity in transferring the 55 crores: 'In the name of the people, our Government have taken a liberal step without counting the cost. What will be Pakistan's countergesture? The ways are many if there is the will. Is it there?'.[66] Instead, the Finance Minister of Pakistan, Ghulam Mohammad, responded, 'I am glad that Mahatma Gandhi's efforts have been fruitful and that he has succeeded in making the Government of India see the error of its ways and save it from a most untenable position'.[67] We might as well ask, where was the counter-gesture? There was none. Perhaps Gandhi was wrong and India had lost one of its key bargaining points with a country whose enmity has continued over the last six-and-a-half decades.

In the last few days of his life, Gandhi continuously emphasized the idea that Hindu–Muslim friendship was the only guarantee to safeguard the future of the two new nations. This became the enduring insight of his experiments in quelling the violence of the Partition. For instance, in his prayer meeting of 18 January, the day he ended his fast, he said:

> My reason and my heart tell me that if for some reason or other we are unable to forge friendship between Hindus and Muslims, not only here but also in Pakistan and in the whole world, we shall not be able to keep India for long. It will pass into the hands of others and become a slave country again. Pakistan too will become a slave country and the freedom we have gained will be lost again.[68]

Internal dissension was the cause of external rule; and if Hindus and Muslims could not get along, the independence of both nations would be lost. In the meanwhile, both communities had to confront all the horrors they had perpetrated on one another and, if possible, repent:

> In the name of God we have indulged in lies, massacres of people, without caring whether they were innocent or guilty, men or women, children or infants. We have indulged in abductions, forcible conversions and we have done all this shamelessly. I am not aware if anybody has done these things in the name of Truth.[69]

If truth were to be told, then the God in whose name such atrocities had been committed was a dangerous idea; truth is God, the reversal of Gandhi's original formula, God is truth, might be a better bet in this case. And the deadly truth was that the God in whose name all these horrors were committed could not be God at all – this, no less, is the radical import of Gandhi's statement.

Gandhi ended his fast only after he was faced with a massive upsurge of public support. A noted historian of the Partition, Gyanendra Pandey, notes:

> On the fifth day of the fast, 100,000 government employees, who had been to the fore in both pro-Pakistani and anti-Pakistani propaganda in Delhi since 1946, signed a pledge promising to work for peace and appealing to Gandhi to break his fast. The police signed a separate pledge. Among others who had more or less openly opposed Gandhi up to this point, representatives of the RSS and the Hindu Mahasabha arrived with leaders of various Sikh and Muslim organisations, the Pakistani High Commissioner, and the chief commissioner and deputy commissioner of Delhi (who signed on behalf of the administration) to pledge their acceptance of the basic demands set out by Gandhi and to urge him to now break his fast.[70]

Gandhi was touched by this wave of concern and solidarity, but he was not entirely convinced about its lasting impact.

On 23 January 1948, Gandhi acknowledged Subhas Chandra Bose on his birthday. Bose had raised an army against the British with Japanese support. Though Gandhi disliked violence and Japanese imperialism, he praised the communal harmony that was the basis of Subhas's practice:

> The soldiers of that army included Hindus, Muslims, Parsis and Christians. He never considered himself only a Bengali. He had no use for parochialism or caste distinctions. In his eyes all were Indians and servants of India. He treated all alike. It never occurred to him that since he was the commander he deserved more and others less. Let us therefore in remembering Subhas think of his great virtues and purge our hearts of malice.[71]

On 26 January 1948, he spoke of the meaning of independence on what had been traditionally observed as Independence Day by the Congress Party, once again insisting that Hindu–Muslim friendship was the only way to preserve the Union. Independence, he admitted, had been disillusioning: 'Now we have handled it [independence] and we seem to be disillusioned. At least I am, even if you are not. What are we celebrating today? Surely not our disillusionment'.[72] Gandhi, spelling out his vision of Svaraj, once again said that villagers and city dwellers would be on equal footing:

> we are on the road to showing the lowliest of the villager that it means his freedom from serfdom and that he is no longer a serf born to serve the cities and towns of India but that he is destined to exploit the city-dwellers for the advertisement of the finished fruits of well-thought-out labours, that he is the salt of the Indian earth and that it means also equality of all classes and creeds, never the domination and superiority of the major community over a minor, however insignificant it may be in numbers or influence.[73]

What is more, he even wished for Indo-Pakistani friendship, a dream that has still not been fulfilled:

> Before leaving this topic of the day, let us permit ourselves to hope that though geographically and politically India is divided into two, at heart we shall ever be friends and brothers helping and respecting one another and be one for the outside world.[74]

On the day he was killed, Gandhi actually admitted that he feared that the fate of quarrelling Hindus and Muslims would be like the legendary Yadavas, whose head and hero was Krishna:

> Wherever I look I find our plight the same as that of the Yadavas who met their doom killing one another. No one

realizes how much harm we are doing to society by being engaged in our personal feuds. But what can you or anyone else do about it? This indicates a failure on my part. What could anyone do when God made me blind to these things?[75]

Gandhi had, it would seem, a premonition that his efforts would not yield results, at least just yet, because not all the members of the two communities had realized that fighting with each other would be self-defeating.

In retrospect it does seem as if Gandhi's was the last, and an almost superhuman, effort to bring about a unity between Hindus and Muslims in the subcontinent. The failure of this effort was evident even to him in his last days. But he did not give up on the somewhat more modest goal of peaceful coexistence, if not friendly relations, between the two communities.[76] Hindu nationalists and supremacists considered Gandhi's efforts at securing Hindu–Muslim amity as attempts to appease and favour the Muslims. Like their Muslim counterparts who wanted to defeat India militarily, these groups also cherished dreams of Hindu dominion and domination over Muslims. While Gandhi did not favour aggression under any circumstances, he did support a principled self-defence, both through non-violent and, failing that, violent means. Non-aggression combined with principled self-defence is the hallmark of Svaraj. We do not wish to rule or dominate others, but this does not mean that we are weak or incapable of protecting ourselves from those who wish to rule or dominate us. But it is a precarious balance, even in favourable circumstances, with the scales easily dipping to one side or the other in times of stress or crisis.

24   The art of dying

While it is untrue to say that Gandhi came to Delhi with the conscious intention to die, it is perhaps not an exaggeration to claim that he was preparing himself for such an eventuality. In his last 133 days he repeated his resolve to 'do or die' probably 50 times. Early on, in a piece in *Harijan* called 'One Step is Enough for Me', published on 22 September 1947, he calmly contemplated the eventuality with remarkable foresight and fortitude, but without any hint of a violent termination:

> My death can take place in three ways: 1. The usual dissolution of the body. 2. Only the eyes move but the mind no longer works. 3. The body and mind may work but I may withdraw from all public activity. The first kind overtakes everybody – some die today, others tomorrow. It demands no consideration. The second variety is to be wished by or for nobody. I for one do not wish for any such imbecile state. It is a burden on earth. The third variety does demand serious consideration. Some readers suggest that the period of my active life should be over now. A new age for India began on 15th August last. There is no place for me in that age.[1]

What is clear is that Gandhi does not want to die helpless and disabled, a burden upon others, but he does not mind withdrawing or retiring from public life. He is quite convinced of his own irrelevance to the new age that has dawned with India's independence and the Partition of the country. Gandhi is also increasingly aware of his sense of helplessness, the waning of his ability to influence policy or change the way the new governments of India and Pakistan behave. As he confesses in his discussion with Kripalani on 25 September 1947, 'I have become useless because I cannot make the Pakistan authorities do the right thing'.[2] Yet it is also clear from this conversation, as it was from his very first prayer meeting on 9 September 1947, that he was far from retiring or quitting. Instead, he was already in the middle of his last *yajna* in which the key assumption was that Delhi was India in miniature; if Delhi could be persuaded to turn around, then the rest of the country might be saved; the repercussions might also cross the border to Pakistan. If that were to happen, Gandhi was prepared to go to Pakistan himself, taking his mission of peace there. As he said to Kripalani, 'If normalcy is restored in Delhi I would like to go and die there'.[3] But the crucial part of this conversation was his assertion about knowing how to die: 'I am not being arrogant when I say that I know the art of dying but I have the courage to say it'.[4] That his remark was not a sign of hubris was clear by his brutal modesty and the exacting self-appraisal that followed:

> But God alone knows if I will run away when I am being shot at or attacked with knives or will get angry with the attacker. If this happens then also there is no harm because the people will come to know that the man they looked upon as a Mahatma was not a true Mahatma. I too shall come to know where I stand. It is possible that I may still utter 'Rama Rama' when I am shot at or attacked. Let the outcome be either; ultimately it will be for good.[5]

When it came to the decisive moment, Gandhi went just as he had predicted, exiting according to his own script right down to the last words.

As the days went by, his inner resolve to make this his final confrontation with the forces of communal hatred and violence became firmer. In the fragment of a letter of 11 November 1947, he said: 'Maybe my end is approaching. I am fully prepared. Everyone should be prepared'.[6] But with this came also the growing conviction that he was on the right track, that the final task he had set for himself was the natural culmination of a life dedicated not only to the building of a nation but also to ensuring a certain kind of future for it with his last sacrifice. As he added in another fragment of a letter dated 15 November 1947, 'The more I look within the more I feel that God is with me'.[7] Again, this quiet inner conviction goes contrary to the view that he was either deeply depressed or delusive in this final phase. Instead, a gradual clarity was emergent within as to what he must do for the cause to which he had dedicated his life. In the *Harijan* of 23 November 1947 he continued his reflections on an appropriate end to a life lived according to certain principles, upholding the kind of values that he had espoused: 'Life becomes liveable only to the extent that death is treated as a friend, never as an enemy'.[8] He had begun, like Socrates, to argue that life was worth living only on certain conditions, not under all circumstances:

> To conquer life's temptations, summon death to your aid. In order to postpone death a coward surrenders honour, wife, daughter and all. A courageous man prefers death to the surrender of self-respect. . . . A beginning is always made by a few, even one.[9]

Postponing death, clinging to an ignoble life, was meaningless. Embracing death as a friend was the only way for a principled man to be able to resist evil without fear. All that someone might threaten you with was your life. Once you were prepared to lose that, nothing could cow you down.

He insisted that he would rather die than be a mute and helpless witness to the fires of hatred and destruction raging all about him. On his seventy-eighth birthday, he asked his listeners to pray that 'either the present conflagration should end or He should take me away'.[10] He had no wish to live on to watch the undoing and destruction of all that he had stood for: 'I do not wish another birthday to overtake me in an India still in flames'.[11] In anguish he asked Patel, 'What sin must I have committed that He should have kept me alive to witness all these horrors?'.[12] In his prayer meeting on 25 November 1947, he admitted: 'Today I am very much disturbed. My life has become a burden to me. I wonder why I am still here. I could become strong if Delhi were restored to sanity'.[13] In a fragment of a letter written on the same day, upon hearing that Khwaja Abdul Majid, President of the All-India Muslim Majlis, was attacked when he tried to intervene to stop the violence, Gandhi replied, 'Had they killed you, I would have danced (with joy). And by dying you would have rendered service both to Muslims and Hindus'.[14] For the *yajna* that he was conducting he wanted others to similarly offer themselves as sacrifice. Only several such pure-hearted self-immolations in the cause of non-violence might bring about a change of heart of the sort he wanted.

In another letter written on 21 December 1947, he said in his prayer meeting,

> I am not certain how long I shall have to be here. I must do or die. And since I am resolved to die I do pray to God that He may fulfil the wish. All of you too should make the same prayer.[15]

He added that he had no doubt, but calm certainty, that his was the right course of action in trying to bring peace and normalcy back to Delhi. He felt that he was merely an instrument of the divine in such an endeavour: 'In the end it will be as Rama commands me. Thus I dance as He pulls the strings. I am in His hands and so I am experiencing ineffable peace'.[16] In a letter written on 2 January

1948, he offered yet another iteration of his view of life and death, before offering up his own life to bring about communal harmony:

> No one can harm another. In my view man is himself the cause of his sufferings. . . . Why is it that the freedom achieved through non-violence is sought to be sustained by violence? I have been searching my heart. I find despair there. Maybe it was the will of God that I should witness this day. Now I have to do or die.[17]

Again, in his in his prayer meeting of 9 January 1948, Gandhi averred:

> We should not fear death. We must fear dishonour and indignity. To save one's honour one must lay down one's life. If someone is asked to embrace Islam or be prepared to die, he must choose death.[18]

If we all lived as if death were preferable to dishonour, the world would be a different kind of place. In the context of the violence of Partition, Gandhi believed that a certain kind of noble death was better than either cowardly victimhood or cowardly brutality. He made Hindu–Muslim rapprochement and the ending of communal violence the precondition of his continuing to live; rather than seeing the freedom so hard-won being squandered away in a blood feud between Hindus and Muslims, Gandhi preferred to die:

> Death for me would be a glorious deliverance rather than that I should be a helpless witness of the destruction of India, Hinduism, Sikhism and Islam. That destruction is certain if Pakistan does not ensure equality of status and security of life and property for all professing the various faiths of the world and if India copies her.[19]

Devdas, his youngest son, had tried to dissuade him from embarking upon his fast. In his reply on 14 January 1948, the day after he had started his fast, he said: 'So long as we are unable to leave aside the question of life and death it is an illusion to think that we can do a particular thing only if we are alive'.[20] Gandhi was already seeing embodiment as a limitation and was considering the possibility of a more effective afterlife when released from the body.

What Gandhi meant, of course, was that the cause that he had spelled out was worth dying for rather than continuing to live having accepted its failure or impossibility. He spoke about the inevitability of death in his prayer meeting of 15 January 1948:

> He who is born cannot escape death. Why then should we fear death or grieve over it? It is my belief that death is a friend to whom we should be grateful, for it frees us from the manifold ills which are our lot.[21]

Death here is a release from the ills of the world.

Meanwhile, with mounting anti-Gandhi feelings in a section of the Hindu and Sikh refugees, there were increased concerns for his safety. G. D. Birla, his host, was also concerned at Gandhi's reluctance to increase the security at his residence, where Gandhi was staying. Gandhi wrote to him:

> it is all the same to me whether there are or there are not all these police and military personnel posted here for my protection. Because it is Rama who protects me and I become more and more convinced that everything else is futile.[22]

Sardar Patel, the Home Minister of India and a close associate of Gandhi, had already received information about a conspiracy to assassinate Gandhi after the bomb explosion on 20 January 1948. He moved to enhance the security cover at Birla House by posting army and police personnel along with plain-clothes men.

But Gandhi refused to allow all those entering the compound to be searched. After the assassination, Patel made a statement in Parliament on 6 February 1948, where he reported:

> the D.I.G. met Gandhiji and represented to him that there was danger and they should be allowed the facilities asked for, otherwise they would be discredited if anything untoward happened, but Gandhiji would not agree. He said that his life was in the hands of God, that if he had to die, no precautions could save him and that he would not agree to anybody being restricted from coming to prayer meetings or anybody being allowed to come between his audience and himself. I myself pleaded with Gandhiji for allowing the police to do their duty in regard to his protection, but without success.[23]

But this justification after the fact seems somewhat weak, if not unconvincing. As Home Minister, Patel should have taken whatever measures he deemed necessary to protect Gandhi without seeking the latter's approval. After all, nowhere in the world is the protection of leaders left entirely to their own whims or oddities.

Gandhi, no doubt, was courting death. He was convinced that if his offering himself to the forces of hatred and violence might save thousands of lives, then it was well worth making. It was as if the monster of Hindu–Muslim enmity wanted some price before it would quieten and he was willing to be the scapegoat. He began to reduce his reliance on human and worldly agencies, placing his trust entirely in God. As he wrote in response to the letter from a young man: 'If God wants to save me He will do so'.[24] But even more importantly, 'The death of a non-violent man will always have desirable consequences'.[25] That such a sacrifice may be insufficient was not lost on him: 'But when Krishna was no more the Yadavas did not become better and purer. They destroyed themselves in fratricidal strife. I shall not weep over it'.[26] To resist evil even with one's own life was a duty, an end in itself, even if it did not yield the desired fruit in the real world. Having done one's best, one had no reason to lament over the failure of one's actions. Gandhi repeated the allusion to the destruction of the Yadavas that is mentioned in the Mahabharata. He feared that like these accursed clansmen of Krishna, the Hindus and Muslims, who were equally dear to him, would also destroy each other after he was gone.

In another letter dated 24 January 1948, he once again asserted that his life was not his any more and that he had already 'arranged' for a certain kind of death: 'I will do His work so long as He wills. I shall have won if I am granted a death whereby I can demonstrate the strength of truth and non-violence'.[27] He reflected on the bomb that was exploded on 20 January 1948 with the intention of killing him. Gandhi had continued the prayer meeting without flinching. Now he refused to take any credit for his courage and heroism:

> I did not display any courage in what happened on the 20th. I thought it was part of some army exercise. Had I known that it was an intimation of my death I cannot tell how I might have reacted. So I am not yet a mahatma. What does it matter if people describe me as one? I am only an ordinary mortal.[28]

But in the very next sentence, he raises the bar for himself when the end really comes:

> Yes, if I have been sincere in my pursuit of truth, non-violence, nonstealing, *brahmacharya* and so on and if I have done all this with God as my witness, I shall certainly be granted the kind of death that I seek. I have expressed the wish at the prayer meeting also that should someone kill me I may have no anger against the killer in my heart and I may die with Ramanama on my lips.[29]

Again, Gandhi is scripting his own death in considerable detail. In a fragment of a letter written a few days before he was murdered, he repeated,

But this can only be if I can joyfully take a volley of bullets. I do not think that I deserve to be congratulated on what happened on the 20th. It was only God's blessing. But I am fully prepared to go when the summons comes.[30]

On 30 January 1948, the day he was murdered, Gandhi gave his energy to another big problem that was confronting the Indian Government: the rift between Nehru and Patel. In *Gandhi's Emissary* Sudhir Ghosh remembers his meeting with Gandhi on the morning of 30 January:

As I sat down he handed to me a letter written to him by Agatha Harrison enclosing with it a clipping from the London *Times*. Agatha's letter said that the whispering campaign about a serious rift between his two lieutenants Mr. Nehru and Vallabhbhai Patel had spread to London and *The Times* editorial on this rift between the two men was a bad omen; was Gandhiji not going to do something about it?[31]

Gandhi himself was aware of this and had already referred to it in one of his prayer meetings, on 20 January 1948. He realized that healing this breach was of fundamental importance not only to the smooth running of the Cabinet but also to maintaining the public perception that the Government was united. Ghosh continues:

'I wonder what I am going to do about it' – as if asking himself a question. I said, 'Well they are so big that nobody dares to talk to them about it; but people talk behind their backs. Some day you may like to talk to both of them about it. You alone can do it.' He pondered over my remark and said, 'Well, there is something in what you say. I think I am going to talk about it. I think I will talk about it after prayers this evening.'[32]

As it happened, Patel was to see Gandhi at 4:00 in the afternoon and Nehru at 7:00. He was with Patel when he was called away to the prayer meeting, on the way to which he was killed. He never got to see Nehru.

But in his death, the two stalwarts of the Congress Party and the most powerful members of the Cabinet were reunited. During the funeral procession and ceremonies both were seen together and were, indeed, together in spirit in Manubehn's account *The End of an Epoch*. Patel sat with the body in the gun carriage while Nehru led the procession and sat in the carriage by turns.[33] Nehru was asked to light the pyre but Ramdas Gandhi, Gandhi's son, did so at Nehru's behest. When the pyre was lit, however, the blaze was so intense that all the onlookers had to step away:

> Very soon, the pyre was ablaze. The wind fanned the fire and the flames soared high. The fire became too hot for people to stay near it. It seemed as if the flames were reprimanding us for our sins and telling us that the great world citizen whom it was now transporting to another world, was a victim of the wicked passions that consume us humans. The flames seemed to be telling us that we had no right to go near one who had tried to rid society of its passions, but had, alas! died in the attempt. And so the flames kept us away from Bapuji.[34]

Gandhi burned alone in his solitary anguish and splendour.

25 From repression to redemption?

Gandhi's life and death have by now entered the realms of legend and myth. The logic and ethos of post-independence India is considerably different from that of the freedom struggle. Ours is an age of disillusionment and cynicism, if the freedom struggle was one of idealism and hope. Writing about the reception of the stories of the Puranas in a later age, R. H. Zimmer says: 'But the myths of the Puranas come down to us reshaped by a definitely post-heroic, anti-tragic age of Indian religion and philosophy'.[1] Similarly, our understanding of Gandhi is also shaped by our own scepticism about the perfectibility of the human condition, both personal and political. Many of Gandhi's ideas, beliefs and projects, therefore, seem not just antiquated, but quaint. The present 'religion' of India, which to all appearances seems to be consumerism, is at considerable odds with Gandhi's virtue-orientation and emancipatory commitment. But both Gandhi's life and his death will continue to disturb, puzzle and challenge us. The latter especially, as we have seen, was designed to provoke and haunt us as only the Oedipal, taboo-breaking patricide of the murder of the Father of the Nation might.

But in the manner and matter of his death, Gandhi not only brought peace to Delhi and to India, but also gave a definite shape to the future of a new nation. As Gyanendra Pandey observes in *Remembering Partition: Violence, Nationalism and History in India*:

> Perhaps Gandhi's arrival in Delhi was the turning point; perhaps his intervention gave to secular nationalist elements the moral strength they needed to renew the fight for the composite and tolerant India that so many had dreamed of; perhaps his very presence stunned the government and an army of stupefied Congress workers into action.[2]

Gandhi's presence and actions galvanized the dispirited and derailed leadership to reiterate its commitment to a democratic and secular country, where many varieties of faiths, ethnicities and cultures could have a place and feel secure. But in the atmosphere of hostility and conflict after the Partition, it was Gandhi's presence in Delhi that ensured that Muslims were accorded the status of full citizens of the Indian Union rather than being looked at with suspicion and pushed out of the country.

Pandey quotes how a Muslim gentleman described Gandhi's arrival in Delhi: '*Sukhe dhanon mein pani pad gaya*' ('Water sprinkled on dry seeds').[3] After Gandhi's arrival in Delhi, no major outbreak of violence or rioting occurred in the city. Pandey continues:

> In the event, the fast, and Gandhi's subsequent martyrdom, did work something like a miracle. The demand for continued Partition, for the driving of every Muslim out of every part of Delhi, lost its immediate appeal; many Muslims were able to return to their homes and mohallas, and perhaps for the first time since late 1946, the people of Delhi began to return to the business of living and of rebuilding their lives, their uprooted city and their future.[4]

Maulana Azad wrote that the impact of Gandhi's fast was 'electric', and Qidwai, another eyewitness that Pandey quotes, observed 'contrition written on people's faces, a stoop in their walk, tears in their eyes';[5] another Muslim, after Gandhi's death, remarked, '*Duniya hi badal gayi*' ('The world itself changed').[6] Indeed, Pandey contends that 'Gandhi achieved through his death even more than he had achieved through his fast':

> His success at this juncture conveys an unusual message about the meaning of politics and the possibility of a new kind of political community. It is an improbable story of how a certain kind of bodily sacrifice in the public sphere – and a refusal by one outstanding leader to give his consent to the particular conception of the political community that was emerging – changed the nature of sociality at the local level. . . . The assassination of Gandhi wiped out the blaze of Hindu-Muslim violence in such a way that 'the world veritably changed'. The fire of sectarian strife that had raged for months, or rather years, died down as if such strife had never occurred.[7]

If we examine the record, we shall have to agree with Pandey and historians like him about what Gandhi accomplished in the kind of death he chose for himself.

But this extended meditation on the death of Gandhi must now be interrupted. A journey like this does not have a destination, or at any rate one fixed closure: if it has a direction then it is from repression to redemption. The whole country, as we have seen, wants to avoid confronting the meaning of Gandhi's death. This patricidal act is 'unbearable' to Hindus in particular and is repressed deep into the recesses of their collective psyche. But the event also had profound implications for the Muslims of the subcontinent, especially for the state of Pakistan. For the one take-away from Gandhi's death is that Hindu–Muslim amity is the precondition for peace in the subcontinent. At the state level this will mean an Indo-Pak entente, spelled out and adhered to sincerely by both parties. Thanks in great measure to Gandhi, India both as nation and people, did not become a mirror image of Pakistan. After 67 years of independence, it is fairly obvious which model is preferred by the large majority of the people of South Asia: India's pluralism, religious tolerance and freedom seem a much more attractive bet, while Pakistan's Islamism, despotism and militarism stand discredited both within that country and in the region. Gandhi's death also ought to make Hindus reflect upon who they wish to be: insecure, defensive, mistrustful, aggressive and domineering, or self-confident, open, trusting, non-aggressive and egalitarian.

Gandhi's murder and the Partition of India, of which it was the most poignant symbol, put the two newly independent nations in a state of permanent pollution, from which the only release is through a process of repentance and commitment to peaceful coexistence. The defilement and impurity wrought by hatred in our hearts needs to be cleansed through a renewed commitment to a non-sectarian, democratic, plural and humane society implied in Gandhi's idea of Svaraj. We have the capacity to recreate our future by revisiting and reinterpreting our past. Such has been the main attempt of this book. But as there are multiple narratives of Gandhi's life, there will also be multiple narratives of his death, with this one far from claiming to be definitive or final. Here, by looking at the manner in which the Mahatma has been memorialized, we have tried to tease out why and how he died. Gandhi died once, though he has been killed many times over, by those who hated him and what he stood for – as if killing him once was not enough or killing him over and over again would actually finish him off. But what did his death mean? It is this question that we have tried to address and answer. Gandhi showed us a way to be modern without denying our traditions, how to be an inclusive and non-hierarchical nation, how to flower as individuals without losing entirely our characteristically communitarian and collective way of living. He also showed us how to be secular and deeply religious at the same time, how to be Sanatani Hindus without hating or disrespecting other religions, how to be Indian, even Asian, without opting out of a universal world culture. Perhaps it is a gynocentric civilization such as ours which will have the strength and the courage to confront and overcome the shame of our patricidal act in slaying the Father of the Nation and turn it into a moment of continuous self-examination and transformation.

Epilogue[1]

At the end of this meditation on the meaning of the Mahatma's murder, perhaps it should become clearer that the question no longer is, 'Who killed Gandhi?' What matters is neither whose finger pulled the trigger nor whose hand did the deed, as much as *what* caused the calamitous fatality.

The facts are reasonably well-known, the evidence documented quite thoroughly. Questions of the wider conspiracy, of course, remain, as does the inconclusive link of the assassins with Vinayak Damodar 'Veer' Savarkar. The Government led by Jawaharlal Nehru, with Vallabhbhai Patel as the home minister – both Gandhi's closest aides and disciples – failed to protect the Mahatma, against whose life an unsuccessful attempt had already been made, by the very same band of assassins, just a few days before. Worse, the bungled police investigation of that attempted murder, marked by lack of coordination and communication between the Delhi and Bombay police, cannot be overlooked. The Congress-led Bombay Government's disregarding of vital information, given by a reliable informant to the then Bombay state premier B.G. Kher, and Home Minister Morarji Desai, himself a staunch Gandhian, specifically naming the conspirators, is even more damaging. The circle of responsibility, it is clear, is even wider, including power-seekers, aspirants for the spoils of office, members of the Congress

High Command, and party workers who considered Gandhi an obstacle to their aims and desires. Beyond these, the millions of Hindus, Muslims, Sikhs, and many others whose causes Gandhi had championed, including women and Dalits, those who regarded Gandhi as obscure, unnecessary, superfluous, obsolete, outdated, better out of, than in, the way – all these, indeed all of us, must shoulder some part of the burden of guilt, must answer in some measure howsoever small to *who* killed Gandhi. At the same time, Gandhi's own role in co-authoring and scripting his own martyrdom cannot be denied.

Yet, *who* killed Gandhi is not as germane after the event as *what* killed him. What killed him, as this book has tried to show, was the Partition of India. The causal link between the two is unmistakeable and incontrovertible. As early as April 1940, soon after the All India Muslim League adopted the so-called 'Pakistan Resolution' in its Lahore session of 22–24 March 1940, Gandhi had declared:

> As a man of non-violence I cannot forcibly resist the proposed partition if the Muslims of India really insist upon it. But I can never be a willing party to the vivisection. I would employ every non-violent means to prevent it . . .

> But that is my belief. I cannot thrust it down the throats of the Muslims who think that they are a different nation.[2]

In the end, despite all his efforts to prevent it, having to witness India divided into two nations, which were still at each other throats, Gandhi wondered why he continued to live, especially now that the vivisection seemed to be repeating itself endlessly in cycles of internecine violence. It might be accurate, therefore, to say that Gandhi put himself in the way of that recurring violence and bloodletting. While Gandhi did not, could not, stop the Partition of India, he did stay the Partition machine playing itself out repeatedly. He thwarted and stopped the calculus of endless violence by offering his life in return. Like the legendary Dadhichi rishi, out of whose bones were fashioned the weapons with which alone the Devas could overcome the Asuras, Gandhi offered his bones against the Rakshasas of Partition and communal violence.

Did he succeed? The subsequent history of the subcontinent shows that the Partition was not the 'final' solution to the problems of Hindus and Muslims. The 'two nation' theory, for all practical purposes, undid itself when Pakistan itself was partitioned into Bangladesh; religion alone, thus, proved insufficient to bond linguistically and ethnically diverse communities. As Gandhi said in the same statement in 1940 quoted above,

> Partition means a patent untruth. My whole soul rebels against the idea that Hinduism and Islam represent two antagonistic cultures and doctrines. To assent to such a doctrine is for me denial of God. For I believe with my whole soul that the God of the Koran is also the God of the Gita, and that we are all, no matter by what name designated, children of the same God. I must rebel against the idea that millions of Indians who were Hindus the other day changed their nationality on adopting Islam as their religion.[3]

But religion continues to be abused for political ends in the subcontinent, not just in India, Pakistan, or Bangladesh, but also in Sri Lanka, Nepal, and, of course, Afghanistan, which is perhaps the worst example of this. What, then, did the Partition achieve? Gandhi was right in resisting it, even in giving up his life to stop smaller scale partitions from replicating themselves all over the region.

Gandhi tried to bring the religious communities of the country together through an inter-denominational national religion which regarded all faith communities to be equally true and valid. But Gandhi's experiment in inter-faith theology failed. Perhaps he did not take seriously enough the doctrinal differences between religions, especially between Hindus and Muslims, nor their historical struggle against one another during the long centuries of Muslim rule in India.

Yet, once again, he was fundamentally right in his belief that there could be no lasting peace in the subcontinent unless Hindus and Muslims learned to coexist peacefully. Post-colonial and post-Partition India and Pakistan have been unable to find a new covenant, a new formula for lasting peace and mutuality, after they rejected the Gandhian invitation. It seems obvious that whenever and wherever efforts are made to find the means for such a pact, Gandhi will have to be remembered and reconsidered. No one tried longer, harder, or experimented more than he did for this cause. Even if his efforts did not succeed, any new ones will have to begin where he ended, taking into account his trials and errors.

What Gandhi also shows is that destroying or driving away minorities from our midst does not really solve communal conflict. In Pakistan, for example, where Hindus have been exterminated, converted, or driven out, Muslims are slaughtering Muslims. This means that when we are done with killing others, we turn upon ourselves. For the simple reason that violence against others is also violence against ourselves; in fact, there are no *others;* only ourselves, in our many plural and diverse varieties. This Gandhi knew well and practised ardently all his life. But we are very far from learning it. We still target those we see as Others not just to shore up our own identities, but to consolidate our notions of who we are or what our identities ought to be.

It is inconceivable that everyone in the world will belong to one religion. Even in one religion, all do not belong to the same sect. Diversity and plurality are therefore the perpetual conditions of human culture. The Indian subcontinent is no exception to this rule, being one of the most linguistically, ethnically, and religiously diverse parts of the world. If so, there is no other way than to learn to live with those who are different from us in religion, language, community, ethnicity, habits, culture, and so on. What, then, are the underlying values, principles, or norms of conduct that can ensure that we all live in relative peace and prosperity? Surely, the basis of such coexistence must be equality, mutual respect, and the recognition of the dignity of all – in a word, the principle of *ahimsa*, non-injury, or to put it even more radically, *love*.

Is there another way? Yes, perhaps a more rational articulation of rights and responsibilities, less demanding of love or any other 'higher' principle. That would be Gandhi's way too, though to him the former would have to be grounded in the latter, the rational in the spiritual, the civic in the heartfelt. But as an expert lawyer and negotiator, he always respected the legal, the constitution, and transactional, recognizing self-interest as a major determinant in human action. To Gandhi, however, sacrifice was superior to self-interest; he believed that sacrifice could conquer self-interest. He routinely expected human agents to rise to the occasion, to undergo suffering for values and causes that were higher than their mere self-interest; he considered such nobility natural to being human, not unreasonable or exceptional. Whether or not we go as far as Gandhi, it is apparent that the alternative, whether it is the domination, decimation, or defeat of others, cannot produce lasting peace or even coexistence between competing groups.

How, then, are ideologies that purport to bully, browbeat, and bludgeon others into submission to be thwarted and overcome? Gandhi devised *satyagraha*, a form of protest against the superior might of a colonial government. He helped destroy the imperial ideologies that undergird the empire. Against non-state actors like marauding or murderous mobs, this methodology did not work as well. This Gandhi realized in his last days. The state had to be strong, had to exercise its impartial authority to quell such communal clashes or outbreaks of violence. In our times, similarly, Gandhian *ahimsa* may not work with non-state terrorist organizations either. Some form of responsible counter-violence against such groups appears inevitable.

More immediately, Congress-style secularism has been rejected because it was perceived as no longer being fair or impartial. Instead, it was seen as hypocritical and cynical in playing community against community, pandering to and appeasing minorities in order to cobble a coalition of expedient and self-serving allies. What remains to be seen is if a majoritarian political formation, such as rules India at present, can deliver better governance and prove more effective in safeguarding the rights of all the stake-holders, including the so-called minorities. That, indeed, is the best-case argument in favour of Hindutva– Hinduism as a better guarantor of religious and cultural pluralism than pseudo-secularism. Similarly, when it comes to our external neighbourhood, will a stronger, more militaristic India be able to demand and enforce better relations with Pakistan? Gandhi was ahead of his times; the subcontinent was not ready for his idealism. But will the new realism of pragmatic majoritarianism succeed better?

Whatever the answers to such questions, it *is* certain that Partition ideologies produce horrors and destroy not just states, but societies. This has been shown not only in India, but in Pakistan, Sri Lanka, Nepal, and Bangladesh. Violence breeds violence; it does not end violence. The Partition killed Gandhi, but by willingly submitting to such a death, Gandhi overturned the mechanics of Partition, countering the engines of hatred, violence, domination, destruction, and death. Just as he did not live in vain, the Mahatma did not die in vain either. This is attested to not only by his life, but much more so by his death and afterlife.

Notes

Preface to the paperback edition

1. This is the view of a minority within the Hindu right. The Rashtriya Swayamsevak Sangh, right from M.S. Golwarkar's condolence letters to Jawaharlal Nehru and Vallabhbhai Patel, not only condemns the assassination, but considers Gandhi one of the greatest heroes of the Hindu nation. His name figures in the litany of Hindu heroes commemorated daily in their *shakhas*. Their ideological affiliate, the Bharatiya Janata Party, has also adopted Gandhian *sarvodaya*, or welfare of all, as one of their foundational principles for the development of the country.

Prologue

1. To the Indian edition.
2. Gandhi 1999, Vol. 10: 243.
3. Ibid.: 243–244.
4. Ibid.: 244.
5. Ibid.

1.   Who killed Gandhi?

1. Erikson 1969: 64.
2. Ibid.: 98.
3. Incidentally, such a title was used by Gandhi himself for Dadabhai Naoroji; see *Hind Swaraj* 20. The Reader asks the Editor, 'What has he whom you consider to be the Father of the Nation done for it?' The Editor replies,

    > I must tell you, with all gentleness, that it must be a matter of shame for us that you should speak about that great man in terms of disrespect. Just look at his work. He has dedicated his life to the service of India. We have learned what we know from him. It was the respected Dadabhai who taught us that the English had sucked our life-blood. What does it matter that, today, his trust is still in the English nation? Is Dadabhai less

> to be honoured because, in the exuberance of youth, we are prepared to
> go a step further? Are we, on that account, wiser than he? It is a mark of
> wisdom not to kick away the very step from which we have risen higher ...
> Such is the case with the Grand Old Man of India. We must admit that he
> is the author of nationalism (CWMG 10: 248–249).

4. The growing interest in Gandhi's death is evident in recent works such as *Speaking of Gandhi's Death* in which a group of scholars, carefully selected from the left-liberal spectrum, congregated at Sabarmati Ashram to reflect on Mahatma's demise.
5. Payne 1969: 646.
6. Malgonkar 1978; 2008: 143.
7. Ibid.: 155.
8. Dr Jagdish Chandra Jain, an Indologist and Jainism scholar, warned the then Home Minister of Bombay, Morarji Desai, of the plan to murder Gandhi. Dr Jain had learned this from Madanlal Pahwa, a refugee from the newly formed Pakistan and one of the conspirators. Government, however, did not follow up effectively on Dr Jain's warnings. After the murder, Dr Jain became one of the key witnesses in the trial, appearing on behalf of the prosecution. See *I Could Not Save Bapu* (1949) for a fuller account.
9. Payne 1969: 572.
10. Or 'the supreme swan', an appellation for self-realized souls.
11. Gandhi 1999, Vol. 98: 333.
12. Ibid.: 334.
13. Gandhi 1999, Vol. 97: 310.
14. Gandhi 1999, Vol. 98: 72.
15. Ibid.
16. Payne 1969: 647.
17. T. Gandhi 2007: xvii–xviii.
18. Nandy 1990: 87.
19. Nehru and Gopal 1988: 63.
20. Ibid.: 65.

2. The event

1. Bob Stimpson, who is mentioned by Sheean, also filed a report for the BBC, which is supposedly available on http://news.bbc.co.uk/2/hi/50664.stm, but the link to the sound file is dead (last access failure on 22 August 2013). The report is also supposedly on the CBC (Canadian Broadcasting Corporation) website (www.cbc.ca/archives/categories/politics/international-politics/india -colonial-past-global-future/the-assassination-of-mahatma-Gandhi.html) where too it fails to play (last access failure on 22 August 2013). Other eyewitness accounts include Dharam Jit Jigyasu's recollection to his grandson in 2000, originally posted on the CBS website, and available on YouTube (Jaitly 2007); but recorded over 50 years after, this account lacks the immediacy of Sheean's

account. The written text from the website by the grandson, Muni S. Jaitly, begins with the dramatic claim, 'Mahatma Gandhi died in my grandfather's arms' (Jaitly 2009), which is not strictly true because it was in Abha Gandhi's arms that the fatally wounded Mahatma drew his last breath. In early 2012, a report by Vivek Shukla of the reminiscences of K. D. Madan, another eyewitness, was published in *The Pioneer* (28 January 2012). However, nonagenarian Madan, who was then an employee of the All India Radio, hardly adds anything new to what we already know about the event.

2. *Traces* 2003.
3. Gandhi 1999, Vol. 98: 318–319.
4. *Traces* 2003.
5. Actually, there were three, not four shots.
6. Sheean, quoted in EyeWitness to History, 15 May 2005.
7. Her name is spelled in at least three different ways: Manubehn, Manuben, and Manubahen. Actually, Manu is the name and 'bahen' the honorific, meaning sister. I have used the first form, which is found in the *Collected Works of Mahatma Gandhi* and also in her own books.
8. Manubehn 1962a: 40.
9. Ibid.
10. Ibid.: 40–41.
11. Ibid.: 41.
12. Ibid.
13. Ibid.
14. Ibid.: 42.
15. Ibid.
16. Ibid.
17. Ibid.
18. Ibid.: 43.
19. Ibid.
20. Ibid.
21. Manubehn 1962b: 43.
22. Ibid.
23. Ibid.: 44.
24. Ibid.
25. Ibid.: 37.
26. Ibid.: 45.
27. Ibid.: 44.
28. Ibid.
29. Ibid.: 46.
30. Ibid.
31. Ibid.: 47.
32. Ibid.
33. Ibid.: 48.
34. Ibid.
35. Ibid.: 49.

36. Ibid.: 49–50.
37. Khan 2011: 62.

3. The post-mortem

1. See Karan Thapar's column in *Hindustan Times* where he reports an eyewitness account of these proceedings (Thapar 2007). Portions of this are reproduced in Tushar Gandhi's book (2007: 644–645).
2. Payne 1969: 643.
3. Ibid.: 645.
4. Dalvi 1997 cited in Phadke 1 February 2001.
5. See for instance, A. G. Noorani's *Savarkar and Hindutva: The Godse Connection* (2002).
6. According to Jean Alphonso Curran, Nathuram was a member of the RSS from 1932–1934; he left because the RSS did not wish to become a political organization (1951; 1979: 18–19). Godse added that he was not against the Congress either: 'I wish to make it clear that I am not an enemy of the Congress. I have always regarded that body as the premier institution which has worked for the political uplift of the country' (Godse 1989: 143). The controversy still smoulders; see for instance Neena Vyas's report in *The Hindu*, 'RSS releases 'proof' of its innocence' (18 August 2004).
7. Payne 1969: 646.
8. See www.nathuram.com. This is a relatively new website, which I have not seen prior to the year 2012. Its motto is 'Ek Hi Laksha – Hindu Rashtra' ('Only one objective – a Hindu nation'). Godse's defence was also available at http://ngodse.tripod.comdefense.htm/ but the link is now dead (access failure 23 August 2013).

4. The memorialization

1. Naidu 2010: 288–289.
2. Khan 2011: 77.
3. Ibid.
4. Nehru and Gopal 1988: 45–46.
5. Khan 2011: 78.
6. Ibid.
7. Gandhi 1999, Vol. 96: 355.
8. Gandhi 1999, Vol. 97: 226.
9. Gandhiserve 2010.

5. The repression

1. See, for instance, Mukherjee, Mukherjee and Mahajan, *RSS, School Texts, and the Murder of Mahatma Gandhi: The Hindu Communal Project* (2008), which tries

to establish a link between the RSS, school textbooks, and the murder of the Mahatma. The omitting of Gandhi's murder, according to the authors, is an attempt to shield the RSS from blame: 'The silence in the historical record is at one with the attempt of all-Hindu communal parties to hide their link with Gandhi's murder by any means possible – dissociating, disowning, dissolving and reinventing' (2008: 48). But as I show at length, all these mechanisms of erasure have also been practised by others; the repression has been so widespread as to be a national practice.

2. Godse 1989: 153.
3. Sondhi 2008: 339–340.
4. Interestingly, the word Nandy uses is 'parricide' rather than *patricide*. The former means the killing of parents and close relatives, whereas the latter specifically refers to the murder of the father by his offspring. My analysis hinges on the 'impossibility' of patricide rather than parricide in the Hindu imaginary.
5. Nandy 1990: 86.
6. Ibid.
7. Ibid.: 85.
8. Ibid.: 83–84.
9. Ibid.: 93.
10. Ibid.: 71.
11. Ibid.
12. Ibid.
13. Ibid.: 72.
14. Ibid.: 74.
15. Ibid.
16. Ibid.
17. Ibid.: 76.
18. For continuing dalit attacks on Gandhi see TNN, 'Mayawati Faces Flak Over Remarks on Mahatma Gandhi' in Works Cited. For Ambedkar and Gandhi see, for instance, Paranjape (2009), *Altered Destinations: Self, Society, and Nation in India*, or 'The "Persistent" Mahatma: Rereading Gandhi Post-Hindutva' in Paranjape (2012), *Making India* (237–251).
19. This arch-enemy of Gandhi and the Congress was once a loyal and valued leader of the party. The Haripura Congress Souvenir of 1938 describes him as 'one of the creators of the Congress triumph in the Central Provinces' who 'strove for a united Congress Party and he succeeded in his effort' (Kamat Research Database 2009). It adds that 'Imbued with Gandhian spirit. . . . He played a notable part in imparting fresh vigour to the Congress movement in C.P.' (ibid.). When the Souvenir was published, Kher was the Premier of the Central Provinces elected on a Congress ticket.
20. See Kapur 1970–71: Vol. II, chapter 13; T. Gandhi 2007: 781–787.
21. See Malgonkar (1978; 2008: 135–137); also see Vinayak Chaturvedi's essay (2003: 155–173) based on his detailed interviews with Dr Upendra Parchure, the son of Dr Dattatraya Parchure of Gwalior, who procured the gun for Nathuram on 28 January 1948. Details of the gun are also found in the Kapur Commission Report, Part 1, Volume I.

Interestingly, the Gwalior royal family had staunch supporters of Hindutva such as the Rajmata Vijayaraje Scindia, who became the president of the Bharatiya Janata Party after being a long-standing member of its predecessor, the Bharatiya Jana Sangh. Her son, Madhavrao, the heir-apparent and then the 'Maharaja' of Gwalior, broke with her and joined the Congress, where he became a senior leader and member of the Union Cabinet. His son, Jyotiraditya, the current 'Maharaja', is also a Congress Member of Parliament from Gwalior, while his paternal aunt, Madhavrao's sister and Vijayaraje's daughter, Vasundharaje, continues with the BJP and was Rajasthan's former Chief Minister.

22. T. Gandhi 2007: 793; Kapur 1970–1971, Vol. II, 15.32.
23. See Malgonkar (1978; 2008: 278); in several places, the army had to be called in to restore order. A fictionalized account of the attacks on Brahmins in the wake of the assassination can be found in Vyankatesh Madgulkar's *Waavtal*, translated into English as *The Winds of Fire*. Admittedly, these attacks were part of older tensions between the Brahmins and non-Brahmins, but the latter found this a convenient occasion to attack the former. For a personal account, see Arvind Kolhatkar's 'Gandhi Assassination Backlash in Satara' (2009). For the rise of non-Brahmin elites, see 'Consolidation of Maratha Dominance in Maharashtra' by S. M. Dahiwale (1995: 336–342).
24. Nandy 1990: 77.
25. Ibid.
26. Ibid.: 78.
27. Ibid.
28. Ibid.
29. It is perhaps time to reveal, for those who do not know, that I too hail from the same community. The power of the Godse myth continues to appeal to sections of the Chitpavans, though its votaries are dwindling. When I was growing up, I myself heard views supporting Godse's stance, particularly the opinion that he had not been given a 'fair' hearing; on the other hand, several members of my family ridiculed these claims as being totally unfounded.
30. Nandy 1990: 42.
31. Dhar 2010: 67–68, emphasis in original.

6.   The unbearability of patricide

1. See W. J. Wilkins, *Hindu Mythology, Vedic and Purānic* (1882; 1913: 164–169).
2. There is actually a book edited by T. S. Rukmini by this title, though it mentions nothing of patricide (Rukmini 2005).
3. Girish Karnad retells this extraordinary story in his play, *Agni Mattu Male*, which he translated himself as *The Fire and the Rain* (1998). It is not clear, however, whether he did so because it has the lone instance of patricide in Hindu tradition. The blurb glibly declares:

This play by one of India's foremost playwrights and actors is based on a story from the Mahabharata which tellingly illuminates universal themes – alienation, loneliness, love, family, hatred – through the daily lives and concerns of a whole community of individuals.

Patricide is nowhere mentioned. The play was very poorly adapted by Arjun Sajnani into a movie of the same name.

4. See Richman (2000: 243–264); apparently there are some Telugu songs that also tell the same story (Richman 1991: 123).
5. See Subhash Mazumdar's *Who is Who in the Mahabharata* (1988: 32); Dowson's *Classical Dictionary of Hindu Mythology* (1897; 1979) remains a handy ready-reference on Hindu mythology and literature.
6. Robert Graves's *Greek Myths* (1955) continues to be a stimulating and absorbing source for these narratives. The stories of the Titans and Gods are mostly derived from Hesiod; see Jenny Strauss Clay's *Hesiod's Cosmos* (2009) for a readable overview.
7. Ramanujan 1999: 385.
8. Ibid.

7. Oedipus in India

1. Freud 1905; 1955; 2000: 92.
2. Freud 1913; 1950; 2001: 149–150.
3. Ibid.: 153.
4. Ibid.: 182.
5. Ibid.
6. Freud 1916–17; 1978a: 337.
7. Freud 1919; 1978b: 193.
8. Freud 1900; 1955; 2010: 280.
9. Ibid.
10. Freud 1913; 1950; 2001: 182.
11. Malinowski 1927; 2001: 137.
12. Ibid.: 129.
13. Freud 1914a: 62.
14. Bose 1964.
15. Hartnack 2003: 10.
16. Hartnack 2001: 148.
17. Bose 1964: 237.
18. Ibid.: 231.
19. Hartnack 2003: 10.
20. Ramanujan 1999: 376.
21. Ibid.: 378.
22. Ibid.: 385.
23. Goldman 1978: 364.

24. Ramanujan 1999: 385.
25. Ibid.: 386.
26. Ibid.: 387–388.
27. Ramanujan 1999: 392.
28. Ibid.: 392.
29. Ibid.: 393.
30. Devereux 1951: 3.
31. Ibid.: 13.
32. Ramanujan 1999: 396.
33. Ibid.
34. See Singh 2008.
35. Ramanujan 1999: 396.
36. Ibid.
37. Ibid.
38. Ibid.
39. Kosambi 1956: 51.
40. Obeysekere 1989: 3.

8.   The pollution

1.   Literally, collective powers, later 'spirits' of the dead; or 'the good people', an anxious euphemism like the Greek name of 'the kindly ones' for the Furies ('Manes', *Encyclopaedia Britannica*).
2.   Euripides 1981: 55–56.
3.   Ibid.: 58.
4.   Ibid.: 56.
5.   Parker 1983: 25–26.
6.   Ibid.
7.   Freud 1913; 1950; 2001: 40.
8.   Byron 2011: 121.
9.   Ibid.: 122.
10. Kane 1962–1975, Vol. IV: 41–42.
11. Kane 1962–1975: 1–11.
12. Buhler 1886, Vol. 11: 45–46.
13. Ibid.: 72.
14. Ibid.
15. Ibid.: 77.
16. Ibid.: 127–146.
17. Ibid.: 144.
18. Ibid.: 75.
19. Douglas 1966; 1984: 114.
20. Parker 1983: 325–327.
21. Parker 1983: 326.
22. Ibid.

9.   The haunting

1.   See Naidu and Paranjape (ed.) *Sarojini Naidu: Selected Poetry and Prose* (2010) for a more detailed engagement with her life and literary works.
2.   Naidu 2010: 285.
3.   Ibid.
4.   Ibid.
5.   Ibid.
6.   Ibid.: 286.
7.   Ibid.
8.   Ibid.: 287.
9.   Perhaps, she (un)consciously echoes Tennyson's famous lines from 'In Memoriam':

> Is this an hour
> For private sorrow's barren song,
> When more and more the people throng
> The chairs and thrones of civil power?

10.   Naidu 2010: 287.
11.   Ibid.
12.   Ibid.
13.   Sarojini's many allusions to Christian traditions are not merely a reflection of her education but also of ready-made templates to reinscribe the meaning of Gandhi's death. See Jonathan Dollimore's *Death, Desire, and Loss in Western Culture* (1998) for a reading of how death is understood in the West, India's most intimate civilizational Other.
14.   Naidu 2010: 288.
15.   Ibid.: 289.
16.   Ibid.

10. The guilt

1.   Jaspers, as he himself acknowledges, was following in the footsteps of Hannah Arendt's 'moving, soberly factual article, 'Organized Guilt', *Jewish Frontier*, January, 1945 (Jaspers 1948; 2000: 78). To my knowledge no one has tried to apply his essay to the murder of the Mahatma or the partition of India.
2.   Jaspers 1948; 2000: 21.
3.   Ibid.: 3.
4.   Ibid.: 29.
5.   Ibid.: 56.
6.   Ibid.: 28.

7. Ibid.
8. Ibid.: 64.
9. Ibid.: 25.
10. Ibid.: 26.
11. Ibid.: 33.
12. Ibid.: 34.
13. Ibid.: 36.
14. Ibid.: 55–56.
15. Ibid.: 27.
16. Ibid.
17. Ibid.: 26.
18. Ibid.: 57.
19. Ibid.: 26.
20. Ibid.
21. Ibid.: 27.
22. Ibid.: 57.
23. Ibid.
24. Ibid.
25. Ibid.: 58.
26. Ibid.
27. Ibid.: 30.
28. Ibid.: 59.
29. Ibid.: 30.
30. Ibid.
31. Ibid.
32. Ibid.
33. Ibid.: 43.
34. Ibid.: 61.
35. Ibid.
36. Ibid.: 63.
37. Ibid.
38. Ibid.: 66.
39. Ibid.: 91.
40. Jaspers 1948; 2000: 97–98.
41. Ibid.: 103.
42. Ibid.: 112.
43. Ibid.: 113.
44. Ibid.: 114.
45. Ibid.
46. Ibid.: 115.
47. Ibid.
48. Nandy 1998: 110.
49. Ibid.

11. The unbearable modernity of patricide

1. Mallik grew up in India, read Philosophy at Calcutta University, worked as a private tutor to the sons of the Prime Minister of Nepal, spent many years at Oxford where he had many influential friends including Robert Graves, and developed his own, unique philosophy and sociology of history. See *Basanta Kumar Mallik: A Garland of Homage* (1961) edited by Winifred Lewis.
2. Sondhi 2008: 273.
3. Ibid.: 275.
4. Ibid.: 276.
5. Ibid.
6. Ibid.: 277.
7. Ibid.: 276.
8. Ibid.
9. Ibid.
10. Ibid.: 278.
11. Ibid.
12. Ibid.
13. Ibid.
14. Ibid.: 279–280.
15. Ibid.: 280.
16. Ibid.
17. Mallik 1948: 280.
18. Sondhi 2008: 280.
19. Ibid.
20. Ibid.: 281.
21. Ibid.
22. Ibid.
23. Ibid.
24. Ibid.: 282.
25. Ibid.: 294.
26. Ibid.: 335.
27. Ibid.: 339–340.

12. The Mahatma's endgame

1. Ramanujan 1999: 387–388.
2. Nandy 1990: 85.
3. Gandhi 1999, Vol. 30: 248.
4. Godse and Godse 1993: 95.
5. Nandy 1990: 114.
6. Payne 1969: 573.

7.   Nandy 1990: 71.
8.   Mahadevan 1978: 1.
9.   Manubehn 1962a: 54.
10. Manubehn 1962b: 28–29.
11. Manubehn 1962a: 55.
12. Ibid.
13. Manubehn 1962b: 28.
14. Manubehn 1962a: 287.
15. Manubehn 1962b: 32.
16. Tendulkar 1951–54, Vol. 8: 287.
17. Pyarelal 1958, Vol. 2: 772.
18. Ibid.: 686.
19. Manubehn 1962a: 284.
20. Nanda 1958: 509.
21. Pyarelal 1958, Vol. 2: 685.
22. Nandy 1990: 90.
23. Gandhi 1999, Vol. 86: 6.
24. Nandy 1990: 87.
25. Ibid.
26. Payne 1969: 647.
27. Nandy 1990: 93.
28. James 1984: 10.
29. Ibid.
30. Bose 1974: 252–253.
31. James 1984: 24–25.
32. Ibid.
33. Malgonkar 1978; 2008: 251.
34. Lal 2001: 38.

13. Gandh*ism* vs. Gandh*igiri*

1.   The subtitle of this section, as of the book, is similar to the subtitle of Claude
     Markovits's revisionist history called *The Un-Gandhian Gandhi*. The book was
     first published in India by Permanent Black with the subtitle '*Gandhi's Posthumous
     Life*', which changed the following year in the Anthem Press London imprint.
     Markovits, attempting a 'non-traditional biography', tries to go beyond – or
     beneath – common perceptions to locate the 'real' Gandhi in history.
2.   Payne 1969: 646.
3.   Among the other feature films on Gandhi, special mention may be made of
     Shyam Benegal's bilingual *The Making of the Mahatma* (1996), Kamala Hassan's
     He Ram (2000), Jahnu Barua's *Maine Gandhi Ko Nahin Mara* (2005), and Feroze
     Abbas Khan's *Gandhi, My Father* (2007).
4.   Gandhi 1999, Vol. 96: 366.

5.   Payne 1969: 509.
6.   Ibid.
7.   Attenborough 1982a: 101.
8.   Cooper 1983: 47.
9.   Orwell 2003: 347; 347–357.
10. Markovits 2003; 2004: 13.
11. Ibid.
12. Ibid.: 15–16.
13. Ibid.: 17.
14. Ibid.: 16.
15. Ibid.: 17.
16. Attenborough 1982a: 68.
17. Hay 1983: 86.
18. Attenborough 1982a: 228.
19. Hay 1983: 87.
20. Ibid.: 87–88.
21. Ibid.: 90.
22. Rushdie 1991: 102.
23. Ibid.
24. Ibid.
25. Ibid.: 103.
26. Ibid.: 105.
27. Ibid.
28. Ibid.: 106.
29. For some hard-hitting criticism against the film, see Duara (2006) and Ganesh (2006).
30. Boxofficeindia.com 2012.
31. Zeeshan 2006.
32. Ramachandran 2006.
33. Gentleman 2006.
34. Sappenfield 2006.
35. Sharma 2006.
36. Gits4u.com 2006.
37. Indo-Asian News Service 2006.
38. Gits4u.com 2006.
39. Chaudhury 2007.
40. Joshi 2006.
41. Ibid.
42. Sen 2006b.
43. Frykenberg 1972: 468.
44. Joshi 2006.
45. Ibid.
46. Sen 2006a.

47. See *Bollywood in Australia: Transnationalism and Culture*, edited by Andrew Hassam and Makarand Paranjape for a more detailed version of this argument.
48. Naidu 2010: 289.

14. Beyond the monument

1. Huyssen 1995: 4.
2. Paranjape 2012: 213–235.
3. Bal, Crewe and Spitzer 1999: vii.
4. Ibid.
5. Ibid.: vii.
6. Ibid.: viii.
7. Ibid.
8. Ibid.
9. Ibid.
10. Ibid.: viii.
11. van der Kolk and van der Hart: 168–169 cited in Bal, Crewe and Spitzer 1999: ix.
12. Bal, Crewe and Spitzer 1999: x.
13. Ibid.
14. Ibid.
15. Ibid.
16. Ibid.
17. Parr 2008: 16.
18. Ibid.
19. Parr 2008: 16–17.
20. Ibid.: 17.
21. Ibid.
22. Ibid.
23. Deleuze 1994: 19.
24. Deleuze and Guattari 1994: 16.
25. Ibid.
26. Ibid.: 177.
27. Ibid.: 184.
28. Ibid.: 211.
29. Ibid.: 183–184.
30. Huyssen 1995: 9.
31. Ibid.: 6.
32. Ibid.: 10.
33. Jameson 1991: xi.
34. Huyssen 1995: 32.
35. Assmann 1992. Richard Terdiman, in addition, makes the useful distinction between memory and history, arguing that the French Revolution marks a breaking point, a 'memory crisis' after which, due to urbanization, industriali-

zation and the ensuing increase in the complexity of life, people lost any implicit or indwelling understanding of the past, and had to rely on historical representation to access the past (Terdiman 1993). I would argue that in India, people may still 'remember' through acts of collective invocation, such as attempted here.

15. Gandhi and *Anti-Oedipus*

1. Sondhi 2008: 294.
2. Ibid.: 377–378.
3. Ibid.: 378.
4. Gandhi 1999, Vol. 98: 343.
5. Deleuze and Guattari 1977: xiii.
6. Ibid.: 190.
7. Rudnytsky 1982: 462.
8. Ibid.
9. Ibid.
10. Goodhart 1978: 67.
11. Ibid.: 64.
12. Rudnytsky 1982: 464.
13. Ibid.: 468.
14. Ibid.: 679.
15. Ibid.
16. Ibid.
17. Ibid.
18. Ibid.: 466.
19. Ibid.
20. Girard 1995: 145.
21. Ibid.
22. Ibid.: 77.
23. Ibid.
24. Ibid.: 145.
25. Ibid.: 146.
26. Ibid.
27. Ibid.: 148.
28. Gandhi 1999, Vol. 98: 284.
29. Ibid.: 86.
30. Manubehn 1962b: 38.
31. Deleuze and Guattari 1977: 23.
32. Ibid.: xv.
33. Holland 1985/1986: 294.
34. Ibid.: 295.
35. Ibid.: 298.
36. Ibid.: 301.

37. Ibid.: 304.
38. Ibid.
39. Deleuze and Guattari 1977: 24.
40. Holland 1986: 305.
41. Deleuze and Guattari 1977: 15.
42. Ibid.: 23.
43. Ibid.: 26.
44. Ibid.: 42.
45. Ibid.: 53.
46. Ibid.: 44.
47. Ibid.: 45.
48. Ibid.: 46.
49. Rudnytsky 1982: 643.
50. Ibid.
51. Deleuze and Guattari 1977: 47.
52. Ibid.: 48.
53. Ibid.: 49.
54. Ibid.
55. Ibid.: 50.
56. Ibid.
57. Ibid.: 189.
58. Ibid.: 190.
59. Ibid.
60. Ibid.: 171.
61. Ibid.: 173–174.
62. Ibid.: 178.
63. Ibid.
64. Ibid.: 265.
65. Ibid.: 264.
66. Ibid.: 270.
67. Ibid.: 351.
68. Ibid.: 352.
69. Ibid.: 353.
70. Ibid.
71. Ibid.: 356.
72. Ibid.: 366.
73. Rudnytsky 1982: 469.

16. Arrival in Delhi

1. Gandhi 1999, Vol. 97: 342.
2. The *Collected Works* do not give the actual Bangla sentence, which according to Umashankar Joshi (1969: 1) was *'Aamaar Jivani Aamaar Vani'*.

3. Gandhi 1999, Vol. 98: 418.
4. The only one who has attempted to do this thus far is Sudhir Chandra (2011), who in his Hindi book, *Gandhi: Ek Asambhav Sambhavana*, treads similar ground.

17. 'Do or die'

1. Gandhi 1999, Vol. 96: 352.
2. Ibid.
3. Ibid.: 353.
4. Ibid.
5. Ibid.
6. Ibid.: 353.
7. Ibid.: 353–354.
8. Ibid.
9. Ibid.: 355.
10. Ibid.: 326.

18. The final *yajna*

1. Gandhi 1999, Vol. 96: 361.
2. Ibid.: 361–362.
3. Ibid.: 362.
4. Ibid.
5. Ibid.
6. Ibid.
7. Ibid.
8. Ibid.
9. Ibid.: 363.
10. Ibid.
11. Ibid.: 374.
12. Ibid.
13. Ibid.
14. Ibid.
15. Ibid.
16. Ibid.: 374.
17. Ibid.: 364.
18. Ibid.
19. Ibid.
20. Ibid.
21. Ibid.
22. Ibid.
23. Ibid.: 365.

24. Ibid.
25. Ibid.
26. Ibid.: 368.
27. Ibid.
28. Ibid.
29. Ibid.: 368.
30. Ibid.
31. Ibid.: 370.
32. Ibid.
33. Ibid.: 362.
34. Ibid.: 373
35. Ibid.: 370.
36. Ibid.
37. Ibid.: 373
38. Ibid.
39. Quoted in Subramanian 2001: 5.
40. Gandhi 1999, Vol. 96: 373–374.
41. Ibid.: 374.
42. Ibid.
43. Ibid.
44. Ibid.
45. Ibid.: 375.
46. Ibid.
47. Ibid.: 376.
48. Ibid.
49. Ibid.: 376
50. Ibid.
51. Gandhi 1999, Vol. 10: 250.
52. Gandhi 1999, Vol. 98: 224.
53. Ibid.
54. Ibid.
55. Ibid.: 240.
56. Ibid.
57. Ibid.: 224.
58. Ibid.: 249.
59. Ibid.: 256.
60. Ibid.: 225.
61. Ibid.: 245.
62. Ibid.: 248.
63. Ibid.
64. Ibid.: 227.
65. Ibid.: 257.
66. Ibid.: 235.
67. Ibid.

19. Partitioning women

1. A key resource is *Borders and Boundaries: Women in India's Partition* edited by Ritu Menon and Kamla Bhasin (1998). Also see 'Women and Partition' (CWDS 2012) in the CWDS Library Reading Lists Series 6 (2012) for a more extensive bibliography.
2. Butalia 1997: 92.
3. Ibid.
4. Ibid.: 92–93.
5. Gandhi 1999, Vol. 96: 362.
6. Ibid.
7. Ibid.
8. Ibid.: 382.
9. Ibid.: 423.
10. Ibid.
11. See, for instance, Anderson's *The Indian Ideology* (2013), Joseph Lelyveld's *The Great Soul* (2011), or Kathryn Tidrick's *Gandhi: A Political and Spiritual Life* (2006).
12. Gandhi 1999, Vol. 96: 399.
13. Ibid.
14. Ibid.
15. Ibid.
16. Manubehn 1957: 75–77.
17. Gandhi 1999, Vol. 96: 414.
18. Gandhi 1999, Vol. 97: 420.
19. Ibid.
20. Ibid.
21. Ibid.
22. Gandhi 1999, Vol. 96: 425.
23. Ibid.
24. Ibid.: 443.
25. Ibid.: 442.
26. Ibid.: 442–443.
27. Ibid.: 443.
28. Ibid.
29. Ibid.
30. Ibid.
31. Ibid.
32. Ibid.: 443–444.
33. Ibid.: 444.
34. Gandhi 1999, Vol. 97: 8.
35. Ibid.: 9.
36. Ibid.: 10.
37. Ibid.

38.   Ibid.
39.   Ibid.: 118.
40.   Ibid.
41.   Ibid.
42.   Ibid.
43.   Ibid.: 317.
44.   Butalia 1997: 105.

20.   Gandhi at an RSS rally

1.   Gandhi 1999, Vol. 96: 380–382.
2.   See also Pyarelal 1958, Vol. II: 441.
3.   Gandhi 1999, Vol. 96: 365.
4.   According to M. G. Chitkara, Gandhi visited the RSS camp near Wardha on Christmas Day, 25 December 1934 (Chitkara 2004: 254). He arrived at 6:00 a.m. and spent an hour-and-a-half there. Volume 66 of the *Collected Works* of Gandhi, which covers this period, has no record of this meeting.
5.   Gandhi 1999, Vol. 96: 380.
6.   Ibid.
7.   Ibid.
8.   Ibid.
9.   Ibid.
10.   Ibid.
11.   Ibid.
12.   Cited in Jaffrelot 2007: 117.
13.   Gandhi 1999, Vol. 96: 380.
14.   Ibid.: 365.
15.   Ibid.: 381.
16.   Ibid.: 380–381.
17.   Ibid.
18.   Ibid.: 381.
19.   Ibid.
20.   Ibid.
21.   Ibid.
22.   Ibid.
23.   Ibid.: 382.
24.   Ibid.
25.   Ibid.
26.   Gandhi 1999, Vol. 97: 231.
27.   Ibid.: 320.
28.   Gandhi 1999, Vol. 98: 256.
29.   Ibid.: 281.
30.   Ibid.

31. Ibid.: 282.
32. Ibid.: 233.
33. Gandhi 1999, Vol. 97: 4.
34. Ibid.: 293.
35. Kapur 1970–1971, Vol. 1: 165.
36. Gordon 1975: 145–204.
37. Jeffrelot 2007: 175–177.

21. Saving India

1. Gandhi 1999, Vol. 96: 382.
2. Ibid.
3. Ibid.: 383.
4. Ibid.
5. Ibid.: 410.
6. Ibid.
7. Ibid.
8. Ibid.
9. Ibid.
10. Ibid.
11. Ibid.
12. Ibid.: 410.
13. Ibid.
14. Ibid.
15. Ibid.: 384.
16. Ibid.
17. Ibid.
18. Ibid.: 385.
19. Ibid.: 386.
20. Ibid.: 387.
21. Ibid.
22. Ibid.
23. Ibid.
24. Ibid.
25. Ibid.
26. Sanyal 1973.
27. Gandhi 1999, Vol. 86: 387.
28. Ibid.
29. Gandhi 1999, Vol. 96: 388.
30. Ibid.
31. Ibid.: 400.
32. Ibid.
33. Ibid.

34.   Gandhi 1999, Vol. 98: 360.
35.   Gandhi 1999, Vol. 96: 408.
36.   Gandhi 1999, Vol. 98: 219.
37.   Gandhi 1999, Vol. 96: 417.
38.   Ibid.: 428.
39.   Ibid.: 430.
40.   Gandhi 1999, Vol. 97: 389.
41.   Ibid.: 343.
42.   Ibid.: 260.
43.   Gandhi 1999, Vol. 98: 38.

22. Ahimsa

1.   Every day, Gandhi heard heart-rending, if not heart-inflaming, stories of the woes of sufferers and victims of the horrors of the Partition. In his speech during the prayer meeting of 4 November 1947 he shares with his audience what severe, even hard-hearted, detachment a votary of non-violence had to cultivate when faced with such narratives of barbarism and brutality if he were to continue to eat, sleep and worship God:

> I also feel the same distress in my heart and am equally hurt. But I would not be truly non-violent if I started shedding tears or became gloomy. If non-violence made me so very soft, I would be crying the whole time, and there would be no time left to worship God, and to eat and sleep [Gandhi 1999, Vol. 97: 228].

That is when he says that a true believer in non-violence has to be 'softer than a flower and harder than a stone' (ibid.: 229).

  See *Gandhi and Non-Violence* by William Borman (1986) for a fuller exploration of this topic. For a collection of Gandhi's views on non-violence, see *Gandhi on Non-violence: A Selection from the Writings of Mahatma Gandhi*, ed. Thomas Merton (New York: New Directions, 1965).

2.   Gandhi 1999, Vol. 98: 158.
3.   Ibid.
4.   Gandhi 1999, Vol. 96: 401–402.
5.   Ibid.: 402.
6.   Gandhi 1999, Vol. 97: 320.
7.   Ibid.: 321.
8.   Ibid.
9.   Ibid.
10.   Ibid.: 322.
11.   Gandhi 1999, Vol. 98: 224.

12. Ibid.: 225.
13. Gandhi 1999, Vol. 96: 433.
14. Ibid.
15. Ibid.
16. Ibid.
17. Gandhi 1999, Vol. 97: 2.
18. Gandhi 1999, Vol. 96: 434.
19. Ibid.
20. Gandhi 1999, Vol. 74: 129.
21. Gandhi 1999, Vol. 96: 435.
22. Ibid.
23. Ibid.
24. Gandhi 1999, Vol. 10: 262.
25. Gandhi 1999, Vol. 97: 238.
26. Ibid.: 239.
27. Gandhi 1999, Vol. 97: 278–279.
28. Ibid.: 279.
29. Ibid.: 108.
30. Gandhi 1999, Vol. 98: 238.
31. Ibid.
32. Ibid.
33. Gandhi 1999, Vol. 97: 151.
34. Fanon 1967: 74.
35. Gandhi 1999, Vol. 97: 453.
36. Gandhi 1999, Vol. 98: 310.
37. Ibid.: 294–295.
38. Ibid.: 293.

23. Hindu–Muslim amity

1. Gandhi 1999, Vol. 96: 417.
2. Ibid.
3. Ibid.: 429.
4. Ibid.: 418.
5. Ibid.: 419.
6. Ibid.
7. Ibid.: 420.
8. Ibid.
9. Ibid.: 421.
10. Ibid.
11. Ibid.: 429.
12. Ibid.
13. Ibid.

14. Ibid.
15. Ibid.
16. Ibid.: 429–430.
17. Ibid.: 432.
18. Gandhi 1999, Vol. 97: 382.
19. Ibid.: 406.
20. Ibid.: 385.
21. Ibid.: 405.
22. Ibid.: 432.
23. Ibid.
24. Ibid.: 433.
25. Gandhi 1999, Vol. 98: 273.
26. Gandhi 1999, Vol. 97: 469.
27. Gandhi 1999, Vol. 98: 59.
28. Ibid.: 74.
29. Ibid.
30. Ibid.
31. Ibid.: 84.
32. Ibid.: 114.
33. Ibid.: 161.
34. Ibid.
35. Ibid.: 192.
36. Ibid.: 81.
37. Ibid.: 114.
38. Ibid.
39. Ibid.
40. Ibid.
41. Ibid.
42. Ibid.: 232.
43. Ibid.: 233.
44. Ibid.: 331.
45. Ibid.: 234.
46. Ibid.: 235.
47. Ibid.: 239.
48. Ibid.: 310.
49. Ibid.: 127.
50. Ibid.: 148–149.
51. Ibid.: 192.
52. Ibid.: 280.
53. Ibid.: 149.
54. Ibid.
55. Ibid.: 157.
56. Ibid.: 198.
57. Ibid.: 229.

58. Both statements are available as Appendices in Gandhi 1999, Vol. 98.
59. Gandhi 1999, Vol. 98: 245.
60. Ibid.
61. Ibid.
62. Ibid.
63. Godse 1971.
64. Gandhi 1999, Vol. 98: 246.
65. Ibid.
66. Ibid.: 247.
67. Ibid.
68. Ibid.: 261.
69. Ibid.
70. Pandey 2004: 144.
71. Gandhi 1999, Vol. 98: 293.
72. Ibid.: 303.
73. Ibid.
74. Ibid.
75. Ibid.: 339.
76. See Rajmohan Gandhi's *Understanding the Muslim Mind* (2003) and *Eight Lives* (1986) for an account of Hindu–Muslim relations, narrated with the sympathy and depth of understanding befitting of the Mahatma's own grandson.

24. The art of dying

1. Gandhi 1999, Vol. 96: 403.
2. Ibid.: 425.
3. Ibid.
4. Ibid.
5. Ibid.
6. Ibid.: 282.
7. Ibid.: 317.
8. Ibid.: 372.
9. Ibid.
10. Gandhi 1999, Vol. 97: 475.
11. Ibid.
12. Ibid.
13. Ibid.: 394.
14. Ibid.: 389.
15. Gandhi 1999, Vol. 98: 90.
16. Ibid.: 90–91.
17. Ibid.: 158.
18. Ibid.: 203.
19. Ibid.: 219.

20. Ibid.: 231.
21. Ibid.: 236.
22. Ibid.: 279.
23. Ibid.: 279.
24. Ibid.: 288.
25. Ibid.
26. Ibid.
27. Ibid.: 298.
28. Ibid.
29. Ibid.
30. Ibid.: 308.
31. Quoted in Gandhi 1999, Vol. 98: 338.
32. Ibid.
33. Manubehn 1962b: 56.
34. Ibid.: 61–62.

25. From repression to redemption?

1. Zimmer and Campbell 1946: 178.
2. Pandey 2004: 141.
3. Ibid.: 142.
4. Ibid.: 143.
5. Ibid.
6. Ibid.: 145.
7. Ibid.

Epilogue

1. Like the Prologue, also written specially for the Indian edition.
2. 'Vivisect me before you vivisect India,' a remark often attributed to Gandhi, does not occur in his *Collected Works*. It is found in *Akhand Hindustan* (22) by K. M. Munishi, who attributes it to Gandhi and cites the 22.09.1940 issue of *Harijan* as the source. Rajmohan Gandhi also cites, possibly following Munishi, this issue of *Harijan*, but the remark is not found there. Similarly, the other famous statement attributed to Gandhi, 'If the Congress wishes to accept partition, it will be over my dead body. So long as I am alive, I will never agree to the partition of India' is not found in the *Collected Works*. This particular version of it occurs in *India Wins Freedom* (186) by Maulana Azad. Such statements have often been used by his critics to argue that Gandhi in living to see India partitioned did not keep his word, whereas I have tried to show, instead, how he did.
3. Gandhi 1999, Vol. 78:132.
4. Ibid.

Works Cited

Anderson, P. (2013) *The Indian Ideology*, London: Verso.

Ashe, G. (1968) *Gandhi*, New York: Stein and Day.

Assmann, J. (1992) *Das Kulturelle Gedächtnis: Schrift, Erinnerung und Politische Identität in frühen Hochkulturen* (The Cultural Memory: Writing, Memory and Political Identity in Early Advanced Cultures), Munich: Verlag C.H. Beck.

Attenborough, R. (1982a) *In Search of Gandhi*, Piscataway, NJ: New Century Publishers.

Attenborough, R. (dir.) (1982b) *Gandhi* [film], USA: Columbia Pictures.

Azad, Maulana Abul Kalam. (1956) *India Wins Freedom*. Calcutta: Orient Longman.

Bal, M., Crewe, J. and Spitzer L. (eds) (1999) *Acts of Memory: Cultural Recall in the Present*, Hanover, NH and London: University Press of New England.

Banerji, S. C. (1999) *A Brief History of Dharmasastra*, New Delhi: Abhinav Publications.

Borman, W. (1986) *Gandhi and Non-violence*, Albany, NY: State University of New York Press.

Bose, G. (1949) 'The Genesis and Adjustment of Oedipus Wish', *Samiksha*, 3, 4: 222–240.

Bose, G. (1964) *Bose-Freud Correspondence*, Calcutta: Indian Psycho-analytical Society.

Bose, N. K. (1974) *My Days with Gandhi*, Kolkata: Orient Longman.

Boxofficeindia.com Trade Network (2012) 'Top All Time Worldwide Grossers Updated 11/5/2012'. Online. Available at: http://boxofficeindia.com/arounddetail.php?page=shownews&articleid=4409&nCat= (accessed 3 October 2013).

Buhler, G. (ed. and trans.) (1886) *Manusmriti: The Laws of Manu*. Oxford: The Clarendon Press. Online. Available at: http://sanskritdocuments.org/all_pdf/manusmriti.pdf (accessed 3 October 2013).

Butalia, U. (1997) 'Abducted and Widowed Women: Questions of Sexuality and Citizenship during Partition', in M. Thapan (ed.) *Embodiment: Essays on Gender and Identity*, Delhi: Oxford University Press, 90–106.

Byron, J. (2011) *Cain and Abel in Text and Tradition: Jewish and Christian Interpretations of the First Sibling Rivalry*, Leiden: Brill.

Chaturvedi, V. (2003) 'Vinayak & Me: "Hindutva" and the Politics of Naming', *Social History*, 28, 2: 155–173.

Chandra, S. (2011) *Gandhi: Ek Asambhav Sambhavana* (Gandhi: An Impossible Possibility), New Delhi: Rajkamal Prakashan.

Chaudhury, N. (2007) 'October 2 is global non-violence day', *Hindustan Times*, 15 June. Online. Available at: www.hindustantimes.com/storypage/storypage.aspx?id=54580f5e-15a0-4aaf-baa3-8f403b5688fa&&Headline=October+2+is+Int'l+Non-Violence+Day (accessed 3 October 2013).

Chitkara, M. G. (2004) *Rashtriya Swayamsevak Sangh: National Upsurge*, New Delhi: A.P.H. Pub. Corp.

Clay, J. S. (2009) *Hesiod's Cosmos*, Cambridge: Cambridge University Press.

Collen, L. (1995) *The Rape of Sita*, Oxford: Heinemann Educational Publishers.

Cooper, D. (1983) 'Untitled Review of *Gandhi* by Richard Attenborough', *Film Quarterly*, 37, 2: 46–50.

Curran, J. A. (1951; 1979) *Militant Hinduism in Indian Politics: A Study of the R.S.S*, New York: International Secretariat, Institute of Pacific Relations.

CWDS Library. (2012) 'Women and Partition', *CWDS Reading Lists Series*, 17 October. Online reading list. Available at: www.cwds.ac.in/library/services/6.Partition.pdf (accessed 10 October 2013).

Dahiwale, S. M. (1995) 'Consolidation of Maratha Dominance in Maharashtra', *Economic and Political Weekly*, 336–342.

Deleuze, G. (1994) *Difference and Repetition*, trans. P. Patton, New York: Columbia University Press.

Deleuze, G. and Guattari, F. (1972) *L'Anti-Oedipe: Capitalisme et Schizophrenie*, Paris: Seuil.

Deleuze, G. and Guattari, F. (1977) *Anti-Oedipus: Capitalism and Schizophrenia*, trans. R. Hurley, M. Seem and H. Lane, New York: Viking.

Deleuze, G. and Guattari, F. (1994) *What is Philosophy?*, trans. H. Tomlinson and G. Burchell, New York: Columbia University Press.

Devereux, G. (1951) 'The Oedipal Situation and Its Consequences in Epics of Ancient India', *Samiksha*, 5, 1: 3–13.

Dhar, A. K. (2004) 'Survival of Violence: Violence of Survival', *Identity, Culture and Politics*, 5: 60–85. Online. Available at: www.codesria.org/IMG/pdf/dhar.pdf (accessed 3 October 2013).

Dollimore, J. (1998) *Death, Desire, and Loss in Western Culture*, New York: Routledge.

Douglas, M. (1966; 1984) *Purity and Danger: An Analysis of the Concepts of Pollution and Taboo*, London: Routledge.

Dowson, J. (1879; 1979) *A Classical Dictionary of Hindu Mythology and Religion, Geography, History, and Literature*, London: Routledge.

Duara, A. (2006) 'Nothing Gandhian about it', *The Hindu*, 1 October. Online. Available at: www.hindu.com/mag/2006/10/01/stories/2006100100110500.htm (accessed 3 October 2013).

Elst, K. (2001) *Gandhi and Godse – A Review and a Critique*. Delhi: Voice of India.

Encyclopædia Britannica (2013) 'Manes', *Encyclopædia Britannica Online*. Online. Available at: www.britannica.com/EBchecked/topic/361788/Manes (accessed 3 September 2013).

Erkison, E. (1969) *Gandhi's Truth: On the Origins of Militant Nonviolence*, New York: Norton.

Euripides (1981) *Medea*, trans. P. Vellacott, New York: Penguin.

EyeWitness to History (2005) 'The Assassination of Gandhi, 1948', *EyeWitness to History*. Online. Available at: www.eyewitnesstohistory.com/Gandhi.htm (accessed 4 October 2013).

Fanon, F. (1967) *The Wretched of the Earth*, trans. C. Farrington, Harmondsworth: Penguin.

Frazer, J. G. (1890; 1951) *The Golden Bough; A Study in Magic and Religion*, New York: Macmillan.

Freud, S. (1900; 1955; 2010) *The Interpretation of Dreams*, trans. and ed. J. Strachey, New York: Basic Books.

Freud, S. (1905; 1955; 2000) *Three Essays on the Theory of Sexuality*, trans. and ed. J. Strachey, New York: Basic Books.

Freud, S. (1913; 1950; 2001) *Totem and Taboo: Some Points of Agreement between the Mental Lives of Savages and Neurotics*, trans. and ed. J. Strachey, London: Routledge.

Freud, S. (1914a) *On the History of the Psychoanalytic Movement*, in *The Standard Edition of the Complete Psychological Works of Sigmund Freud, Volume XIV*, trans. and ed. by J. Strachey, London: Hogarth.

Freud, S. (1914b; 1955) 'Some Reflections on Schoolboy Psychology', in *The Standard Edition of the Complete Psychological Works of Sigmund Freud, Volume XIII*, trans. and ed. by J. Strachey, London: Hogarth, 239–244.

Freud, S. (1916–1917; 1978a) *Introductory Lectures on Psycho-Analysis*, in *The Standard Edition of the Complete Psychological Works of Sigmund Freud, Volume XV & XVI*, trans. and ed. by J. Strachey, London: Hogarth.

Freud, S. (1919; 1978b) 'A Child is Being Beaten', in *The Standard Edition of the Complete Psychological Works of Sigmund Freud, Volume XVII*, trans. and ed. by J. Strachey, London: Hogarth, 177–204.

Freud, S. (1943) *A General Introduction to Psychoanalysis*, New York: Garden City Publishing Company.

Freud, S. (1986) *The Complete Psychological Works of Sigmund Freud*, Standard edn, 24 vols, New York: W.W. Norton.

Frykenberg, R. E. (1972) 'The Partition of India: A Quarter Century After', *The American Historical Review*, 77, 2: 463–472.

Gandhi, M. K. (1999) *The Collected Works of Mahatma Gandhi*, 98 vols, New Delhi: Publications Division. Online. Available at: www.gandhiserve. org/e/cwmg/cwmg.htm (accessed 4 October 2013).

Gandhi, R. (1986) *Eight Lives: A Study of the Hindu-Muslim Encounter*, Albany, NY: State University of New York Press.

Gandhi, R. (1995) *The Good Boatman: A Portrait of Gandhi*, New Delhi: Penguin.

Gandhi, R. (2003) *Understanding the Muslim Mind*, New Delhi: Penguin.

Gandhi, R. (2007) *Mohandas: A True Story of a Man, His People and an Empire*, New Delhi: Penguin.

Gandhi, T. (2007) *Let's Kill Gandhi*, New Delhi: Rupa.

Gandhiserve (2010) *Abha Gandhi Talks about Mahatma Gandhi's Assassination (Hindi) – 01 – Footage*. 30 July. Video online. Available at: www. youtube.com/watch?v=xUjna9vkUBk (accessed 4 August 2014).

Ganesh, S. (2006) '"Lage Raho Munnabhai": History as Farce', *Economic and Political Weekly*, 4317–4319.

Gentleman, A. (2006) 'Does Urbanized India have room for Gandhi?', *International Herald Tribune*, 20 September. Online. Available at: www. nytimes.com/2006/09/20/world/asia/20iht-letter.2875619.html?_r=0 (accessed 4 October 2013).

Ghosh, T. (1973) *The Gandhi Murder Trial*, New York: Asia Publishing House.

Girard, R. (1977; 1995) *Violence and the Sacred*, London: Athlone Press.

Gits4u.com (2006) '*Lage Raho Munna Bhai* – Gandhigiri', *Gits4u.com*. Online. Available at: www.gits4u.com/misc/misc10.htm (accessed 4 October 2013).

Godse, G. V. (1989) *Gandhihatya Ani Me*, Mumbai: Surya-Prakashan.

Godse, G. V. (1971) *Panchavanna Kotinche Bali*, Pune: Raviraj Prakashan.

Godse, G. V. (1989) *Gandhiji's Murder and After*, trans. S. T. Godbole, Delhi: Surya Prakashan.

Godse, N. (1977) *Mahatma Gandhi Murder Case, Volume II, Criminal Appeals No. 66 to 72 of 1949*, Simla: Punjab High Court.

Godse, N. (1989) *May It Please Your Honour*, Delhi: Surya Prakashan.

Godse, N. and Godse, G. V. (1993) *Why I Assassinated Mahatma Gandhi*, Delhi: Surya Bharti Parkashan.

Goldman, R. P. (1978) 'Fathers, Sons and Gurus: Oedipal Conflict in the Sanskrit Epics', *Journal of Indian Philosophy*, 6, 4: 325–392.

Goodhart, S. (1978) 'Ληστὰς Ἔφασκε: Oedipus and Laius' Many Murderers', *Diacritics*, 8, 1: 55–71.

Gordon, R. (1975), 'The Hindu Mahasabha and the Indian National Congress 1915 to 1926', *Modern Asian Studies*, 9, 2: 145–203.

Graves, R. (1955) *Greek Myths*, London: Penguin.

Guthrie, W. K. C. (1954) 'Purity and Impurity', Review of *Le pur et l'impur dans la pensée des Grecs* by L. Moulinier, *The Classical Review, New Series*, 4, 3/4: 235–237.

Hartnack, C. (2001) *Psychoanalysis in Colonial India*, New Delhi: Oxford University Press.

Hartnack, C. (2003) 'Freud on Garuda's Wings: Psychoanalysis in Colonial India', *IIAS Newsletter*, 30: 10.

Hassam, A. and Paranjape, M. (eds) (2010) *Bollywood in Australia: Transnationalism and Culture*, Crawley: University of Western Australia Press.

Hay, S. (1983) 'Attenborough's "*Gandhi*"', *The Public Historian*, 5, 3: 84–94.

Hirani, R. (dir.) (2006) *Lage Raho Munna Bhai* [film], India: Yash Raj Films.

Holland, E. W. (1985–1986) 'The Anti-Oedipus: Postmodernism in Theory; Or, the Post-Lacanian Historical Contextualization of Psychoanalysis', *Boundary*, 2, 14.1/2: 291–307.

Howard, V. R. (2013) 'Rethinking Gandhi's Celibacy: Ascetic Power and Women's Empowerment', *Journal of the American Academy of Religion*, 81, 1: 130–161.

Huntington, S. P. (1996) *The Clash of Civilizations and the Remaking of World Order*, New York: Simon & Schuster.

Huyssen, A. (1995) *Twilight Memories: Marking Time in a Culture of Amnesia*, New York: Routledge.

Indo-Asian News Service (2006) 'UN Members Laughed and Applauded at "Lage Raho"', *glamsham.com*, 14 November. Online. Available at: www. glamsham.com/movies/scoops/06/nov/14_lage_raho_Munna_bhai _rajkumar_hirani.asp (accessed 4 October 2013).

Jaffrelot, C. (ed.) (2007) *Hindu Nationalism: A Reader*, Princeton, NJ: Princeton University Press.

Jain, Jagdish Chandra. (1949) *I Could Not Save Bapu*, Mumbai: Jagran Sahitya Bhandar, 1949.

Jain, Jagdish Chandra. (1961) *The Murder of Mahatma Gandhi: Prelude and Aftermath*, Bombay: Chetana.

Jaitly, M. (2007) *Eyewitness: Mahatma Gandhi Assassination*. Online video. Available at: www.youtube.com/watch?v=34jm36ZloOA (accessed 4 October 2013).

Jain, Jagdish Chandra. (2009) 'Mahatma Gandhi and My Grandfather', *CBS News*. Online. Available at: www.cbsnews.com/stories/2007/01/30/ world/main2415455.shtml (accessed 22 August 2013).

James, K. E. (1984) 'From Mohandas to Mahatma: The Spiritual Metamorphosis of Gandhi', *Essays in History*, 28: 5–20. Online. Available at: www.lib.virginia.edu/area-studies/SouthAsia/Gandhi. html#n1.51 (accessed 4 October 2013).

Jameson, F. (1981) *The Political Unconscious: Narrative as a Socially Symbolic Act*, Ithaca, NY: Cornell University Press.

Jameson, F. (1991) *Postmodernism, or, The Cultural Logic of Late Capitalism*, Durham, NC: Duke University Press.

Jaspers, K. (1948; 2000) *The of Question German Guilt*, trans. E. B. Ashton, New York: Fordham University Press.

Johnson, A. and Price-Williams, D. (1996) *Oedipus Ubiquitous: The Family Complex in World Literature*, Stanford, CA: Stanford University Press.

Joshi, A. (2006) 'How Gandhigiri Found a Place in Munnabhai', *Rediff.com*, 26 September. Online. Available at: www.rediff.com/movies/2006/ sep/26joshi.htm (accessed 4 October 2013).

Joshi, Umashankar. (1969) *Gandhi Katha*, trans. Divya Joshi, Mumbai: Mumbai Sarvodaya Mandal.

Juergensmeyer, M. (1987) 'Saint Gandhi', in J. S. Hawley (ed.) *Saints and Virtues*, Berkeley, CA: University of California Press, 187–203.

Kakar, S. (1978; 2004) *The Inner World: A Psycho-analytic Study of Childhood and Society in India*, Delhi: Oxford University Press.

Kakar, S. (1982) 'Fathers and Sons: An Indian Experience', in Cath, S. H., Gurwitt, A. R. and Ross, J. M. (eds) *Father and Child: Developmental and Clinical Perspectives*, Boston, MA: Little, Brown and Company, 417–423.

Kamat Research Database (2009) 'Biography: N. B. Khare', *Kamat Research Database*. Online. Available at: www.kamat.com/database/biographies/n_b_khare.htm (accessed 28 August 2013).

Kane, P. V. (1962–1975) *History of Dharmaśāstra*, Poona: Bhandarkar Oriental Research Institute.

Kapur, J. L. (1970–1971) *Report of Commission of Inquiry into Conspiracy to Murder Mahatma Gandhi*, 6 vols, New Delhi: Ministry of Home Affairs.

Karnad, G. R. (1998) *The Fire and the Rain*, Oxford: Oxford University Press.

Khan, Y. (2011) 'Performing Peace: Gandhi's Assassination as a Critical Moment in the Consolidation of the Nehruvian State', *Modern Asian Studies*, 45, 1: 57–80.

Khosla, G. D. (1963) *The Murder of the Mahatma*, London: Chatto and Windus.

Kolhatkar, A. (2009) 'Gandhi Assassination Backlash in Satara', *Dadi Nani Foundation*. Online. Available at: www.dadinani.com/capture-memories/read-contributions/major-events-pre-1950/145-Gandhi-assassination-backlash-by-arvind-kolhatkar (accessed 28 August 2013).

Kosambi, D. D. (1956) *An Introduction to the Study of Indian History*, Bombay: Popular Book Depot.

Kübler-Ross, E. (1969) *On Death and Dying*, New York: Macmillan.

Kulkarni, S. (2012) *Music of the Spinning Wheel: Mahatma Gandhi's Manifesto for the Internet Age*, New Delhi: Amaryllis.

Lal, V. (2001) '"Hey Ram": The Politics of Gandhi's Last Words', *Humanscape*, 8.1: 34–38. Online. Available at: www.sscnet.ucla.edu/southasia/History/Gandhi/HeRam_Gandhi.html (accessed 4 October 2013).

Lelyveld, J. (2011) *Great soul: Mahatma Gandhi and His Struggle with India*, New York: Alfred A. Knopf.

Lewis, W. (ed.) (1961) *Basanta Kumar Mallik: A Garland of Homage*, London: Vincent Stuart.

Madgulkar, V. (1974) *The Winds of Fire*, trans. P. Kale, Delhi: Hind Pocket Books.

Mahadevan, T. K. (1978) 'Godse versus Gandhi', *The Times of India Sunday Magazine*, 12 March: 1.

Malgonkar, M. (1978; 2008) *The Men Who Killed Gandhi*, New Delhi: Roli Books.

Malinowski, B. (1927; 2001) *Sex and Repression in Savage Society*, London: Routledge.

Mallik, B. K. (1948) *Gandhi – A Prophecy*, Oxford: Hall the Publisher.

Manubehn (1957) *Ekla Chalo Re*, Ahmedabad: Navajivan.

Manubehn (1962a) *Last Glimpses of Bapu*, Delhi: Shiva Lal.

Manubehn (1962b) *The End of an Epoch*, trans. G. Gandhi, Ahmedabad: Navajivan.

Markovits, C. (2003; 2004) *The Un-Gandhian Gandhi: The Life and Afterlife of the Mahatma*, London: Anthem.

Mazumdar, S. (1988) *Who is Who in the Mahabharata*, Mumbai: Bharatiya Vidya Bhavan.

Menon, R. and Bhasin, K. (1998) *Borders & Boundaries: Women in India's Partition*, New Brunswick, NJ: Rutgers University Press.

Merton, T. and Gandhi (1965) *Gandhi on Non-violence, A Selection from the Writings of Mahatma Gandhi*, New York: New Directions Publishing Corp.

Moulinier, L. (1975) *Le pur et l'impur dans la pensée des Grecs d'Homère à Aristote*, New York: Arno Press.

Mukherjee, A., Mukherjee, M. and Mahajan, S. (2008) *RSS, School Texts, and the Murder of Mahatma Gandhi: The Hindu Communal Project*, New Delhi: Sage Publications.

Munshi, K. M. (1942) *Akhand Hindustan*. Mumbai: New Book Company.

Naidu, S. and Paranjape M. R. (ed.) (2010) *Selected Poetry and Prose*, revised 2nd edn, New Delhi: Rupa.

Nanda, B. R. (1958) *Mahatma Gandhi: A Biography*, Boston, MA: The Beacon Press.

Nandy, A. (1983) *The Intimate Enemy: Loss and Recovery of Self under Colonialism*, Delhi: Oxford University Press.

Nandy, A. (1990) *At the Edge of Psychology: Essays in Politics and Culture*, Delhi: Oxford University Press.

Nandy, A. (1998) 'Adorno in India: Revisiting the Psychology of Fascism', in *Exiled at Home*, Delhi: Oxford University Press, 99–111.

Nehru, J. and Gopal, S. (ed.) (1988) *Selected Works of Jawaharlal Nehru*, 2nd series, vol. 5, New Delhi: Oxford University Press.

Noorani, A. G. (2002) *Savarkar and Hindutva: The Godse Connection*, New Delhi: Left-Word Books.

Orwell, G. (2003) *Shooting an Elephant*, Harmondsworth: Penguin.

Pandey, G. (2004) *Remembering Partition: Violence, Nationalism and History in India*, Cambridge: Cambridge University Press.

Paranjape, M. R. (2009) *Altered Destinations: Self, Society, and Nation in India*, New Delhi: Anthem Press.

Paranjape, M. R. (2013) *Making India: Colonialism, National Culture, and the Afterlife of Indian English Authority*, Dordrecht: Springer.

Parker, R. (1983) *Miasma: Pollution and Purification in Early Greek Religion*, Oxford: Oxford University Press.

Parr, A. (2008) *Deleuze and Memorial Culture: Desire, Singular Memory and the Politics of Trauma*, Edinburgh: Edinburgh University Press.

Payne, R. (1969) *The Life and Death of Mahatma Gandhi*, London: Bodley Head.

Phadke, Y. D. (1998) *Nathuramayan*, Mumbai: Akshar Prakashan. English translations of excerpts are available online. Available at: www.mkGandhi-sarvodaya.org/godse.htm (accessed 4 October 2013).

Phadke, Y. D. (2001) 'Myth and Reality', *mkgandhi-sarvodaya.org*, 1 February. Online. Available at: www.mkgandhi-sarvodaya.org/godse.htm (accessed 23 August 2013).

Pyarelal, N. (1958) *Mahatma Gandhi: The Last Phase*, 2 vols, Ahmedabad: Navajivan Press.

Rajagopalachari, C. (1978) *Mahabharata*, Bombay: Bharatiya Vidya Bhavan.

Rajan, R. (2009) *Eclipse of the Hindu Nation: Gandhi and his Freedom Struggle*, New Delhi: New Age Publishers.

Ramachandran, S. (2006) 'The Mahatma Goes Hip', *Asia Times*, 29 September. Online. Available at: www.atimes.com/atimes/South_Asia/HI29Df01.html (accessed 4 October 2013).

Ramanujan, A. K. (1999) 'The Indian Oedipus', in V. Dharwardkar (ed.) *The Collected Essays of A.K. Ramanujan*, New Delhi: Oxford University Press, 377–397; reprinted in A. Poddar (ed.) (1972) *Indian Literature*, Simla: Indian Institute of Advanced Study; and also in L. Edmunds and A. Dundes (eds) (1983) *Oedipus: A Folklore Casebook*, New York: Garland, 234–349.

Richman, P. (ed.) (1991) *Many Ramayanas: The Diversity of a Narrative Tradition in South Asia*, Berkeley, CA: University of California Press.

Richman, P. (ed.) (2000) *Questioning Ramayanas: A South Asian Tradition*, Berkeley, CA: University of California Press.

Rolland, R. (1924; 2003) *Mahatma Gandhi*, New York: Kessinger Publishing.

Rudnytsky, P. L. (1982) 'Oedipus and Anti-Oedipus', *World Literature Today*, 56, 3: 462–470.

Rukmini, T. S. (2005) *The Mahabharata: What is Not Here is Nowhere Else;* (Yannehasti na Tadkavacit), Delhi: Munshiram Manoharlal.

Rushdie, Salman. *Imaginary Homelands: Essays and Criticism, 1981-1991.* London: Granta, 1991.

Sanyal, J. M. (1973) *Srimad-Bhagvatam of Krishna-Dwaipayana Vyasa*, New Delhi: Munshiram Manoharlal.

Sappenfield, M. (2006) 'It Took a Comedy to Revive Gandhi's Ideals in India', *Christian Science Monitor*, 3 October. Online. Available at: www.csmonitor. com/2006/1003/p01s04-wosc.html (accessed 4 October 2013).

Sen, R. (2006) '*Lage Raho* will make you laugh with moist eyes', interview with R. Hirani, *rediff.com*, 4 September. Online. Available at: www. rediff.com/movies/2006/sep/04hirani.htm (accessed 4 October 2013).

Sen, R. (2006) 'Munna and Circuit are Divine Fools', interview with R. Hirani, *rediff.com*, 4 September. Online. Available at: http://in.rediff. com/movies/2006/sep/01hirani1.htm (accessed 4 October 2013).

Sharma, S. G. (2006) 'How Gandhi Got His Mojo Back', *The Boston Globe*, 13 October. Online. Available at: www.boston.com/news/globe/editorial_opinion/oped/articles/2006/10/13/how_Gandhi_got_his_mojo_back/ (accessed 4 October 2013).

Sheean, V. (1949) *Lead, Kindly Light*, New York: Random House.

Shukla, V. (2012) 'When Gandhi Breathed His Last', *The Pioneer*. Online. Available at: http://archive.dailypioneer.com/sunday-edition/sundayagenda/people-agenda/38411-when-gandhi-breathed-his-last. html (accessed 22 August 2013).

Singh, U. (2008) *A History of Ancient and Early Medieval India: From the Stone Age to the 12th century*, New Delhi: Pearson Education.

Sondhi, M. S. (2008) *Intercivilizational Dialogue on Peace: Martin Buber and Basanta Kumar Mallik*, New Delhi: Indian Council for Philosophical Research.

Spratt, P. (1966) *Hindu Culture and Personality: A Psycho-Analytic Study*, Bombay: Manaktalas.

Subramanian, V. K. (2001) *Introspection for India: A Paradigm for Progress*, New Delhi: Abhinav Publications.

Suhrud, T. and De Souza, P. R. (eds) (2010) *Speaking of Gandhi's Death*. New Delhi: Indian Institute of Advanced Study and Orient Blackswan.

Tendulkar, D. G. (1951–1954) *Mahatma: Life of Mohandas Karamchand Gandhi*, 8 vols, New Delhi: Publications Division.

Terdiman, R. (1993) *Present Past: Modernity and the Memory Crisis*, Ithaca, NY: Cornell University Press.

Thapar, K. (2007) 'How Nathuram Godse Died', *Hindustan Times*, 4 February. Online. Available at: www.hindustantimes.com/News-Feed/NewsMartImportedStories/How-Nathuram-Godse-died/Article1-203779.aspx (accessed 4 October 2013).

Tidrick, K. (2006) *Gandhi: A Political and Spiritual Life*, London: I.B. Tauris.

TNN (2009) 'Mayawati Faces Flak over Remarks on Mahatma Gandhi', *Times of India*. Online. Available at: http://articles.timesofindia.indiatimes.com/2009–06–16/india/28193938_1_dalits-mayawati-general-secretary#ixzz0zr01nMxG (accessed 28 August 2013).

Traces.org. (2003) 'Vincent Sheean', *traces.org*. Online. Available at: www.traces.org/vincentsheean.html (accessed 4 October 2013).

Van der Kolk, B. A. and Van der Hart, O. (1995) 'The Intrusive Past: The Flexibility of Memory and the Engraving of Trauma', in C. Caruth (ed.) *Trauma: Explorations in Memory*, Baltimore, MD: Johns Hopkins University Press, 158–183.

Vera, H. (1978) 'Review of *Anti-Oedipus: Capitalism and Schizophrenia* by G. Deleuze and F. Guattari', *Contemporary Sociology*, 7, 3: 310–311.

Vyas, N. (2004) 'RSS Releases "Proof " of its Innocence', *The Hindu*, 18 August. Online. Available at: www.hindu.com/2004/08/18/stories/2004081805151100.htm (accessed 4 October 2013).

Wilkins, W. J. (1882; 1913) *Hindu Mythology, Vedic and Purānic*, Calcutta: Thacker, Spink & Co.

Zeeshan, J. (2006) 'Groove to Gandhi, Get it? – Books on Bapu Fly off Shelves, Schools Block Bulk Tickets', *The Telegraph*, 22 September. Online. Available at: www.telegraphindia.com/1060922/asp/calcutta/story_6766052.asp (accessed 3 October 2012).

Zimmer, R. H. and Campbell, J. (eds) (1946) *Myths and Symbols in Indian Art and Civilization*, New York: Pantheon.

Index

A Note on the Type

This book was set in Adobe Caslon Pro, a variant of Caslon designed by Carol Twombly. Caslon was originally designed and engraved by William Caslon of William Caslon & Son, Letter-Founders, in London, and first released in 1722. Caslon's types were based on seventeenth-century Dutch old-style designs and met with instant success, becoming popular throughout Europe and the American colonies. For her revival of the typeface, Twombly studied specimen pages printed between 1734 and 1770.

A Note on the Type